"A touching glimpse of the pain and longing felt by a child who doesn't quite belong to anyone, this unsentimental journey through the star-studded vacuum of her various families is unexpectedly tender and forgiving. She writes with an artist's eye for detail, with the clear gaze of a small outsider, searching forever for love."

—Joanna Lumley, actress, *Absolutely Fabulous*, and author of
No Room for Secrets

"I loved the book, which was not only fascinating, but beautifully put together and written. I was enormously impressed by the way [Huston] managed to think herself back into her state of mind and emotions as a child, and to present the world as she saw it then in the kind of images and notions that would have struck a child. And by the fact that she managed to be kind."

—Adam Zamoyski, author of *1812: Napoleon's Fatal March on Moscow*

"Allegra Huston has written an extraordinary book about her complicated life, which succeeds in being brave, generous, lyrically written and wholly devoid of self-pity. A considerable achievement."

—Hugo Vickers, author of *Cecil Beaton* and
Vivien Leigh: A Biography

"As an adult, [Huston] realized how special her circumstances were. . . . [*Love Child* is] a memoir about her nomadic, singular life."

—Susan King, *Los Angeles Times*

"Allegra Huston's memoir, *Love Child*, takes the reader inside her odyssey and reveals a young girl trying to make sense of family and life."

—David Steinberg, *Albuquerque Journal*

"The most beautifully written book about identity and memory that I have read this year."

—Antony Beevor, *Daily Telegraph* (UK)

Praise for Allegra Huston and *Love Child*

Shortlisted for Best First Biography by the Biographers' Club (UK)

"So bravely written, so clear and intensely vivid, so unsentimentally honest, so deeply humane about the whole cast of characters . . . a magnificent achievement."

—Simon Schama

"This extraordinary book reveals the all but unendurable sorrow of loss and the courage of those unwilling to live in a world without love. Allegra Huston's memoir glimmers with triumphant wisdom. She has, above all, a great conscience, understanding that it is only what is mysterious that survives."

—Susanna Moore, author of *Light Years: A Girlhood in Hawai'i,*
The Big Girls and *In the Cut*

"At its core, *Love Child* is about an innocent little girl, wandering in deep, shadowy chasms but surrounded by sun-drenched peaks of wealth and fame. How she emerged as an [adult] is a tribute to her own considerable inner resources, not to the often shabby efforts of inconstant adults who passed in and out of her childhood . . . a dishy read."

—Alan Peppard, *The Dallas Morning News*

"A masterpiece of astute and unshrinking compassion, an encouragement to all of us to face the turmoil and complexities of our past with forgiveness, humble self-knowledge and openness to the mysterious and often paradoxical rhythms of healing. Allegra Huston has written a book that will last and inspire, and I salute her for her art and her courage."

—Andrew Harvey, author of *The Hope: A Guide to Sacred Activism* and
The Way of Passion: A Celebration of Rumi

"[Y]ou will not read anything so sublimely felt and exquisitely written in a good many years. . . . It's a highly satisfying moral tale and a surpassing delight to read."

—Melik Kaylan, Forbes.com

"[*Love Child*] is an authentic 'poor little rich girl' story . . . life in [her] family appears precarious, slippery. . . . Allegra has cast her nets high and wide and succeeded in creating a durable . . . family."

—Carolyn See, *The Washington Post*

"Skillfully written and rich with personal detail, this is a tumultuous story of loss, healing, and redemption."

—Larry Cox, *The Tucson Citizen*

"I was entranced by *Love Child*, Allegra Huston's irresistible memoir . . . a close-up view of a glittering world tempered by an outsider's sense of just how off-kilter that land of money and megafame is . . . fluent, vivid and gripping."

—Caryn James, *The Huffington Post*

"[A] marvelous memoir . . . Huston reconstructs a remarkably tangled web of relationships with candor and understanding—a life of being and becoming."

—Scott Eyman, *Palm Beach Post*

"[A] beautifully written memoir . . . *Love Child* is written with such emotional restraint that the reader aches to protect [Allegra]."

—Carol Nigrelli, *The Buffalo News*

"Allegra Huston's life story sounds as complex as the plot of *The Maltese Falcon*, a movie, not coincidentally, directed by the man who raised her. . . . In her candid and incisive new memoir, *Love Child* . . . [Allegra] writes with loving detail about the many branches of her family."

—Daniel Bubbeo, *Newsday*

"Huston . . . skillfully integrates her childhood memories . . . with great sensitivity. . . . Where many memoirists compete to see who's had the most outrageous life, this story stands out in its quiet poignancy."

—*Publishers Weekly* (starred review)

Love Child

A MEMOIR OF
FAMILY LOST AND FOUND

Allegra Huston

Simon & Schuster Paperbacks
New York   London   Toronto   Sydney

SIMON & SCHUSTER PAPERBACKS
A Division of Simon & Schuster, Inc.
1230 Avenue of the Americas
New York, NY 10020

First Simon & Schuster trade paperback edition April 2010

SIMON & SCHUSTER PAPERBACKS and colophon are registered
trademarks of Simon & Schuster, Inc.

For information about special discounts for bulk purchases,
please contact Simon & Schuster Special Sales at
1-866-506-1949 or business@simonandschuster.com.

The Simon & Schuster Speakers Bureau can bring authors to
your live event. For more information or to book an event,
contact the Simon & Schuster Speakers Bureau at
1-866-248-3049 or visit our website at www.simonspeakers.com.

Designed by Suet Y. Chong

Manufactured in the United States of America

10 9 8 7 6 5 4 3 2 1

The Library of Congress has cataloged the hardcover edition as follows:

Huston, Allegra, 1964–
Love child / Allegra Huston.
p. cm.
1. Huston, John, 1906–1987—Family. 2. Huston, Allegra, 1964—Family.
3. Huston, Allegra, 1964—Childhood and youth.
I. Title.
PN1998.3.H87H87 2009
791.4302′33092—dc22
[B]
2009003141

ISBN 978-1-4165-5157-7
ISBN 978-1-4165-5158-4 (pbk)
ISBN 978-1-4391-5926-2 (ebook)

*for Rafa
and for Stella*

Love Child

1

I am playing on the parquet floor of the drawing room. The wood is golden, with dark lines that swirl like puddles when you jump in them. The wax gleams dull. It must be a cloudy day.

There are grown-ups in the room, but I don't pay them much attention. The atmosphere is somber. I feel like I'm the only one who's entirely alive, so I slide my feet across the smooth floor to prove it. I'm wearing woolly tights and no shoes. I want to make some noise because the silence is getting loud, but I'm a good girl so I don't.

"I want you all to come up to Ricki's room."

I don't have to look up to know whose voice that is: precise, almost fussy, with a funny lilt. It's my godfather, Leslie Waddington. He has tight curly hair and a nose like a bird's beak. One of my favorite books is a field guide to birds.

His words clang a sour note in my ears. Why, I wonder, should everyone barge into my mother's room when she's not there? She's been away for a few days, and won't be back for days more. You don't go into people's rooms without permission. Still, I've already realized that there are many odd things in the world. I look up to see if there's anything especially odd about this one: any clues to what's going on.

Leslie doesn't look at me as he disappears out the door. Nor does anyone else. The sour note dies away: obviously whatever is going on doesn't include me. I relax. Vaguely I take notice of their backs, leaving.

"I think he means you too," says a woman's voice. It startles me. I thought they'd left me alone.

It's Leslie's wife, Ferriel, sunk in a low chair. Her blond hair hangs down as if it has invisible weights on the ends. She looks blue-gray, the same color as the walls. The light has gone out of the portion of space she's in.

Her eyes are flat. She doesn't "think." She knows he means me too.

I jump up, wanting to catch up before anyone notices that I didn't go with them. I hate being in the wrong. Also, I hate being late. I run out of the room.

This is where the memory ends. Upstairs, I will be lifted onto Mum's bed to sit between my brother, Tony, and my sister, Anjelica—two dark heads flanking my little blond one. They're much older than me: eighteen and seventeen. I am four.

Leslie will sit on a low chair opposite us. He will tell me that my mother has been killed in a car crash while driving across France on her way to her father's house in northern Italy for a holiday. She will not come home. I will never see her again.

Anjelica and Tony already know. Leslie has taken on the task of telling me because Mum asked him to look after me if anything ever happened to her. He has choreographed this scene in her bedroom especially for me.

In the silence that followed his words, I let out a sound that my sister describes as a banshee wail. It went on much longer than the amount of breath I could possibly have held in my small lungs. It was unearthly, she says, like no sound she'd ever heard. It chilled her. I didn't cry.

I didn't cry on my first day at Stepping Stones nursery school, either. My best friend, Lionel Smith-Gordon, did, and I was mortified. I kissed my mother good-bye and edged away from Lionel, trying to pretend that I didn't know him. He was clinging to his mother, howling. We were two years old. I was very impressed by the children who were three.

I was a proper little English girl, with patent-leather shoes and a navy coat and clothes perfectly pressed by Nurse, my Irish nanny. There was a gilt A on the door of my room, for Allegra, and on the same landing a T for Tony and a K for Nurse. I thought it should have been an N, even after Nurse told me that her real name was Kathleen. I didn't see what that had to do with it. Everyone called her Nurse.

Every morning, Nurse gave me my breakfast in the pine-paneled kitchen, which opened onto the garden behind the house. One day, the mother who was supposed to pick me up and take me to school didn't come. I heard Mum's feet running down the stairs. She was still in her pajamas—blue, my favorite color—but she had real shoes on her feet, dark and square-toed. "I'll have to take you," she said. She grabbed a raincoat from a peg by the front door and tied the belt around her waist. I don't think it was raining.

I watched her as she drove: the bones of her hands sticking up above the steering wheel like little mountains, her eyes fixed on the road. The side of her nose and her cheek shone pale against her dark hair. She didn't look at me where I sat beside her in the passenger seat; she was concentrating on the road. We had waited too long for the mother who didn't come.

Her left hand reached over and slotted the gear stick down,

across, and down again, slowing for a corner. It always amazed me that she didn't have to look. I could just see, under the sandy-colored raincoat, the pale blue edge of her pajamas where they fell into the hollow of her collarbone. I was wearing a kilt, I think: warm winter clothes, certainly. Woolly tights again. I was probably four by then, old enough to be carpooled to school. Mum died in January 1969. This can't have been long before.

I started to worry. She's driving too fast, I thought. The police will see us and stop us for speeding. They'll make her get out of the car. They'll take her to the police station. And there she'll be, with nowhere to hide and all those policemen, wearing only her pajamas and a raincoat.

I liked things to be correct. My favorite pastime was to practice writing, which I did in lined exercise books. Nurse would write out the alphabet for me, a letter to a page, in a column along the left side, and for hours I would form laborious *a*'s, *b*'s, and so on. If I messed up I would throw out the book and start a new one at *a* again. I made it as far as *r*—Nurse's cursive, lowercase *r*'s had fat loops at the top, and an angle of descent that for some reason I thought of as especially Irish. Line after line, I couldn't get mine to match hers. I was English, and obviously that had something to do with it; but I wasn't trying to write English *r*'s, I was copying Nurse's. It drove me mad that I couldn't do it.

No one wanted perfection but me. Mum would have had more sympathy with the way my own son writes letters, adding extra cross-pieces to an E or leaning an R forward and telling me it's running. She had grown up with a ballet dancer's ferocious discipline and obsession with detail. She didn't raise her children the same way.

In my room she hung a silvered glass ball, mottled dark like a planet of strange metals, and every night I fell asleep to the sound of Chopin on the record player. Her closest friends were artists. Often she took me to visit her friend Gina Medcalf, whose painting studio was a big open space with a window seat I loved to nestle in. Once we brought a Lego kit with a picture of a house on the box, whose regular windows, red-tiled roof, and solid-looking chimney were, to my eyes, perfect. I started putting it together, but it was hard, because you couldn't see the joins between same-colored blocks in the picture. Gina started playing around, seeing what other shapes she could make with the blocks we had: more fun, she urged me, than my mulish devotion to doing what the Lego people wanted us to do. I was having none of it. I'd chosen this Lego exactly because the blocks could make—were supposed to make—the house that was pictured on the box.

I didn't like things to be free-form; it unsettled me. I preferred paint-by-numbers and drawing by join-the-dots. I peered at the picture, figuring out how many blocks went between the window and the roof, and what it should look like on the other side. I could feel Mum's frustration. Her disappointment bled toward me, though she tried to conceal it. I knew she wished I was imaginative like Gina. I refused to feel it was my failing. I knew, as she and Gina obviously didn't, that there was a right way and a wrong way to do Lego. I was someone who did things right.

It's Mum's turn to carpool home from school. There are two of us, so we're in the back seat. Mum has stopped to buy something. She's left the car double-parked. The other cars have to edge around us.

My friend and I are bouncing as hard as we can on the springy seat while Mum is in the shop. It's the sixties; we don't have child seats. We're giggling and shouting: two little girls having the time of our lives.

Suddenly Mum's face is at the passenger-side window. She's angry. "Stop it! Right now! The brake isn't on and you'll make the car roll down the hill!"

We subside. I can feel the seat quivering. I'm embarrassed in front of my friend, having my mother tell us off. I'm silently indignant. It wasn't my fault she didn't put the brake on, and if she parked on a hill, why didn't she put it on instead of blaming us?

It intrigues me to think why some memories stayed when others were lost. In the years after Mum's death, most of my images of her faded away; but a few seared tracks in the electric labyrinth of my brain. It was pride that preserved the memory of being given a book, aged two, by a woman who said, "Of course she won't be able to read it yet," and I knowing that I could, and sitting on the top step of the stairs with Nurse and reading it as Mum showed the woman to the door. And fear that preserved others, such as the time we watched a friend of Mum's walk like a circus performer along the high rafter of a barnlike room in Kent; or the time Mum and I got out of a train on the way to Cornwall to buy something to drink, maybe, from the kiosk on the platform. As we walked back toward our compartment, the train started to move. I tugged at her, straining for the nearest door. I couldn't understand why she still walked calmly down the platform while the train was gaining speed and about to leave without us—why she didn't at least run. When we got to our door, which was still open, I put my hand on her wrist to climb the steps. She climbed them behind me.

And memory after memory of Mum and a car.

"Your mother's new car is here, Allegra! Come and see it!"

I'm in the drawing room again, alone for some reason. Usually I'm with Nurse. I don't remember who the woman was who called me; she rushed out immediately. A friend of Mum's.

I run to the window and climb up on the square, ranked iron tubes of the radiator. I know they're cold, they won't burn me; it must have been spring or summer. Outside, the sunlight is cut into shafts by the green leaves, as big as plates, of the tall, spreading trees that line the road. Opposite, beyond a black iron railing, is a canal lined with painted houseboats. Flowers spill out of pots on their roofs.

I look from side to side for Mum, and the car. There she is, below me. The top of her head is divided in two by the part in her hair. She's wearing a billowy skirt. The car she's next to is red. I know she had the car repainted—it's not really new—and I'm annoyed that she chose red. I hate red. My excitement drains away like bathwater.

All my life I've returned to these memories, familiar and unquestioned, their anguish smoothed away by use. They've been solid, like way posts seen out of the corner of my eye. But now, when I look at them head-on, they turn slippery, like fish. Sometimes the whole picture slithers away into a murky doubt, and I'm not sure I even remember it at all.

The angle at which I looked down on Mum's head isn't the angle from the drawing-room window, but from my bedroom two stories above. I picture the car to the right—then suddenly it's away to the left. A stick-shift car parked on a hill without the parking brake must be in gear—so it can't roll down a hill. Mum must have been afraid that we'd bounce the car off the brake, but my memory insists those are the words she said.

I think all these remembered cars must be the same one, though Anjelica remembers Mum's car as dark gray, and my godmother Gina says blue or—if it has to be red—maroon, not the bright red I'm sure I saw. Maybe the red that wasn't really the car is the red of the cake I got for my birthday, in the shape of a train. Not only did I hate red, but red icing meant cinnamon, and I loathed cinnamon.

I was offended and furious, and I held on to my hurt even during the trip on the Water Bus along the canal to the zoo. I loved the Water Bus, but that day it felt like a bribe, and I wasn't buying. My cake had obviously been meant for someone else; I didn't even like trains. How could Mum have chosen it for me? Did she not know me at all?

I'm hungry for every scrap of the life my mother and I shared. I can see her love for me in pictures of the two of us, in the photo of me that has a big pink heart superimposed on it; in my collages and drawings that she had framed, in the scraps of paper that record my first words and my first tooth. But I don't carry it inside me. Why didn't those memories—whatever they might have been—survive?

The harder I flex my memory, the more the stories dissolve. It makes me sick to my stomach. I feel as if I'm somehow playing myself for a fool. How many of the few, delicate threads that bind me to my mother are fictions? In the blue-pajamas-and-a-raincoat memory I'm wearing a red tartan kilt with a big safety pin—but a demon in my head whispers that I just added this in the remembering. I'm trawling my brain, and I can't tell from which part of it the fragments come. Maybe I did just make that kilt up, or more likely I borrowed it from some other time and place. Maybe these borrowings of memory were done a long time ago.

One memory doesn't shape-shift or dissolve. It's cold and immovable, like a stone. I don't remember it directly. I remember remembering it.

It's the evening of the day on which Leslie told me my mother was dead. It's about six-thirty. I know that because Nurse is about to come into my bedroom to start getting me ready for bed. I'm playing with my favorite toy: a map of Britain with place-names on little sticky transparent labels; or maybe it was my farmyard, with wooden animals and fences and barns. I'm utterly content as I play. Not a care in the world.

I see myself from outside, as if Nurse's sight of me has become my own from the vantage point of a year or so in the future. My bedroom then, where the memory lived with me, had a dark wood bed with blue-and-green bed curtains, not the pink-and-white candy-cane-striped iron bed I had in Mum's house. I still had those toys, though, set up in a corner: the map pinned to the wall, the farmyard arranged on the sloping, green-carpeted floor.

How could I have played? The same day.

Secretly I scalded myself with that memory. How unfeeling I was, how self-centered. How just plain stupid, not to have understood. How unworthy of love, not to have cried for the entire day when I knew that my mother was dead. I deserved to lose her.

Already, a year later, I had no memory of actually being told. I blamed myself even more: that hard-hearted little girl who *played* didn't care enough to carry the actual loss with her. I shocked myself, and the self that was shocked had no sympathy for the self that obliterated the truth in the only way it could.

Very soon, I lost all memories of the aftermath: the return to school and the looks I must have got, the house being packed up, my stay with Nurse at the house of my mother's friends the O'Tooles. I erased every shadow of my own misery, of Aujellas, of Tony's. All I remembered was the playing before, and the playing after. As if a chasm hadn't opened up in between.

2

"This is your father."

I'm at Claridge's hotel in London. I'm not sure who has brought me there: not Mum. She may already be dead.

I'm led into a room through a dark wood door by a woman I don't know. Her pale blond hair is pulled tight over her round head. It makes me think of the moon.

The hotel room has a white shag rug. (Which seems unlikely, in Claridge's.) I sit on it, fiddling with the toys Nurse has brought for me. My nerves strain to pick up information. The corner of a coffee table is so close I can almost feel its point against the skin of my cheek. On the far side of the coffee table, on a sofa, sits a man with long fingers holding a long brown cigar. Cigar smoke must have hazed the room, but my memory has cleared it. Every detail is as sharp as the corner of that table.

My father's knees make peaks under the dust-colored twill of his trousers. His shoes curve elegantly around his feet, the color of the hard round chestnuts I pick up in the park. Fine socks cover the knobbly bones of his ankles like shiny skin. I think I can even see the bones on the corners of his shoulders sticking up under his white turtleneck. He has a wide mouth and an open face that looks soft, as if the bones are made of sponge. With his long arms, he reminds me of a monkey at the zoo. I can imagine him hanging from branches, except that he seems so dignified and important. There are other people in the room, and they wait for him to speak and laugh at his jokes.

He's talking with them, but I feel him watching me.

I'm not sure what to do. I don't know how you're supposed to behave when you meet your father. So I play warily until it's time to go.

When I leave, I have no sense that I will ever see this imposing, disconnected father again. I don't understand that he is Tony and Anjelica's father too.

I'm pretty sure I hadn't felt the lack of a father before this. Fathers were remote beings in upper-middle-class London in the 1960s. I think the only one of my friends' fathers I even met was Pat and Kate O'Toole's father, Peter, a smoke-swathed, glittering presence in the middle part of the house, between their rooms upstairs and the basement kitchen where their Welsh grandmother, Mamgu, with her bony witch's nose, held long, low-voiced, deliciously sinister conversations with Nurse, a teapot smothered in a knitted cozy steaming between them.

I didn't ask about this man with his cigar like a king's scepter, his tall knees and voice like dark treacle. I was shy—by nature, or because Mum's death arrested me in the shy phase of a four-year-old. And I was afraid—of lively dogs, of falling off swings, of missing trains, of doing the wrong thing. The only questions I asked were play ones, like any small child. "Why is the sky blue, Nurse?" And when she came up with some answer, I'd ask "Why?" again, and "Why?" until she tired of the game.

The man was John Huston, the husband my mother had left. She had asked Leslie to take me because she didn't want me to grow up in the Huston world. Did Mum know, somehow, that she was going to die? The question haunts me. Perhaps it was every single mother's fear; I think it was some omen that settled with brutal certainty in her heart. She didn't make a will, as if she didn't want to admit to it publicly. But when her safe-deposit box was opened, there were small tags tied to her best pieces of jewelry with red string, each one labeled in her sloping print with one of three names: Tony, Anjelica, Allegra.

This father I met at the age of four was a man who pulled everything into orbit around him. Mum, with great force of will, had put a small sea between them; now that she was gone, he pulled me in. Even though, as Mum had wished, I was to live with Leslie whom he knew, since Leslie had been Tony and Anjelica's tutor for a season—I spent that first summer after she died in Ireland.

At Shannon Airport, Nurse and I were met by a weather-beaten man named, she told me, Paddy Lynch. They talked all through the long drive about people I'd never heard of, and half of Paddy's words I couldn't understand. Silently, I looked out at the patchwork of small fields stitched together by walls made of lacy gray stones. The green saturated my eyes so that they almost hurt. I thought I'd never seen anything so green, not even in Kent or Cornwall, where Mum had taken me for weekends and holidays.

I was amazed by how much Nurse and Paddy had to say to each other. Until this moment, I'd seen Nurse as a kind of extension of me, and myself as an extension of her. Even when Mum was alive, Nurse had tended to all my needs, and it was Nurse whom I was with if I wasn't with somebody else. I knew Nurse was Irish, but I

13

was shocked, and a bit affronted, that she knew this place and I did not. I felt as if we'd been cut into two people. I was different, and alone.

At last we went over a crossroads into a long drive through a wood, lined with lanterns on high black poles, like streetlights. It was daytime, so they weren't lit, but still they were friendly. I learned later that my mother had set them there.

We drove through a pair of tall iron gates into a courtyard. The car lurched as its wheels sank into deep gravel. When I got out, I found myself standing in front of a house exactly like the houses I drew: a door in the middle with a window on either side, three windows across the top, a sloping roof, and a chimney in the middle with smoke curling out. The front door was open, and waiting outside it was a man with wild black hair. He almost ran to Nurse. They took each other's hands.

I hadn't fully understood that Nurse had once lived in the place where we were going—my father's house. It looked like she was coming home.

Two girls my own age came out of a house on the far side of the courtyard, and some older boys, followed by a heavy woman who embraced Nurse. These were the Lynches, Paddy's family, come out to see this new daughter of Mr. Huston's. It was a whole world I'd come into, and suddenly I was grateful that Nurse knew it even though I didn't. She led me into a stone-floored kitchen and sat me at a round table in front of the window. I watched while she made me a sandwich and got me a glass of black-currant Ribena, my favorite drink. She knew exactly where everything was.

"This is the Little House," she told me. "Mr. Huston lives in the Big House."

She didn't say any more about it. And she didn't call him "your father."

She led me upstairs to a bedroom that looked out over the courtyard. "This used to be Anjelica's room," she said. "Now it'll be yours."

The whole house felt familiar, and I sank into its embrace, not wondering why. The Little House had been my mother's house, though I didn't know it then. The soft gray-blues and greens were like those in Mum's house on Maida Avenue. Even though Mum had not wanted me to be here, her spirit remained to cradle me. I understood that this house was ours: just for Nurse and me.

The next day, Nurse took my hand. "I'll take you up to the Big House," she said.

We walked out of the courtyard and farther up the drive. We crossed a bridge, with a little waterfall on the upstream side and on the downstream side a wide pool thick with watercress, and in it an island, and on the island a little hut, like a picture in a storybook.

Beyond the bridge, we met someone coming toward us: the woman with the moonlike hair. She crouched down beside me.

"You should call him Daddy," she said.

We rounded a corner. Looming ahead of us was the back of a tall gray stone house. The drive turned to gravel and curved around the house, the side of which was rounded into a semicircle. We didn't follow it. Instead we crossed a flagstone courtyard and entered through a back door.

Inside was a big space, with a ping-pong table. I'd never seen one before. We skirted it, and climbed a narrow staircase. At the top of the staircase was a door. Nurse opened it and pushed me gently through.

We were in a big, wood-floored hall, underneath a high curving staircase. The ceiling was higher than any I'd ever seen. Beyond, I could see another hall, that one floored in black marble, and in the far wall the inside of what was obviously the front door. It was strange to have come in from the back and up through the bowels of the house, as if I was sneaking into a world where I might or might not be welcome. I reached for Nurse's hand.

She led me through another door, into a huge, high-ceilinged kitchen, with pots hanging down, little niches lined with bright blue-patterned tiles, and, between two tall windows, a shadowy painting of a lady pulling aside her dress to show her heart pierced with arrows. At a table in the center was a woman in a white uniform, her hands floury with baking. Her face was soft and round like the dough.

"This is Allegra," said Nurse.

Mrs. Creagh wiped her hands and bent down to me. I felt like crying. I was overwhelmed: too many people, too many houses, too many rooms. I wanted to run and hide. But I held myself together, too proud to cling to Nurse's skirts.

"You'll be looking for Miss O'Kelly," said Mrs. Creagh to Nurse.

Another woman came in, with masklike makeup and firmly set hair. "You may call me Betty," she said to me. "Your father is in the study. Come." Nurse didn't follow.

On the far side of the hall, Betty opened a door. Inside it was another door; the walls were so thick all the doors came in pairs. Suddenly the house wasn't scary anymore. Those double doors pocked it with deliciously secret spaces.

The inner door stood open. Betty led me through.

On a green sofa sat the man I'd met in the hotel room at Claridge's. The long arms and legs were the same, the bony knees and elbows, the cigar, whose ash he tipped into a stone bowl a foot high. He put down the pages he was reading.

"Come over here, honey," he said to me. I had stopped just inside the door, next to Betty. Behind him, on shelves, sat three big stone men, cross-legged, with square-cut headdresses over blank, frightening faces. The low fire in the grate gave off thin wisps of smoke, but no flames. It smelled sweet, like grass. Through the windows I could see horses in a field.

I walked over to him. Betty stayed by the door. He took my hands and kissed me on the forehead. "Welcome to St. Cleran's, Allegra," he said. "I hope you'll be happy here."

He went away soon after that, and I found myself living one of those stories where there aren't any parents, and the children run free. I played with the Lynch girls, Jackie and Caroline, in the big walled garden behind the Little House, thick with climbing roses and lilacs. We swung on the trailing branches of a weeping willow, and jumped in the piles of new-cut grass. We snuck into the kitchen garden and ate peas fresh from the vine, cracking the pods like eggs under our fingernails and pulling out the peas slowly enough to hear the tendon snap.

It was light way past my bedtime. For months I never saw night.

Betty—Betts, as I was soon calling her—was the estate manager, and the spinner of the tale. She took us into the woods to look for fairy rings, faint circles in the mossy ground where the fairies' dancing feet had trod, surrounded by mushrooms which they used for chairs when they got tired. If it was raining, she set up one of Daddy's giant stone ashtrays at the foot of the stairs for staircase golf. She led us on walks with the dogs, straight out across the fields, climbing over the low stone walls to special places where we searched for lucky four-leafed clovers among the shamrocks. She showed us how to soothe nettle stings with dock leaves. She insisted that the ha-ha—a wide trench in front of the Big House that kept the cows in their field—had been dug all the way through the earth to China. I used to imagine hordes of little yellow men with swords emerging from it, come to conquer us.

One warm day she piled us into the car. "We're going to the beach," she said.

We drove for hours. There were few cars on the roads. Mostly we saw tinkers, their horse-drawn wagons parked by the side of the road, sometimes a woman cooking on a fire and lots of red-haired, dirty-faced children staring stonily as we passed by. In Connemara, wild ponies leaped across the craggy outcrops, and the few fields were as small as rooms, dug in among the rocks. Betty drove fast around the corners, and we girls flung ourselves from side to side on the back seat, in fits of hysterical giggles.

We drove down a lane so narrow that a car could barely fit through, and stopped at a thatched cottage. An old couple were waiting for us, with a pot of tea and fresh bread. They spoke only Irish, a craggy language that matched their faces, so lined and weathered and toothless that I could only tell which was the woman and which was the man by their clothes.

We put on our bathing suits and walked on down the lane—and there, hidden in an inlet of the rocky shore, was a perfect little beach of yellow sand. Seaweed-shrouded rocks shielded it from the waves. The water was icy cold but we got in anyway, and Betty put her hands under my stomach and taught me to swim. I have a photo of myself from that day, sitting on a rock, pointing at something far in the distance.

There were no family photographs at St. Cleran's, nothing tangible to recall Mum, just the half-understood relics of her presence here sometime in the past. Nobody at St. Cleran's spoke of her: not the Lynches nor Paddy Coyne with the wild black hair, not Betty O'Kelly, not Mrs. Creagh. Even Nurse rarely mentioned her. Nurse knew the sadness that had dogged Mum when she lived here, and she knew that Mum hadn't wanted this for me. She was, I know now, privately angry at Betty for enchanting me, for taking my mother's place. Old-fashioned as she was, she thought it wasn't her place to say anything, so she fumed silently and avoided the subject.

In the long slanting light of that Irish summer, Mum became a kind of ghost to me. Not a real ghost like the one that paced the Big House at night, which Betty told tales of to scare us; nothing so definite as a warmth or a presence nearby—more like a whisper that you're not sure you've heard. She became my secret. I knew that the back bedroom in the Little House, at the top of the stairs, had been hers. The door was always closed. Every time I passed it—every time I went to my room—the sensation of her washed through me. Sometimes, if Nurse wasn't there, I put my hand on the doorknob and pretended to turn it. One day I did turn it, and opened the door. My heart pounded as if I was doing something forbidden, even though I knew I was not.

Inside was a sunny room overlooking the beautiful garden I loved; a bed with a beige bedspread, impersonal and, if anything, masculine; and shelves of books. I felt silly for fearing, or hoping for, something that I couldn't even name.

Back in London when the summer ended, I climbed the stairs of Leslie's house to the room that was to be mine. There was my pink-striped bed, the paint nubbly on the iron rods. The blue-striped bed was in Nurse's room, as it had been in Maida Avenue. Instantly I felt resentful. I didn't want to live here. I wanted the blue bed, and nobody had cared enough to know that and give it to me. I had lost my mother. I deserved the blue bed, but I wouldn't expose my hurt by asking for it. Anyway, nothing would make me feel better enough.

Aged five now, I was one of the big girls at Stepping Stones, in the Dolphins class upstairs. When I was younger, I had gazed up those right-angled stairs to the heights where the Dolphins and the Eagles were, and longed for the day when I would be important enough to climb them. Now that I had made it, I didn't care. Aside from the blue-striped bed, I didn't care about anything.

I can't blame Leslie for writing to Ireland to say he couldn't keep me. Ferriel had a new baby, and my sullen gloom must have strained her nerves. I was the child of a woman with whom, she probably knew, her husband had been at least half in love—a woman adored by many for her beauty, wit, and intelligence, now haloed by a sudden and gruesome death. In Ferriel's place, I would have felt obscurely judged and found wanting.

Mum had wanted me to grow up a little English girl. She chose Leslie to look after me instead of her own parents, who lived outside New York City. Leslie tried his best, and the guilt of his failure scorched him. He disappeared from my life for twenty years, until finally, out of the blue, he found the courage to call me and ask, tentatively, if I would let him back in.

3

High in a tower of Houghton Hall, in the low eastern hump of England, my mother's letters lay locked in a trunk. Tony took charge of them when she died and stored them there, in his brother-in-law's house, when he left England. On a midsummer day in 2006, I went to find them.

Houghton is probably a hundred years older than St. Cleran's, and was built by the first prime minister of England. It has a tower at each corner, with a fat, pointy roof like the tents you see in old paintings of tournaments. I took an elevator, then stairs, to climb up into one of the tower attic rooms. It was octagonal, its high pointed ceiling ribbed like the inside of a strange fish. The plaster was bare and finely cracked, softened by centuries and yellowed by smoke. An arc of low, square-paned windows looked out onto the pillowy tops of old trees and, far below, smooth grass glittering in the sun.

There were angular piles draped in heavy canvas dust sheets and, in a corner opposite the windows, a cluster of tin trunks and leather suitcases. I found a bunch of keys in a chest of metal drawers, but they fit only some of the locks. A paper clip sprang the locks of others. Trunk after trunk contained sweaters, falconry equipment, children's report cards and letters, random odds and ends.

The last trunk was navy-blue tin, with steel corners and a tarnished brass lock. It had to be the one. No key opened it; not the paper clip; not a corkscrew. I went downstairs and asked for a screwdriver.

The trunk breathed out the air it had held since 1969, the year Mum died. The dusty sweet smell of old paper flooded up into my face, stopping my hands where they rested on the manila folders that topped the pile inside. That smell had followed me from Ireland through all the houses I lived in, buried deep in the gutter of an old paperback of *Alice in Wonderland*, which I believed had once been Mum's. As a child, as a teenager, I opened the book and pressed it against my face so that its pages blotted out the light, and inhaled, along with the delicious weirdness of the story, the melancholy of my old, accustomed loss.

I didn't read the letters there, in that beautiful, octagonal, sun-washed room. They came back with me to New Mexico, where they sat in a suitcase at the foot of my bed for almost a year. Finally, in another big, sunlit house—this one built by my husband that I'm not married to, as they say in Taos—surrounded by the snowy fields of a bitterly cold winter, I laid them out, and explored, very gently, the hinterlands of my mother's life.

Almost all the letters from the trunk were written to her. There is a box of girlish back-and-forth with her ballerina schoolmate Tanaquil LeClercq, a card "from the desk of Jean-Paul Sartre," a thank-you note from Lauren Bacall for Mum's condolences on Bogie's death, picture postcards from Truman Capote, a mountain of rambling scrawls from her father, terse telegrams from Dad . . . and some names I'd never heard of before, letter after letter mounting into high piles of passionate longing. Relics of her shadow life.

But even with this suitcase of letters spread around me, still I can't touch her. Father, friends, lovers tell her how well she writes, but all I have is a filigree of gaps where her letters should be. I found only two letters in her hand, never sent, full of pain and blame of herself, and three tiny scraps of diary, one humorous, one anguished, the third clear-eyed and rational. I feel as I am hearing her voice across a vast distance, a word here and there intelligible, the rest sucked away by the dull air.

Most of the letters she wrote are gone. Her parents' house burned down. Dad's papers didn't survive him for long. The lovers, mainly, returned to their own married lives. The friends are mostly dead, and Mum means nothing to their heirs.

As I read through elliptical remarks on indecipherable problems and mundane accounts of daily life, frustration chafes against the sense of thievery I've never managed to shake. Fate—or chance, or the blind carelessness of the universe stole her from me. I had hoped to catch her again in these letters, but I feel like I'm snatching at the hem of her coat as she flies unknowingly away.

Still, there are motes of insight, single stars that break through a clouded sky. On Mother's Day, my grandmother writes that my mother is her first child, "and who needs to know that you were five when I married Daddy." I knew that, like me, Mum had lost her mother when she was young, but I'd always thought she'd been a toddler, barely conscious of it. Now I saw, on a hazy mirror of tears, that she'd been a little girl. With two small children to be tended, Grampa wouldn't have waited long before marrying again. Let's say he waited a minimal, decent year—which makes Mum four when, probably, she was taken in to see her mother on her deathbed and hear her last words. Four: the same age as I was when I sat on my mother's bed in a room that had suddenly become her shrine. In that second, as I held Nana's letter in my shaking hands, I felt my heart change shape.

Mum, who had been my imperfectly healed wound, became my ally, my twin. She and I had had the same strength of understanding when we were told that we would never see our mothers again.

As Dad told the story, he and Mum each saw St. Cleran's separately while out hunting: an elegant Georgian half ruin, graciously proportioned, its big windows inviting, nestled amid green pastures crazed by stone walls, the fairy-tale woods bisected by that storybook river. This part is true. The implied excitement of a married couple discovering their first family home—the "Shall we?" and "Oh, let's!"—is not. They had been married for about five years, together for another year or so before that, but when the decision to buy St. Cleran's was made, Mum and Dad were, at best, doing a kind of stately dance around each other, a flow of synchronized avoidance through geography and time.

When she was barely eighteen, Mum had appeared on the cover of *Life* magazine, for no reason other than her breath-stopping beauty. She was, at the time, a dancer with the New York City Ballet. The producer David O. Selznick put her under contract and brought her to Hollywood. She appeared in *Life* again as one of the young starlets of 1949, identified as Rick Soma, the name she went by then; sitting front center in the photograph is Marilyn Monroe.

Mum never made a movie. Selznick sent her to acting classes and paired her with actors being screen-tested, but she seems never to have been given a screen test of her own. She performed on stage in La Jolla, outside L.A., and made two shorts for the Red Cross. When her contract came up for renewal, Selznick dropped her.

Her father urged her to stand on her head and sing in Selznick's office, to show what she could do. He was Italian and owned a restaurant in Manhattan called Tony's, where film and theater people liked to go, perhaps because the *padrone* would stand on his head and sing operatic arias on request. He fancied himself a yogi and sent out Christmas cards with messages like "May the spirit of Prana be with you." In his mind *prana*, breath, was a kind of elixir of the superhuman.

Until this point, Mum had always met with success. Not only did she dance for Balanchine; she was a soloist at the age of seventeen. As the beautiful daughter of the restaurant, her autograph book full of good wishes from patrons such as Zero Mostel, she grew up in the knowledge that a place in that pantheon of glamour and artistic accomplishment was reserved for her, and all she had to do was claim it. I can hear, between the lines of the letters her father wrote to her, echoes of her baffled despair. She didn't know what to do in Hollywood; she didn't know what she was doing wrong. Did the loss of her mother teach her—as it taught me—that it's useless to struggle? Mum was not as determined, not as single-minded, not as convinced of her superiority to the rest of humanity as her father thought she should be.

He barraged Mum with letters full of exhortations to become ever more flexible and disciplined, to be always bright and delightful and never show weakness or sorrow, to become a Nietzschean superhuman like himself. He told her that nobody could judge her but herself, that exalted humans like themselves were always right— though reading his letters, I wonder if Mum felt she was ever good enough. I imagine her walking to the mailbox in the lobby of her apartment building and seeing her father's scrawl on yet another fat envelope, and steeling herself to open it.

She was his firstborn and favorite. His moods swung from fury when she didn't write often enough, or long enough, to an embarrassingly detailed appreciation of every beauty of her physical and mental form. He admonished her constantly on everything from how to be prepared to escape from a blazing hotel to the exact position in which she should hold her lips when she sang or read aloud— away from her teeth, with her voice projected from her diaphragm. I sense her losing her bearings under the onslaught. How could she be natural on-screen or onstage when she was forced into a pricklingly minute self-consciousness by her father's fusillade of instructions?

Still only nineteen, she was by this time involved with the legendarily hell-raising director John Huston, twenty-three years her senior. He was exactly the sort of man my Grampa dreamed of for his daughter: celebrated, artistic, intellectual, larger than life, and the son of an even more famous actor, Walter Huston. Grampa knew them both, from the restaurant. Grampa was thrilled, too, by the news that Mum was pregnant, even though Dad was still married to the actress Evelyn Keyes, his third wife. There was no scandal in his eyes; all he saw was a grand meeting of dynasties. A divorce would be obtained and a marriage performed just in time, a month before my brother Tony was born.

Again and again, Grampa refers to "the Soma-Peppa strain": the genes Mum has inherited from him and his sainted mother, whose name was Peppa. He puns on the Greek meaning of *soma*—the physical body—as somehow expressing the idea that the Somas are the ultimate humans. Occasionally he extends this to the "Bona-Peppa-Soma strain." Grampa's grandfather was a foundling, and Grampa was convinced he was descended from Napoleon Bonaparte.

He makes constant swipes at his first wife's materialism, her shallowness, her general inferiority to the Soma-Peppa strain. How anguished and confused Mum must have felt, alone on the treacherous soil of Hollywood, as she read her father's cutting words about her mother. Like me, she had memories of her mother—but fitful ones. She knew she hadn't known her really, hadn't known what kind of a person she was. Even if she tried not to believe what Grampa said, his insults must have thrown shadows on her memory. Which side of herself, which half of her blood, did Mum want to be? In Grampa's eyes, every complaint, every worry, every sign of weakness, betrayed the insidious mediocrity of her mother's heritage.

Grampa made swipes at his second wife too, my Nana, who loved Mum like her own daughter. In response, evidently, to Mum's complaints about her husband, he placed Nana and Dad together in the category of introverted, cold Anglo-Saxons, in contrast to the life-affirming extraversion of the Italian Bona-Peppa-Soma strain. They were the inferior mates that he and Mum, the exalted Somas, were doomed to suffer. It can't have been much comfort. I imagine Mum isolated and lonely in Malibu (then even farther north of L.A. than it is now), fighting a grim and silent resistance against her father's attempts to alienate her from the mother she'd lost and the stepmother she loved, and yet, by force of habit and training, wanting to please him; buffeted by the hormones of pregnancy and Grampa's violent swings between adulation and fury; with a husband cavorting from California to the Congo, and a career for which she had spent her short life preparing dying in her hands.

By the time she was twenty-two, Mum had two children: Walter Anthony, named for his two grandfathers, and Anjelica. No "Rhea," for Dad's mother, or "Dorothy," for Nana. Dad was filming *The African Queen* and reachable only by tom-tom when Anjelica was born, so Mum had a free hand with the birth certificate. She named her daughter firmly for her own lost mother—with Nana's blessing, for she had suggested it with genuine delight in how beautiful the combination "Angelica Huston" sounded. But Mum chose to spell it differently, with a "j" instead of a "g."

Was it superstition, like the tags on her jewelry and the lack of a will? This baby would not do what the first Angelica did. She would not die and leave Mum behind—nor would she repeat the past and lose her mother as Mum had.

When Mum died, my sister Anjelica was seventeen. I was the little half-orphaned girl that Mum had been—the daughter named Allegra, Italian for "happy," the daughter whose name promised, in an Italian proverb, the protection of the gods. *La gente allegra i dei proteggono.* A friend of Mum's, the *padrona* of an Italian restaurant in London, wrote it out for me twenty years after Mum died.

Anjelica was only a month old when Dad insisted Mum go with

him to London, where he was to do postproduction work on *The African Queen*. She left her babies with Nana and Grampa. I read the letters from Nana describing their progress—Tony's walking, Anjelica's babbles and smiles—and I feel the wrenching anguish Mum must have felt at leaving them, every maternal instinct screaming against it, but the two men who ruled her life insisting she go. She was Mrs. Huston, and it was her duty to live up to it.

Dad was a difficult person to be married to, and Mum was the fourth woman to attempt it. He was unfaithful, egocentric, impatient, judgmental, cuttingly sarcastic, and a gambler. The role of Mrs. Huston—"you know, he directed Moulin Rouge or Moby Dick or whatever the film is," as she put it in her diary, with the bluntness of a stick to the head—gave her prestige in the world, but it was barren. Grampa, in his cruelly boastful superiority, needled her for expecting that marriage should bring happiness; while he obviously wanted her to be with a famous man, he seemed to believe that she would be better off as a courtesan than a wife. (He was, by now, writing that her biggest mistake had been to marry Dad.) I don't believe she really believed him; but in her darker moments, he must have seemed right.

The first mention of lawyers comes in 1954, the first clear mention of a lover in 1956, though later letters show that he was not the first. When Mum and Dad were together, as Ray Bradbury recalls in *Green Shadows, White Whale*, their fights approached violence. One letter from Nana to Mum mentions casually that "Daddy still knocks me around a little"—and it makes me sick to realize that this is an expression of sympathy for Mum telling her that she is suffering the same.

Mum wrote to her parents—in letters I don't have—of her despair at the vast commitment St. Cleran's represented. Both Nana and Grampa firmly referred to it as "John's fantasy castle." Mum and Dad had been renting a huge pile of a house called Courttown, outside

Dublin; with Dad away making movies, Mum had a reasonable life there, hunting to hounds, going to the races and parties and balls. Galway was in the crude west, the width of Ireland away from her friends, and St. Cleran's, ruinous as it was, required a vast expense of energy and imagination. All this, for a house she doubted she'd ever live in.

She seems lost—and worse, not to know what she is searching for. In one scrap of diary she writes of her "squirrel-cage brain." I can see her in that cage, running in circles, trapped by comfortless wire, cold and exposed, frantic to escape, her tormented and tormenting brain holding her in a small squirrel body which her spirit yearns to transcend. She has been raised to be one of two things, or perhaps both of them, one leading to the next: a performer, or the mate and muse of a great man. Both hopes have turned to ash—one in failure, the other in poisoned success—but still she spends her breath on them, trying to restart the fire.

In 1956, as work on St. Cleran's was starting, Mum wrote to Otto Preminger asking to be considered for the lead role in *Saint Joan*. She had fallen in love that winter, while skiing in Klosters, but the man was young and still struggling to make his place in the world. Though Mum had been cherishing fantasies of leaving Dad, she couldn't conceive of it without some other ready-made identity to slip on. The young man could not provide it; perhaps she could make it for herself. Preminger's politely uninterested reply must have hit her like the slam of a door.

Two years before, Dad had shown no sign of wanting to cast her in *Moulin Rouge*, despite the fact that, as a dancer, she was a natural for the part. Obviously, he too thought she couldn't act—and his new mistress, Suzanne Flon, could. What did she have to offer him, now that the first flush of enthusiasm for her beauty was past and motherhood and marriage had grounded the adventure? I am sure she longed for respect. Ballet was ten years in her past. She had talent as a writer, correspondents less partisan than her father told her so—but how could she dare set herself up as a serious writer when men such as Ray Bradbury, Jean-Paul Sartre, Truman Capote, and Arthur Miller paraded regularly through Dad's doors?

She knew that she had an intoxicating effect on men, and she used it, probably less cynically than she accused herself of, for ego boosts in her darker times. She congratulated herself sarcastically for captivating a party. But much as she craved it, she couldn't convince herself that love alone was enough.

Dad, meanwhile, had the best of both worlds: a beautiful wife to show off, to keep his house and bring up his children, and freedom to cavort openly with other women as he pleased. "Dad didn't like to let go of anything," my brother Tony says when we talk about why Mum didn't leave Dad earlier. He controlled the money, and he could be delicately seductive in pursuit of his own wishes. In the midst of Mum's turmoil, he wrote from location in Tobago suggesting that she and the children come and visit, or—the silken rope, this—just send the children with Nurse so that she can take some time for herself. She is, in the scrap of diary, virtually bewitched by this throwaway offer—which I had barely noticed when I read Dad's telegram. I can hear her convincing herself that life as Dad's wife isn't so bad after all. "No *reason* for divorce," she writes. "A pit I am sure, a reluctance for the big irrevocable, a shrinking from decision. I am so warmed by John's letter . . ." Twice she circles back to how kind his letter is, how thoughtful. Dad's shadow may be cold and lonely, but it is safe.

She did go to Tobago. However enticing the thought of a month or more of freedom, she refused to be away from Tony and Anjelica for so long again. She rented a separate cottage on the beach for the three of them. According to Tony, they barely saw Dad at all.

For three decades, since I started to understand something of Mum's history, I felt like a traitor to her for having been happy at St. Cleran's. I knew she hadn't wanted me to live there. To me, it was Dad's world, printed everywhere with the marks of his travels and obsessions. But reading the letters, I came to see that it was Mum who created the St. Cleran's I loved, the serene world sheltered by walls and open gates. She polished the surface, ready for the stamp of Dad's hand—and even then she held the hand so that its placement would be right.

Once she began work on this huge project, Mum found herself ambushed by happiness. The Little House was completed first. It was entirely hers; when Dad came, he slept in his studio on the far side of the courtyard. Then she turned her energy to the Big House, which would be his. With the deadening plaster knocked off the facade, the gray stone glowed in the intermittent blazes of Galway sun. She traveled to estate sales around Ireland and combed antique shops in Dublin, London, and Paris in search of treasures. Dad's letters to her, from film sets around the world, consist entirely of requests for news of the children and ideas for the house.

Suddenly, maybe surprisingly, she became for the first time Dad's equal and his partner. She loves the romance of the tumbling stones of the stableyard, and with Dad's enthusiastic agreement she leaves them in a tumble and plants roses to climb over them. She has found the perfect fireplace for his room; he is having hand-blocked Japanese wallpaper made for the dining room (he is in Japan making a film, but it's obviously St. Cleran's that excites his imagination). He sends bonsai trees for the hall, which will travel by ship with their own nursemaid; he asks Mum to pull strings at the Ministry of Agriculture to get an entry permit for them. Specifications arrive for the Japanese bath to be excavated in a room in the basement.

Dad urged Mum to buy the best, whatever it cost. He trusted her taste. He believed in her power to effect a transformation. Perhaps she no longer needed his respect. She could see the evidence of her hard work and her unerring aesthetic judgment for herself, as first the Little House, then the courtyard and stableyard, then the Big House, blossomed into striking and comfortable beauty.

She had, I think for the first time in her life, found real creative expression. I suspect that ballet never gave it to her: hypercritical, perfectionist, regimented, and prescriptive—and she was, then, too young and protected to feel the longing for her own creative identity. (Though she continued to love ballet and later served on the board of Sadler's Wells ballet company in London, she didn't send me to ballet class—in an era when that's what well-brought-up little English girls did.) Suddenly, in the letters from the trunk, there is talk of her opening an interiors shop in Dublin, of selling Irish tweeds to Chanel and Aran sweaters and shawls to the chic boutiques of Paris. Taste has become her currency, and she feels herself rich.

The search for perfect pieces for St. Cleran's gave her excuses to go to Paris. There, she spent as much time as possible with an Argentinian diplomat, with whom she had fallen cataclysmically in love.

Mum wrote in her scrap of diary that she hated to sleep alone. It was true, if cruel. She longed for loving arms not just in bed, but in the daily pursuits of life. A year and a half had passed since the relationship with the struggling young man had withered into an uncertain friendship.

Lucio Garcia del Solar was a member of the Argentinian delegation to UNESCO in Paris. She met him in Klosters too. His letters are charming, intelligent, mischievous. I'm not surprised Mum fell in love with him; I am drawn to him across the decades. He refers to her as "the soon-to-be-ex-Mrs. Huston" and talks about consulting lawyers himself, but I can't tell if the consultations were about his own possible divorce. He echoes words that must come from her own self-critical confessions: "those years of café society dizziness and superficial love affairs," in contrast to the "deep feelings" that she has for him.

She seems to be less needy than she was with the struggling young man. She is more confident, more sure of herself—able to fall in love fearlessly, for the sake of it. There has been a sea change in her—and she has St. Cleran's, "John's fantasy castle," to thank for it.

It's strange to read the evidence of this double life. It wasn't dishonest. She and Dad were married in name only; much was agreed, and unspoken, between them. Deception was not part of her nature. In fact, the struggling young man wrote that he wished she were more able to disguise her feelings; her openness about her connection with him embarrassed him and made him nervous. Still, it must have been a fierce emotional strain. I wonder how she rationalized it to herself, and I long for her missing words to tell me. I sense that she was, somehow, paying a debt to Dad, which, once paid, would release her.

In 1959, Mum is in hospital terminating the life of an unformed, minuscule creature who would have been her third child—who might have been me.

The love affair with Lucio fizzled. Mum had obviously hoped to marry him, but it became clear that he was not going to leave his wife. She wrote him an anguished letter, which she never sent. I found it where she kept it, among his letters to her. She tells him, almost defiantly, that being in love is "a painful malady, for me . . . a sickness which I shall get over, as indeed, I have before." She longed to be in love, ached from the lack of love; but never yet had love brought her peace. In the earlier scrap of diary, which she wrote upon returning to Ireland after two weeks with the struggling young man, she describes seeing a sweater which reminds her of him, and writes that being in love is "in a way . . . a state of blessedness—all the anguish worthwhile for the heightened sensitivity." The desperate bravery of this makes me want to fold her in my arms and stroke her hair—as, in the throes of my own anguished love affairs in my twenties, I longed for someone to hold me and stroke mine.

4

I was standing next to Betty as she made herself a drink in the hall of the Big House. The smooth marble top of the desk that served as a bar was level with my chin. The footwell was filled with bottles, colorful labels with bright liquids inside. Betty's black cigarette holder, its gold tip stained with lipstick, rested on a glass ashtray.

Betty ran her fingers along the dark wood, where it came out past the marble. "When your father comes home he'll be this color," she said. "Mahogany. He's been in Mexico."

When the day came, she lined us up on the front steps of the Big House: Mr. and Mrs. Creagh and their daughter, Karen; the maids, Mary and Mary Margaret, in their pink uniforms; Jackie and Caroline Lynch, and me. Betty stood on the top step beside the open door. Faithful subjects forming a processional route to welcome the king home.

I was nervous. I was "Mr. Huston's daughter" now, in second position next to Betty, but I felt like a fraud. I barely knew him. Should I run to him, the way daughters did in books? It didn't feel right, and I didn't think I ought to break up the ceremonial symmetry. But what if he expected me to, and I didn't?

It seemed like we waited on the steps for hours, until wheels scrunched on the gravel. The car, with Paddy Lynch driving, came around the side of the house and drew to a halt perfectly centered between the stone lions at the foot of the steps. The passenger door opened. Long legs unfolded themselves. I saw the same soft, chestnut-colored shoes. Like a jointed puppet Daddy stood up—far taller than I remembered him. I felt scared suddenly, of this looming stranger. But Betty was wrong: he wasn't as dark as the wood of the bar.

He greeted everyone individually as he came up the steps, a nod or a shake of the hand to one side and then the other. My greeting was no different: just "Hello, Allegra," before Betty ushered him inside. She beckoned to me, so I followed.

He went straight into the study while Betty fixed him a drink. I hung around her. "Go in to your father," she said.

He asked me questions, and I answered in monosyllables, shy and uncertain. Yes, I was happy in the Little House; yes, Nurse was well; yes, school was fine; yes, Jackie and Caroline and Karen were my friends.

"Very good, honey," he said. The words, like everything he said, came out slowly and deliberately, as if he'd thought them over carefully before speaking them.

In the shadowy depths of the archway leading to the stableyard were identical openings with staircases winding up through the thick walls. In the mornings when I didn't have school, I would climb the left-hand one, knock on the door at the top of the stairs, and wait for that rich, singsong voice, which awed and thrilled me, to call, "Come in."

Daddy's studio had skylights and small round windows at knee height that peeped down onto the courtyard and the Little House on the far side. Its air was sweet with oil paint and turpentine, and grassy with the scent of the matting on the floor. Every color I could imagine was there, splashed softly on the matting and in wet, wormy clumps on the palettes. I watched, almost holding my breath, as Daddy swirled the colors together with his brush. I loved to see them combine, and tried to catch with my eyes the exact moment of alchemy, when the two colors became one. Sometimes it never happened: my eyes burned with not blinking, and still the colors threaded through each other, each still itself, held at the exact moment before it was lost—as if Daddy's brush, like a magician's wand, had stopped time.

On the easel was Saint George, his face corpse-pale and green-tinged, faceted like a diamond. His gold halo made a perfect circle around his head. He rode a horse broken into planes like he was, which reared up on thin, angular legs. They reminded me of Daddy's pointy elbows and knees. His left hand held a spear, which stabbed a lizardlike dragon through the throat. A fish curled near his feet, a hanging circle in the orange-red air. I could sit on the floor for hours and watch him work on that painting, adding brushstrokes so tiny that I could barely see what difference they made, or picking up cans of spray paint to make little squirts into the fiery background.

When he reached a stopping place we played pelmanism. I laid the cards out on the floor at his feet, a full pack in orderly rows face-down, and when it was his turn, he would lean down between the wings of his folded knees to choose two cards, turn them over, and turn them back again if they didn't match. Talking to me was a duty he performed gracefully; but he seemed to actually enjoy playing a game which pitted my wits against his—even such a simple one. Usually I won, and he liked that. He wasn't the kind of man who played child's games.

Intelligence was my currency now. I felt I had to earn Daddy's interest, and I was pleased that I could. I asked nothing of him but to let me watch him paint, and play pelmanism with me. I was doing well at having a father.

"I have something to tell you, honey," he said one morning, his eyes resting on the canvas as he touched it with his paintbrush, as softly as you'd touch an eyelash with your finger. "Your brother Danny is coming to visit. He's a couple of years older than you. I'm sure you'll love him, as I do."

I didn't know I had a brother besides Tony. For a moment, I didn't know what to think. I wasn't clear, yet, about how children came into being, but I had an obscure sense that I should be shocked. This was, somehow, a clue to the mystery of why my mother and father hadn't lived together—why I'd met him recently, without her.

Daddy presented it so calmly, though, so casually, that it seemed the most natural thing in the world. And I felt a glimmer of excitement. I was an only child now, with Tony still in London and Anjelica off somewhere far away. There were seven Lynches; I liked the thought of a brother to play with. Additions were fine. What I dreaded, never quite consciously, was something—or someone— being taken away.

Anjelica was becoming mythical to me: the princess of St. Cleran's, who had had my room before me. I barely remembered her. She was a distant, not quite real ideal. She had inherited our mother's beauty, I knew, and was modeling in Paris and New York. More real was Angelica Healy, whose parents owned the shop next to Carrabanne, the local school. Betty sneered at the Healys' presumption in giving a common Irish girl such a fancy, borrowed name.

When Tony came to visit, he taught me to riffle cards when I shuffled them. But he called me Fattypuff, relentlessly. I hated him for it. I wasn't really fat, but I was pudgy, not tall and long-limbed as he and Anjelica were. When he gave me a book called *Fattypuffs and Thinifers* for my birthday, it was more than I could forgive. Birthday presents were supposed to be things that the birthday person liked, not mean jokes.

Every evening as I sat at the kitchen table eating my supper or memorizing the catechism (I went to the convent school in Loughrea), Tony strode in, a blast of energy like the wind crashing open a window. A falcon sat on a bloodstained leather gauntlet on his left hand, blinded by a little leather hood with a silly topknot, which bothered me because it robbed the bird of its dignity. He parked the falcon on a perch—the back of a chair, sometimes—and pulled a bloody carcass out of the satchel slung across his chest: a rabbit, or a smaller bird. He slit it open in the kitchen sink and gave the falcon tidbits of innards to eat. It turned my stomach, but the ease with which he carried out the ritual, his sense of comfort in the kitchen with Nurse and me, made me feel like I was part of his life, not an only child. Sometimes he'd start plucking the dead bird and feathers would drift around the kitchen, and then Nurse would shoo him outside.

He didn't come during the holidays. That's when Danny was there.

It was Easter time, gray-skied and rainy. Danny arrived like the sun. He had skin the color of honey, dark curls tinged with gold, and a constant smile. He had a slight Italian accent too, since he lived in Rome. He slept in the bedroom at the top of the stairs—the one that held the empty space where Mum ought to be—and filled it with life. Every morning I ran into Danny's room, as I now thought of it, and jumped on his bed.

His mother, Zoë, was young and beautiful and exotic: half Indian and a quarter Persian, she told me, though her accent was English like Danny's, flavored with Italian. I loved that she had two dots over the "e" in her name. Her last name wasn't Huston, as I somehow understood that it couldn't be, but Danny's was. We, the Hustons, were so different from everyone around us that I didn't expect us to follow the mother-father-children pattern of the Lynches and the Creaghs or even the O'Tooles. I didn't ask. If everyone else was content with the way things were, so was I.

Zoë had met Dad before he started filming *Freud*, but pregnancy prevented her from playing the part he cast her in (two years later, she played Hagar in his film of *The Bible*). She slept in the Napoleon Room at the Big House. It was called that after the spectacular gilded bed that Napoleon was supposed to have slept in. (I always thought it was so like Dad to have such a bed. In fact it was Mum, the scion of the Bona-Soma-Peppa strain, who found it. A letter from Dad expresses his worry that it may be too short.) I had never gone upstairs at the Big House much before, since I was intimidated by Daddy's majestic suite and the art-filled rooms for important guests. Unlike other women who came to stay—Marietta Tree, Baroness Pauline de Rothschild—Zoë didn't give off the air that she should be approached with care. She laughed easily, and her clothes were floaty and strange, glittering with metallic threads. She let me play with her jewelry. The fact that the Napoleon Room was on the half landing, not all the way up the stairs, somehow fit her. I was in and out of the Napoleon Room, which delighted me because it had a washbasin hidden behind a door that was papered to match the wall, and because I could run circles through the bathroom that it shared with the Bhutan Room just above, and back down the stairs.

In the mornings I went up to the Big House with Danny—first to the Napoleon Room to say good morning to Zoë, then on up the stairs to Daddy's room in the far corner above the drawing room. Daddy would be sitting in his kingly bed, with a red velvet canopy, having breakfast and reading the newspaper. It was a long way across the room from the door. Danny ran straight across the vast distance to kiss Dada, as he called him—which I thought was babyish—while I lingered at the door, running my fingers against the forest-green cut-velvet wallpaper and onto the polished brass of the light switch. Through the curved window near me I could see Daddy's favorite horse, Frisco, grazing in the field. If I looked the other way, beyond the bed, I could just see the armchair in the bathroom upholstered in white terry cloth, as if the chair itself were a towel. I loved the opulence of that room, and though I was welcome, I always tiptoed into it: Daddy's private preserve, with no quarter for anyone to share it. It never occurred to me that Mum might once have slept in it too. In fact, she never did.

I envied Danny his fearlessness, and how bright the world was for him. He loved to ride, even though he fell off his pony, Sixpence, and had to have his arm in a sling. Nothing fazed him. When he stuck his hand in a wasps' nest and got stung all over, he was laughing about it by dinnertime.

I wasn't like that. I knew Daddy wanted me to learn to ride, but when Paddy Lynch put me on the donkey, I clung to its mane and my knees couldn't squeeze the saddle tight enough to hold the sixpences that Paddy put there. I was terrified of falling. When I ran through the woods with Jackie and Caroline, I'd come to a halt at the stream that had carved a little chasm in the damp ground. The earth of the path sloped down on either side, where years of jumping feet had packed it firm, and the stream was probably only a foot or so below. Jackie and Caroline jumped it without breaking stride—then one of them would have to come back and hold out a hand for me. I wasn't just afraid of hurting myself. It was a metaphysical fear. It would break my spirit if I fell.

Danny's presence made me braver. He and Jerry Lynch led us girls into the ruined castle: a thirteenth-century tower which loomed stark and ragged against the sky. We weren't allowed in there; the loose stones were dangerous, and even though its enclosure was surrounded by St. Cleran's, it didn't actually belong to Daddy. We had to climb a tree to get over the wall. I clung to the tree, edging along on my hands and knees, while the others just leaped from branch to wall and down to the forbidden ground. Even though I knew how feeble I was in comparison, once I reached that ground—with Danny helping me—I felt adventurous and strong.

The castle was smothered by dark green ivy. Inside, steps led up in a mossy spiral to a slit with a sloping lower edge, which the boys said was for pouring boiling oil on the enemy attacking below. It was damp and slippery underfoot, and dark. The only light came through arrow slits, until the steps ran out and the walls caved away, leaving the rubble open to the sky.

I felt like I was in one of Enid Blyton's Famous Five books, my favorites. Nurse always bought me a new Enid Blyton at the station bookstall when we took the train to Dublin for the dentist. Daddy disapproved of Enid Blyton, as was the fashion among intellectual parents. It was Gladys—his secretary, the low-voiced woman with the moonlike hair—who told me this, and told me not to tell him about them. I knew he would never see them for himself, as he never set foot in the Little House. Even when he came to play tennis on the court beside the kitchen garden, he always used the garden gate.

Gladys was, in her quiet way, my ally. She had been assigned to tell me, at Claridge's, that Daddy was my father; but when she bent down in the drive and told me to call him "Daddy," I felt it not as a task but as a kindness. She understood my fears. She didn't live at the Big House, as Betty did, but in a studio on the opposite side of the archway from Daddy's. There, in her private space, she wore loose caftans, and sometimes her hair was untied. She was too Anglo-Saxon to look foreign, but she seemed to come from a slower, softer world. I would knock on her door and wait for the calm, deliberate "Come in." Her voice was strangely musical, like a cello idly stroked. She never called me pet names like "darling" or "honey," and had a way of treating me like neither a child nor a grown-up, but simply as a being whom she took on its own terms. Like Daddy, she collected pre-Columbian art, but her pieces were small and friendly, dogs and funny creatures, not like the fearsome idols in the study at the Big House or the museum-quality antiquities immured behind glass. She let me touch them where they stood on shelves in front of her books, and she let me use her typewriter, which was surrounded by high stacks of paper. She seemed to type all day long. I, who traded on cleverness, admired her for it.

❧

I'm looking up at Mum, perched on something high. She's reaching for the top of a Christmas tree, and fiddling something into a knot with the tips of her fingers. Frustrated, she balls it up and hands it down to someone to throw away. It's a piece of sticky tape. I can't figure it out. I saw her twist it up deliberately, so why is she angry and throwing it away?

That's the only memory I have of Mum's Christmases. Did I remember more of them when I was six? I don't know.

At St. Cleran's, Christmas was a performance orchestrated by Betty. One day, as if by magic, a gigantic tree appeared, rising up through the well of the staircase in the Big House, already dripping with balls of silver and gold. Mounds of presents filled the space beneath. They didn't increase as the days led up to Christmas; they appeared all at once with the tree. Like everything at the Big House, it was perfectly done. It was not a family enterprise.

Galway is a long way north. In winter it was dark by five five. On Christmas Eve, everyone squeezed into the hall, bright under the huge chandelier: me and Nurse, Danny and Zoë, Daddy, Mr. and Mrs. Creagh and Karen, all the Lynches, Mary and Mary Margaret and their families, wild-haired gypsy-dark Paddy Coyne, other families from round about, so many I didn't know them all. Everybody talked in whispers.

Bells jingled outside the front door. Betty ran to it, and looked outside. "Santa Claus is here!"

There was a great commotion of more bells and snorting and a lot of "ho-ho-ho"s, and Santa came in through the heavy door. He was big and fat and bearded, exactly as he was supposed to be. His "Merry Christmas!" echoed around the edges of the ceiling. He added, to us children: "The reindeer are waitin' outside. You might give 'em a carrot or two."

I didn't believe in Santa, or at least I thought I didn't. I tried to figure out who this man was, standing by the tree and calling everyone's name in turn to come forward and get their present. Every possible Santa I could think of was there, accounted for, in his regular clothes. In that case, perhaps Santa really did exist. Of course, if there was a Santa, he would come to St. Cleran's exactly when he was wanted, to dish out the presents that I knew Betty had prepared. If I ran into the dining room and looked out the window, would I see reindeer? I didn't want to risk it. What if I wasn't in the hall when Santa called my name?

The first Christmas Eve, I wheeled my doll in her new pram back through the darkness to the Little House. That was what I'd written to Santa to ask for; it was all I wanted, and I was happy. We didn't have a tree in the Little House and all the presents from beneath the Big House tree had been handed out, so I thought that was it, Christmas was over, even though the day itself hadn't yet arrived. The next morning, Nurse gave Danny and me our breakfast, then told me to go with him to the Big House for "family Christmas."

I felt suddenly scared again, and out of place. This was a ritual which families did all over the world—and I didn't know how to do it. I had liked being part of the crowd in the hall. Now I would be on display as Daddy's daughter again. Danny had Zoë for support, and anyway he always knew what to do. Nurse wouldn't be a part of this. I was on my own.

I'd snuck into the drawing room a few times when Daddy wasn't there, just to see what it was like—it was only used by the grown-ups in the evenings. The carpet was cream, and so were the sofas, so that I was afraid of marking them, and on the ceiling was a starburst of gold. The study—the room we usually used—was a deep blue, comfortable and inviting. The drawing room was elegant and formal. Every room in the house held art, but here were the finest pieces. Once there had even been a Monet water-lily painting. Daddy's friend Billy Pearson, a jockey who was his usual partner in escapades, later told me the story of how he had got it.

They had all been in Deauville: Billy and his wife, Mum and Dad and Tony and Anjelica, who were still small. Dad, as he loved to do, had explored the antique shops and seen the painting: dusty, shoved into a corner, vastly underpriced. But he didn't have the $18,000 he needed to buy it, even so. In fact, he had almost none, just what they were living on, and he'd given that to Mum. He demanded it back: he couldn't leave Deauville without the Monet, and the only way to get enough money to pay for it was at the casino. So Mum insisted on going too.

Off they all went, and Dad was on a roll. The chips piled up in front of him at the roulette table, higher and higher—until finally the moment came, and he lost. According to Billy, Mum's face crashed as she saw the croupier's hook pull the whole pile away.

Dad turned to her, and revealed a little stash of chips she hadn't seen him hide.

"It's all right, honey," he said. "We won the Monet."

He'd lost it again a few years before I arrived at St. Cleran's, during another cash crisis. But still the room was filled with treasures: gold objects in cases, iridescent Etruscan glass bottles and Egyptian pieces, and a mysterious painting of an angular, leaping horse, that seemed to be a picture not so much of a horse but of its spirit.

Daddy was sitting on a sofa, holding a tall thin glass with lacy gold patterns around the rim. I couldn't take my eyes off the bubbles in the golden drink inside it. They weren't like the bubbles in orange Fanta, which I once drank enough of to make myself sick; they were small, so small that if they were any smaller I didn't think I'd be able to see them. They made a continuous little explosion, as if the essence of the glass itself were erupting into Daddy's hand.

Zoë was there, in the shimmery clothes I loved, and Betty. They both held bubbling glasses as well. Danny went straight to Daddy, where he sat on the sofa, to be embraced. I did too.

"Merry Christmas, darlings," he said. Betty handed him a wrapped present, which he gave to Danny. Then she went to the door into the marble hall, disappeared, and came back wheeling a bicycle with a ribbon on it—for me.

I felt trapped. The only presents being given out were the "big" presents for Danny and me, and it was up to us to accept them properly, the way sons and daughters were supposed to do on Christmas Day. I was tongue-tied, conscious that I didn't look happy enough about the bicycle, but I was too afraid I'd do the wrong thing in this room. That was wrong too; dimly I dreaded that Daddy might think I was ungrateful. As Danny chattered along, sunny and charming as he always was, all I could think of was the lunchtime gong. When it clanged, the ordeal of "family Christmas" would end.

When Daddy was away, which he was most of the time, we prepared for his return. Betty organized an ongoing drawing competition among us girls, which Daddy would judge when he came home, and award prizes. She told us not to write our names on the back, just our ages, so that the judging would be fair. It never occurred to us that he could tell whose drawing was whose by the age on the back. Only Caroline and I were the same age.

Karen, the oldest by five years or so, was a champion Irish dancer. The Creaghs had an apartment in the basement of the Big House, and once Karen led me inside to show me her four boxes of medals, lined in green velvet. She pointed to two first-place medals in the all-Ireland championship; then she picked out the world championship medal, which she'd won for Ireland. She showed me her competition dress, made of heavy green wool, with a long flap hanging from one shoulder down her back embroidered with complicated knotty patterns. For competitions she did her hair in ringlets. I begged Nurse to roll my hair on sponge curlers overnight so I could have ringlets too.

Karen decided to teach Jackie and Caroline and me to dance so we could put on a performance for Daddy. Betty had matching red skirts and white blouses made for us, and Karen drilled us in the one-hand reel, a two-hand reel for me and Jackie, and a three-hand reel for the finale.

We waited still as statues in the black marble hall, right toes pointed out, hands clasped in fists by our sides. Daddy and his houseguests ranged themselves in the doorway to the inner hall. The Creaghs and Nurse and Mary and Mary Margaret clustered in behind them. Betty started the cassette, and we sprang into motion, like windup toys. We danced with our arms rigid by our sides, no smiles or eye contact allowed, somber in spite of the hopping steps and slow spins as we circled one another and made figure eights on the floor. I danced in the center, pudgy and blond, between buck-toothed Jackie and Caroline with her thick dark-rimmed glasses.

"Wonderful, girls, wonderful," Daddy pronounced as applause echoed around the hall and died away.

Soon I added a double jig to my repertoire—much harder and faster. The fact that I could do Irish dancing proved that I was becoming Irish, which I knew pleased Daddy. I'd named my pet rabbit after a mythical Irish warrior, Oisín, which I thought was the most beautiful name I'd ever heard. When I got a female, Tony named her Gubnit, the stupidest-sounding Irish name he knew. Tony made fun of everything Irish, and I resented it. I felt protective of Ireland, which I loved. My favorite joke, which Nurse told me, was of an Englishwoman asking a train conductor, "Could you tell me when we're at At-henry?" This was our local station. I thought it was hilarious, because the proper pronunciation was "Ath-en-rye." I was in the in crowd now. Not only could I pronounce the place-names, but I laughed at the English.

Still, I knew I wasn't like the other Irish girls. I didn't go to church every Sunday, I didn't get a frilly white dress and make my first Communion. I didn't think of entering Irish-dancing competitions, like Karen, for, even if I'd had the courage, I wasn't at all sure they'd be open to me.

One day I came into the Little House thirsty from the golden dust of the hay barn, where I'd been playing with Jackie and Caroline. The kitchen was empty. I heard noise from the garden room, where the TV was. I was allowed an hour of TV a day: *Skippy the Kangaroo* at five o'clock, and *Sesame Street* after that, and on Tuesdays Nurse would allow me an extra five minutes so I could watch the big wave breaking at the start of *Hawaii Five-O.*

The TV was on—which it never was in the Little House in the middle of the day. I stopped in the doorway, astonished. Nurse was jumping up and down in front of it. Her face was deep red, like a raspberry, with the gray fuzz of her hair on top. She was shouting, and her voice was so hoarse I knew she'd been shouting for a while. I'd never seen anyone so excited, not even when the TV in the staff sitting room at the Big House set the curtains on fire in the middle of a horse race. Nurse was always perfectly controlled—I could hardly believe this was her. I stared at her, fascinated and a little scared, trying on an experimental disapproval. I wondered if I would ever care as much about anything.

Tony was there too. "It's the Ireland–England rugby match," he told me. "It looks like Ireland is going to win."

Nurse didn't look at me. She couldn't drag her eyes from the screen for a second. I'd never known her to watch rugby before, and I knew that she wouldn't care half as much if Ireland were beating Scotland or Wales or France. Her wild excitement was specifically anti-English; and the part of me that wasn't Irish was English still.

I fit in in Ireland, as much as a local celebrity like "Mr. Huston's daughter" ever could. My favorite song was "The Men Behind the Wire," which I thought was the Irish national anthem but was in fact the anthem of the IRA. But I had a British passport and I'd been born in London, so that meant I was a Brit. (I wasn't sure about my mother. She was American but she'd lived in London; still, I didn't think she'd taken British nationality, so she wasn't a proper Brit.)

It hit me: you couldn't actually be both Irish and English. If you were really Irish, you hated the Brits.

When Nurse and I had gone back to London after that first summer at St. Cleran's, I'd seen white letters scrawled on soot-stained bricks: BRITS OUT. On the way to the airport as we returned to Ireland for good, I saw it on the dark steel of railway bridges: BRITS OUT. Those two words were everywhere, and suddenly I felt that they were aimed at me. Everyone I knew in Ireland wanted the Brits out, and one of the men who worked at St. Cleran's was rumored to actually be in the IRA. Daddy was officially Irish—even though he was American, he'd taken Irish nationality. Ireland was, for all I knew, my permanent home, but I was still a Brit—the only one among them. Once a Brit, always a Brit. It was a taint that could never be erased. Maybe even Nurse held it against me.

It was around this time that I started seeing flames in the corner of my bedroom. They were always high up, where the walls met the ceiling, and curiously gentle: not raging, not crackling, but silently lapping, as if they were made from some insubstantial golden-red water freed from gravity. I was awake when I saw them, on the verge of sleep. I know they weren't real, they were halfway between imagination and hallucination. Still, they frightened me. I was very afraid of fire; but the knowledge that the flames were visions frightened me even more. I was conjuring them up, and I couldn't stop myself. I never told Nurse that I saw the flames, never even called out to her that I couldn't sleep. I lay awake in a strangely comfortable terror. The flames weren't going to get worse, the house wasn't going to burn down. The intensity of feeling was almost luxurious.

My mind was unreliable—I knew it was starting to betray me. I had a vivid memory of running around the table in the middle of the kitchen in Mum's house on Maida Avenue, when I tripped and fell against the table. My thumb was sucked into a knothole in the wood, so that I had to yank it free. The knothole pulled up a lump in the middle of the knuckle, like a wart, which never went away. Betty didn't believe me; she said the lump came from sucking my thumb. Nurse had no recollection of that scene in the kitchen, which

I remembered so completely. I was ashamed that I sucked my thumb, and tried not to do it when anyone could see. I was torn about the lump. I wanted it to go, because it looked like I sucked my thumb, but secretly I treasured it as a relic of my life before Mum died, and I knew that thumb-sucking had nothing to do with it. And then, when I did stop sucking my thumb, the lump went away.

How could I have made that memory up? It was so detailed, so explicit. I could feel the grip of the vacuum as my thumb was held in the knothole, hear the pop and flinch with the pain when I yanked it out. My faith in myself, in my knowledge of what was real and what wasn't, shattered. And yet another thread snapped that had connected me to the house on Maida Avenue, and my mother.

5

When I was three, Mum took me to her father's holiday house on Lago Maggiore, in northern Italy. I think we flew. A year and a half later, she decided to go by car, and she didn't take me. That's when she was killed.

Grampa's house was tall and white-painted, with a terrace overlooking the lake's edge. It was summer, and the tile floors felt cool and dry under the sweaty soles of my feet. Sometimes waves would lap against the rocks below the house, and excitedly I would trace the line of white foam out to the middle of the lake until my eyes landed on the speedboat that had caused them. Time moved slowly there; even at three, I felt it.

One day, as we lingered around the lunch table, the doors to the terrace half shut against the heat, there was a thud from upstairs. I jumped half off my chair.

I stared up at the chandelier, its glass diamonds jangling, tinkling, falling silent—waiting for the crash I was sure would come.

"Don't worry, it's fixed tight," said Nana as she fished a fat drop of crystal out of the bowl of peaches on the table. She chuckled, like the sound of water rumbling when you turn on the hot-water tap. "It's just Grampa coming down from standing on his head."

Mum is only a shadow in that memory, though I know she was there.

I remembered Nana well when I saw her again in the summer of 1971, the summer I would turn seven: her broad smile, her short waves of gray hair swept back from her forehead as if she were facing into a brisk wind. She was standing outside the customs hall of JFK Airport, in a sleeveless dress which left her strong arms bare.

"Welcome to America!"

She hugged me, her large handbag bouncing against my back. Her laugh rang against the hard marble floor. Nana's laugh burst like a mortar shell, shattering the membrane that separated me from the world. At first I felt assaulted by it—but I grew to love it for what it said about Nana: her lack of inhibition, her imperviousness to embarrassment, her devil-may-care willingness to have fun. I was dogged by shyness and second thoughts, and whenever Nana laughed—which was often—they lost a little of their power.

I found out later that Dad hated Nana's laugh. He thought it manic and unladylike. I got the impression that somehow it scared him.

The air outside the terminal was thick and sticky in my nose as Nana led Nurse and me to a long blue Cadillac. I'd never known air like that, so heavy I could feel its weight on my skin. On top of the long flight from Ireland, it made me feel fuzzy-headed, and I struggled to focus as we drove east along the Long Island Expressway.

There were no roads that big and crowded in Ireland, and the Cadillac went fast, with a low growling roar.

My uncle Fraser drove. He wore black mirrored sunglasses, held by thin wire frames, which made him look casually sinister, like a villain in *Hawaii Five-O*—as I imagined one, never having seen it past the opening titles. He didn't talk much, which I soon sensed was due not to dark intentions but to a kind of diminishment of spirit. He seemed to have no work other than to attend to Grampa, driving him back and forth from the city (as it was always referred to), doing whatever errand needed doing. He'd married a woman with six children— tiny Aunt Rose, who marched for women's lib and burned her bra at the state capitol—and even in his own house he seemed overwhelmed. He was the youngest of Grampa's five children, and I wondered if he'd spent his childhood being constantly told to shut up.

Finally we reached the town of Miller Place, and turned up a dirt driveway, bordered by long grass and high hedges of honeysuckle. We passed a house with a garden in front, then the road plunged into the shadows of a thickety wood. On the far side of the wood, up a little hill, stood Nana and Grampa's house: flat-roofed, with an upper story like the pilot's cabin of a ship surrounded by a wide skirt of roof. There on the roof was Grampa, on his head.

He was wearing shorts. I could see his bare, broad back and his legs, crossed at the ankles, confidently reaching into the sky. His face was turned away from the driveway, as if it didn't matter to him when we arrived, or if we did at all. When the car stopped, I could hear him:

OH what a BEAU-tee-full MORRR . . . NING!
OH what a BEAU-tee-full DAY!

"There's Grampa," said Nana for my benefit, barely looking at him herself. He didn't come down off his head, or show any sign that our arrival might be a reason to stop what he was doing and do something else, like say hello. That was pretty much how I remembered him from the house on Lago Maggiore—self-contained and upside down. This time I was old enough to wonder why he was singing about the morning when it was already afternoon.

Grampa spent most of his waking hours on the throne of his own triangled arms. Like an obsessive, crazy version of Dad, he expected his world to shape itself to him.

"We're having a real American barbecue for your first day here," Nana said to me as we went inside. "Have you ever had a hamburger?"

I had, the kind that Nurse made in the kitchen of the Little House, ground beef with diced onions and parsley, held together with egg, and I liked them a lot. I wondered how an American hamburger could be different, but I was shy of asking. Besides, I had an Irish accent now and Nana was barely able to understand me.

"Have a rest, then we'll go down to your uncle Nappy's house."

I couldn't believe my ears. In England and Ireland, a nappy was what babies peed and pooped in. I'd never be able to call him that. I settled on "Uncle Nap," but it never felt quite right, so I tried not to call him anything.

He had actually been christened Anthony, after Grampa, but when he was a baby Grampa decided he looked like Napoleon. Of course, a lot of babies look like Napoleon. But nothing could argue Grampa out of a conviction once he got it into his head, and here was visible evidence of his own grandfather's Bonaparte heritage. I'm sure, if he was alive, he'd look at a photo of my own son as a baby with his hand stuck between the buttons of his shirt and see only further proof of the impressive strength of the Bona-Peppa-Soma strain.

Uncle Nap was in the garden in front of his house, wearing shorts and a shirt unbuttoned all the way, a big spiky fork in one hand. Smoke leaked out of a shiny contraption in front of him. His French wife, Aunt Dani, was laying out platters of coleslaw and other salady things in the kitchen. I was handed a plate made of paper. Its floppiness worried me.

"This," said Uncle Nap, forking it off the grill and onto the bun that Nana had laid open on my plate, "is a real American hamburger."

It was weirdly flat and compacted, as if an elephant had sat on it. I wasn't at all sure how to handle it.

"Put the top on and pick it up! Wait a minute, don't you want some ketchup?"

My cousin Martine, two years older than me, was staring in amazement, as if she couldn't believe that anyone could never have seen a hamburger bun before. Self-consciously I bit into it. The bun was cottony and cardboardy at the same time, how a box of Q-tips would taste if it had been ground up and baked. I could barely swallow it. I saw Nana's face as she watched me pick at the hamburger patty with a fork, and I knew I'd disappointed her.

I'd never been in a house as informal as Uncle Nap's. The kitchen bled into the living room (no "drawing room," no "study"), and my cousins had the run of it, getting their own food when they wanted it and eating with the grown-ups as if that were normal. The Lynches' house at St. Cloran's was the closest to it that I'd known, but that was different: the Lynches worked for us and they had seven children, which I realized was, in Mum's and Daddy's world, unseemly. In the houses I knew, the children had their separate spaces and separate routines—and it was the same in the books I read, like *Peter Pan* and *The Secret Garden*. I'd always felt peripheral: not unwanted or unloved, but I knew my place. I was drawn to my cousins' freedom, but I knew it wasn't mine.

I felt like a freak. My voice, my clothes, the food I was familiar with: nothing fit in here. This was my family, I knew, but I was a stranger. I'd never get the hang of being American, I thought, and I decided I didn't want to. I was only there for the summer, anyway.

On Sunday mornings, all the cousins would come up to Nana and Grampa's house. Grampa would kneel in the middle of the living room, lace his fingers tightly together with his forearms flat on the floor, nestle his head into the cradle of his hands, curl into an upside-down fetal position, and finally, methodically, power up into a headstand. Six or seven or eight pairs of legs would fling themselves up into the air next to him, in a raggedy line. Grampa would kick it off with the enthusiasm that was his almost delusional spiritual practice:

> *"OH what a BEAU-tee-full MORRR . . . NING!"*

As Grampa blasted it out, the tempo thudding like a battering ram, the cousins droned along dutifully: "Oh what a beautiful day . . ."

One verse was all that was required. I'm not sure I ever heard Grampa sing beyond that, even by himself. Then seven or eight or nine pairs of feet would hit the floor, and Grampa would dole out a quarter to each cousin in pocket money. It seemed measly, even to a little girl who had never had pocket money before.

Nana tried to teach me to stand on my head so that I could join in this family scene. I could barely put my head on the floor. When I finally built up the courage to kick up my legs, with Nana holding my ankles, it was the worst combination of feeling lost in space and on the verge of crashing to the earth. I was afraid of Grampa's contempt, so after that first Sunday I made sure I wasn't in the living room when my cousins arrived.

The singing was for the benefit of *prana*, because it encouraged deep, regular breathing. When Grampa was right way up, he hawked up mucus from his throat every few minutes and spat it with great force and satisfaction. Old newspapers were spread out all around him—changed daily by Nana, I suppose, as I can't imagine Grampa doing anything so menial for himself. They covered great swathes of his room, which took up the whole of the upstairs. (Nana slept in a room off the kitchen, as far as possible from Grampa.) When he came down to watch television, the coffee table and the floor around it, along with half the sofa, disappeared under drifts of yellowing newsprint.

This was, for Grampa, pretty much what yoga amounted to: standing on your head and singing, and sitting in lotus position and spitting. It was, as far as I could see, more or less what his days amounted to; and he was as contented as a cat. Uncle Nap ran the restaurant in the city. Nana cooked his meals and did his laundry, and aside from that, she more or less ignored him.

Every day, in late morning, Nana packed us all into her wood-paneled station wagon to go to the Beach Club. The house actually had its own beach, at the base of the cliff on which it sat: but it was a long way down—and up. It was solitary, too, and—though he never went down there—part of Grampa's domain. The Beach Club was Nana's. She would sit under a big umbrella in a folding chair, or wade into the calm water and float on her back. Nurse didn't swim, just sat under the umbrella looking hot, with *Reader's Digest* on her lap. Aunt Dani lay on a lounge chair in the sun, with the straps of her bikini top undone and pebbles wedged between her toes. There was something intensely feminine about Aunt Dani's routine, as if she were doing something in public that ought to be private. I put it down to her being French.

I'd been to the beach a few times in Ireland, at the cottage in Connemara and at the O'Tooles' house in Clifden, but the water was so cold it made my teeth chatter. The Long Island Sound was a bath in comparison. There were no waves, except on stormy days. I could see Connecticut on the far side.

Martine and Nancy—Uncle Fraser's stepdaughter, the only girl among Aunt Rose's seven children—taught me to swim out to the raft moored offshore. We jumped off in cannonballs, and caught little stingless transparent jellyfish and stuffed them down one another's bathing suit. We did the dead man's float, face-down, and pulled our bathing suits aside to compare our tans.

Both Martine and Nancy had dark Italian skin, and I roasted myself trying to be like them. Every night I sprayed on Solarcaine to soothe the burn.

When we were tired of swimming, or in the hour after lunch during which we were forbidden to go into the water, we'd walk up and down the pebbly shore looking for beach glass. It came from bottles thrown overboard from boats, we figured, but it was transformed by the gentle, relentless action of the ocean into something mystical and strange: the hard surfaces sandblasted into a translucent fog of color, all jagged edges worn away so that the shards were rounded like cabochons. The pieces lay everywhere among the ordinary stones, the way you'd find jewels in an Enid Blyton story. Any pieces that weren't perfectly smooth and misted over we threw back into the water as far as we could.

Most of the beach glass was white, green, or brown. Occasionally we'd find a piece of blue, always tiny, as bright as a sapphire. We decided the blue had to come from Milk of Magnesia bottles, though it was hard to believe that something so rare and precious came from such lowly beginnings. Once I found a piece of red, about the size of my pinkie fingernail. I thought it was more beautiful than the ruby in the ring Martine wore sometimes, which had been found on the sink in the ladies' room at the restaurant in the city.

On August 26, I told everyone at the Beach Club that it was my birthday. One man replied that it was his birthday too, and he was seventy-seven—exactly seventy years older than me. I was amazed, almost, that it could be possible for the two of us to be there, in the same place; I felt the hand of destiny. Two days later, the seventy-seven-year-old man appeared with a present for me: a jewelry chest about the size of a shoe box, with dovetailed joints and three drawers lined with red felt. He'd made it himself, like a woodcarver in a fairy tale. It came back to Ireland with me and sat on the windowsill, where the early sun, slanting across the courtyard, made the wood glow. I had little to keep in it, but that didn't matter; the chest itself was the treasure, since it had been made especially for me. Fingering its tiny knobs, pulling open the smooth-sliding drawers, I was the princess. I sat beside my little chest every morning, practicing my knitting—casting on, unraveling, casting on, unraveling—while Nurse brushed my hair.

"You're going to come and live in the Big House, Allegra," Betty O'Kelly said to me soon after we got back. "The Little House is being sold. Your father can't afford to keep it anymore."

I felt like the earth was falling away from under me. I had thought St. Cleran's was forever and unchanging; it had existed as the Hustons' home for longer than I'd been alive. The idea that Daddy didn't have enough money to keep it was terrifying. He was the king here, and kings didn't have to sell. And a child—me—was going to live in the grown-ups' house.

"Where will Nurse sleep?"

"In Mary Margaret's room. We've had to let Mary Margaret go."

I didn't dare ask about everyone else: the Lynches, Paddy Coyne. Their homes were part of the Little House courtyard. My world was being broken in two.

My toys and clothes were moved into the Bhutan Room, across from Betty's room at the top of the stairs—the room I had run through on my circuit from the Napoleon Room, when Zoë slept there. At seven, I was a bit old for running in circles, and I felt very grown-up to have this beautiful room for my own. No changes were made to it for me—for a child. Its identity was fixed, and I stayed in it like any other guest. The walls were dark blue, and the bedspread and curtains were made of golden-orange embroidered squares which, Betty told me, were Bhutanese wedding cloth. Daddy had brought them back from Bhutan himself. It was a Himalayan kingdom closed to outsiders, misty and mythical. The sort of place where Daddy, unlike mere mortals, could go.

I ate breakfast at the round table in the bay window of the dining room, and sometimes Daddy would come down to eat buttered toast and read the newspaper across from me. I'd hear the crunch of gravel and see Paddy Lynch drive around the corner below me, then I'd lug my book bag down the steps from the front door, proud of how big and heavy it was. I got to school half an hour earlier than the other girls for my French lesson with Sister Annunciata, which consisted of a walk through the halls of the convent singing "Frère Jacques" and "Alouette"—which were probably the only French she knew.

My school friends didn't come over to play anymore. Even Jackie and Caroline grew distant. The chest of dressing-up clothes, which was our favorite thing to play, hadn't come to the Big House with me. I did my homework, properly, in the study; my books stayed in my room. This wasn't a house where dolls or games could be left lying around.

At night I would hear Seamus, the Irish wolfhound, patrolling up and down the stairs. He spent his days sleeping on the first half landing, and you had to pick your way across him to get up- or downstairs. He was so big that once, when I was four, Paddy Coyne had held me on his back and let me ride him around the kitchen of the Little House. His long, old legs plodded in a rhythm slower than you'd expect from a dog. Dad loved it that guests would hear those padding footfalls and think it was the ghost.

The ghost's name was Daly. For some reason he'd been hanged, and the women of the house had watched from the upstairs windows. After that the windows had been blocked up. Dad and Mum had unblocked them, and let Daly's ghost back in. Dad claimed that one woman houseguest actually saw Daly, when everyone else had gone out with the hunt and she'd been sitting alone in the study reading: the door had opened to admit a man dressed in eighteenth-century costume, who saluted her wordlessly and left again.

I'm sure Dad provided the ghost, though he never admitted to it: a not-very-local man, an outfit from the film costumers Bermans

& Nathans, a briefing on what to do and when to do it. He loved practical jokes, and wouldn't have let an opportunity like that slip by. At the time, I was never sure whether to believe Betty when she said Daly's ghost was real. My brain and my instincts rebelled against it. My mother's absolute vanishment proved that the dead didn't come back to any kind of life. I never heard her voice, smelled her scent, saw her shadow disappearing around a corner, or felt her presence watching over me. There were no signs of her in the material world. The only traces I had left of her were disappearing into the treacherous depths of my memory.

That Christmas, the *Irish Times* ran a coloring competition, a big drawing of Santa with presents that filled half a broadsheet page. I entered it, mainly because Karen Creagh was doing it. She had a red-and-blue color scheme, which I thought was perfect. It would have been cheating to copy it, so, feeling unimaginative and second best, I used purple and yellow. I won: I'd been judged the best colorer in all Ireland. I didn't believe it. Karen's entry, for one, was much better than mine, and there had to be hundreds more. I decided it was a fix. I'd only won because I was "Mr. Huston's daughter" and he was such a huge celebrity in Ireland that they—the *Irish Times*, the people who were in charge of Ireland—wanted to make him happy. My prize was a beautiful wooden case filled with artist's oils, like the ones Daddy used.

Nothing could convince me that I was artistic. Mum had been— Betty showed me the place in the basement of the Big House where she used to arrange flowers—and obviously Daddy was. I knew that those paints were not legitimately mine. I never touched them.

In the Little House the previous Christmas, Tony had made a Nativity. He'd gone out to the thicket of bamboo at the far end of the garden, where the fox lived, and cut stalks for the stable—it was going to look like a log cabin. I watched as he held them upright, slicing them lengthways with a kitchen knife, straight down, one, then the next, until the knife caught on a joint of the bamboo and slid diagonally across the pad of flesh between the thumb and forefinger of his left hand. First there was just a long red line, then blood started to pulse out of it. The skin pulled apart. Tony stared down at his hand as if it belonged to someone else. Nurse jumped up and ran, sloshing through the gravel, through the gates, across the bridge, up to the Big House. I raced after her. We found Betty, who put Tony in her car and took him to the hospital in Galway. Nurse couldn't drive.

While Tony was gone, Nurse told me the story of when he'd fallen off a horse and been dragged through a wood, his foot caught in the stirrup. He'd needed nearly a hundred stitches in his head that time. I began to enfold lack of creative skill into my identity, along with physical cowardice. Carving knives wouldn't slice me open, and fallen branches wouldn't tear at my skull.

Lying in bed in the Bhutan Room with a fever, I felt guilty. Nurse was in Dublin, on her annual week's holiday. It wasn't anyone else's job to take care of me, so I ought to be able to take care of myself. I'd been allowed to come live in the Big House with the grown-ups; I wasn't supposed to be sick.

Dr. Payne came from Loughrea to examine me. He diagnosed spots on my tonsils.

Before he went down to dinner, Daddy came into the Bhutan Room to see me. He was wearing a velvet jacket and a silk shirt with a plain front and a high rolled collar. The silk, when I touched the cuff, was softly magnetic under my fingertips. He sat on the bed beside me, and laid out the crossword from the newspaper. I loved crosswords, and he loved that I was good at them. Each clue I solved was a rush of warmth, as I felt his pride in me. When Betty came in, also dressed for dinner, he kissed me on the cheek and they went downstairs.

I could hear the talk floating up from below, then hollow footsteps as people crossed the wood-floored hall to the dining room. I couldn't sleep; I was too hot with fever. There were the footsteps again, clattery this time, crossing the marble hall to the drawing room. Then the door opened, and it was Daddy.

Maybe I was dreaming him. I was amazed that he had remembered me, amazed that he had left the laughing and drinking to come upstairs and sit on my bed again, draw a hand across my clammy forehead and make sure there was a glass of juice beside me. We were in a cocoon, just the two of us: in this high, dark, quiet space. Did they notice, downstairs, that he wasn't there? Of course they must. But no one would guess that he was here in the Bhutan Room, with me.

A few months later, just as suddenly, Nurse and I were moved back into the Little House. Talk of selling vanished. All was back to normal. When school finished, I packed my blue suitcase again—the one that went with me everywhere, which had my initials, A.H., stenciled on it in white—and we went back to Nana and Grampa's house for the summer. I left my treasure chest behind.

6

{ornament}

Grampa's restaurant was in a brownstone at 150 East Fifty-fifth Street, with an awning over the sidewalk reading, in cursive script, *Tony and Tony's Wife*. I thought it was insulting—but characteristic of Grampa—that he had a name and Nana didn't. I've since learned that it was originally just called *Tony's Wife*, and was a spin-off of Grampa's first restaurant, *Tony's*. When they closed the first one, they merged the names.

I imagine Nana at the time she married Grampa. It was during Prohibition, and the restaurant was a speakeasy; he had two motherless children, officials to charm, policemen to bribe, and liquor to hide. Scottish as she was, Nana was swept off her feet by Grampa's swashbuckling canniness, along with her own maternal instincts. It was a strange marriage; not devoid of affection, but marked by emotional and physical cruelty.

In his letters to Mum, Grampa swings between contempt for Nana and dependence on her. In his eyes, she existed either to enable his glory or as a drag on it. She, not surprisingly, was prone to depression, and turned to Mum as an ally. She told Mum about going in front of some city board for a liquor license and being asked if she'd ever been convicted of a crime. "Marrying Tony Soma," she answered, which made the liquor-board guys laugh. It made me laugh too—until I sensed Mum's silently pleading misery at being caught in the battle between her father and her stepmother: on one side, blood, the man to whom she owed everything, and on the other, no blood, but the only mother love she'd consciously known.

There was never any question of Nana leaving her life with Grampa, and by the time I knew her, she'd carved out her own space. I liked seeing her in the city, being served a solitary, queenly dinner at the round table in "Nana's sitting room" on the first floor above the restaurant by a waiter in formal jacket and bow tie. It was only when I saw the waiter bowing slightly as he set the plate in front of her, shaking out her napkin for her, that I realized that I didn't like how Grampa treated her. Grampa saw himself as an unusually wise and spiritually evolved being, and, so very pleased with himself, he considered himself above the demands of common kindness. I didn't buy it.

No one said it, but I got the idea that Grampa hated Daddy. I picture the two of them as chimpanzees tussling over Mum, with Grampa thrashing in fury as he, the old alpha, was toppled by the new. As Daddy's daughter, I took it personally. I was loyal to him. I couldn't help comparing him to Grampa: each was a king in his own realm, surrounded by a court. But Daddy's world had been run for everybody's happiness, while Grampa's had one transcendent purpose, which was himself. Grampa set himself above the world; Daddy enthusiastically took part in it. When Daddy looked at me, sketched me, I was a person, flesh and blood in front of him. I was real.

On one trip to the city sometime in August, Martine and I were dressed up in our best clothes and taken to Radio City Music Hall for the premiere of Daddy's latest movie, *Fat City*. It was a story of down-and-out boxers, and way over the heads of two little girls (though later Martine excitedly told me she knew what it meant when one of the characters said, "He threw me down on that bed and he raped me!"). Afterward, there was a party at the Metropolitan Museum of Art. Martine and I ran around among the tall statues. The white marble floor was pale and cold, hard beneath our feet. Everything glittered: the marble, the lights, the beaded dresses and jewels. Daddy was at the center of it; it was like seeing his power source, flashes of electricity whizzing around him. It energized him; it made the kingdom of St. Cleran's possible.

Standing beside Daddy was a woman unlike anyone I'd ever met. Her hair fell back from her face in waves, like a lion's mane. Her shoulders were bare, and her skin was tanned and freckled by the sun. She was much younger than him—and younger than the grand women who had visited St. Cleran's and stayed in the Gray Room, those ladies with thick lipstick, pale skin, and patronizing hands. She didn't wear that slashing lipstick, and she was wearing a dress that none of those women would have worn: covered all over in pale lavender sequins and held up only at the back of her neck, like a bathing suit. Those women had carried hard, invisible shells around themselves, like display cases; she gave the impression of hiding nothing.

"This is Cici," said Daddy. She sank down so that our faces were level, and took both my hands for a moment, as if to see whether I was prepared to be hugged. I wasn't—she'd taken me completely by surprise. Even Zoë hadn't done anything like that.

Cici's smile was square, seeming to turn down at the corners because it didn't turn up. There was something wonderfully casual and self-possessed about it, as if she were smiling for nobody's pleasure but her own. If you shared it, you were sharing a joke, or a secret. I didn't know what the secret was, but I loved the complicity of her smile.

When we said good-bye, Cici embraced me. This time I let her, willingly. I couldn't understand why she was genuinely pleased to meet me, but I accepted wholeheartedly that she was. I had no idea what connection she had to Daddy—or might have to me. My universe had fixed points: Daddy, Nurse, Betty, Gladys, Nana and Grampa. It didn't occur to me that the stars might shift their courses, or that the very shape of my universe might change out of recognition. I'm not sure I even wondered whether I would see Cici again.

Not long afterward, Daddy wrote to tell me that he and Cici had been married. I think the letter said that he hoped we would become close. He didn't use the word "stepmother"—and I didn't think of her as a replacement for Mum since I had no conception of Mum as Daddy's wife. In any case, Daddy was virtually a different species from the husbands-and-wives-and-children whom I knew. Theirs was not a pattern that I expected Daddy—or Daddy and me—to follow.

He also told me that I wouldn't be going back to St. Cleran's. Nana and Grampa's house was my home now.

I didn't ask him, or anyone else, why I'd been exiled from St. Cleran's. His marriage to Cici obviously had something to do with it, but I didn't blame her. I couldn't picture her at St. Cleran's, with its rainy skies and headscarf-wearing women and a butler banging a gong to announce lunch. I didn't know much about her, other than that she was from Los Angeles, and she was clearly at home in Daddy's world of money and famous friends. She wasn't an actress; it didn't occur to me that she might "be" anything other than herself. I understood why Daddy was entranced by her. I was. Somehow I had the sense that she knew who I was, too. Maybe she had convinced Daddy that I was better off in Long Island with my cousins than as a solitary Irish princess with the groom's children for friends. Fleetingly I wondered whether I should have put more effort into becoming friends with the other girls at the convent school in Loughrea.

Still, after a second summer collecting beach glass with my

cousins, I wasn't unhappy with the change. I sensed that Daddy was starting off on a new life and leaving the old one behind. It seemed natural that I would be left in his wake. Other people had been found to look after me, and nobody seemed to think I would have any feelings about it at all—so, conveniently, I didn't. If Daddy and I weren't both living at St. Cleran's—which had happened only in short bursts, anyway—I had no conception of what life with Daddy could possibly be.

Great chasms shivered the cliff below Nana and Grampa's house, scoring its surface into deep wrinkles like tissue paper that's been used too many times. It was, visibly, falling away. When Grampa had built the house—when Mum was a girl and first living on her own in California—he'd built a bocce court between the house and the cliff edge: a long narrow rectangle of sand rimmed with boards. Now it was half gone, and the cliff edge crept closer to the house every day. The wooden staircase that led down to the beach ended in midair.

The certainty that one day the house itself would tumble too fascinated me, the way disasters do in a country you've barely heard of. It was neither sad nor frightening, just inevitable and satisfyingly dramatic. I didn't like the house much. Despite all its windows, it felt dark, and it was flimsy after the thick stone of St. Cleran's. The Irish windows that I loved were set deep, so that looking through them felt like looking through a telescope or a peephole, and the golden-gray light ran liquid through the old, swirling glass. The Long Island glass was as flat and featureless as plastic, and marred by ugly screens. I was offended by the miserly shallowness of the windowsills.

Nurse and I slept in the guest bedroom—she in the double bed, which I soon joined her in, and I, theoretically, in the single one beside it. The white candlewick bedspreads were thin, like the windows: worn and saggy by nature, they pulled my spirit down. I'd grown accustomed to rooms Mum had furnished with deep colors and strange objects enriched by the marks of age. Here, old things were just old: tired and visibly ready for their end.

And here too there was talk of selling up. The place was too big; Grampa couldn't support all these households. I bridled inwardly, on everyone's behalf but my own. Uncle Nap worked hard running the restaurant in the city, and I didn't see how it could be his fault that its heyday was past. Uncle Fraser didn't have a real job—but Grampa required a flunky, and if it wasn't Uncle Fraser, who would it be?

I didn't miss St. Cleran's, in the sense of longing to be back there. There was no point. That temporary move to the Big House had shut me down. I was to be housed where convenience dictated; I had felt, in the heart of my family, like a guest. I would always stay in other people's rooms, so I might as well get used to it. I'd just been moved on again—and somewhere in my mind I knew it wouldn't be the last time. I didn't think of asking for a poster or a bright bedspread, or color on the walls. I had a nomad's indifference. But I didn't have a nomad's soul.

A few of my things from Ireland caught up with me five or six years later. I never saw my treasure chest again.

Grampa descended from his upstairs realm every night for dinner, and to watch the news on TV. It was 1972: every night, flag-draped coffins came home from Vietnam, families cried over MIAs and POWs, angry people marched against the war. Then, during the Olympics—which Nana and I watched fervently—the Israeli athletes were murdered. The world outside was full of death, mourning, hijacked planes and cruise ships—and I was comforted. I wasn't the only one who had seen someone they loved disappear into nothingness; my mother wasn't the only one who died. What had happened to me was important enough to be on the news—but multiplied so many times that it was normal. It cheered me that there were protests:

people who wouldn't accept it and wanted it changed. Still, I felt wiser than they were. I knew that death was unjust, and didn't care.

Mum was visible in the house, but never spoken of. On the wall near the fireplace was a vertical row of oval black silhouettes of Grampa's five children, as children. On the mantelpiece rested a big, unframed print of Philippe Halsman's famous photograph *The Act of Creation:* Mum's face and bare shoulders framed by a carved picture frame held in the crook of a naked man's arm as he lies on his side, his elaborately muscled back to the camera, while the artist Jean Cocteau reaches through the frame to draw a paintbrush along Mum's eyebrow. It is, in its way, everything Grampa wished for his beautiful daughter to be: a muse, an object of art. A three-dimensional human as the punch line of an artist's joke.

It bothered me that the photograph wasn't framed. I knew it ought to have been; neither Mum nor Dad would have left it leaning against the wall, bending under its own weight, fading and staining in the humid air. Maybe Grampa was angry at Mum for having died, I thought, and in revenge he was letting her photograph molder away.

There was no sign of Mum the person with a life of her own: no photos of her grown-up and inhabiting her life; no photos of her with Tony and Anjelica or me. I wondered if for Grampa she'd died—or been embalmed—long before: when she left New York, left him. It nagged at me that the unreal Mum in this house—her face blacked out in the silhouette, objectified in the photograph—was more materially real than the Mum whose image faded and flickered inside my head. It was as if one Mum was the shadow, or the echo, of the other. When I looked at that photo—as I did many times a day, every time I walked through the living room—I couldn't be sure which was which.

I was retracing Mum's footsteps—but backward. From Maida Avenue to St. Cleran's to Long Island—and with each step I took, the last place disappeared into Mum's future. I brought nothing with me but my clothes and my blue suitcase, which was mine because it had my initials on it—and Nurse, who was so much a part of me (now that she and I were equally foreigners) that I hardly conceived of her as a separate person. She never talked of the past. I had no tangible evidence that my previous worlds had ever existed, no proof of Mum's future and her death, but me. I felt dizzy sometimes, as if I were hovering near the ceiling and watching my mind turn actual memories into illusions, or wipe them away.

I was, I sensed, the living shape of Grampa's loss of Mum, and the cascade of disappointment and fury he had felt when her life didn't turn out to be as grand and historic as he had hoped. Like my dead mother—like every person in Grampa's world—I was more abstract than real. Something like affection emanated from him occasionally, in my direction. It felt impersonal, a condition of his blood pumping, like body heat or breath.

Most of the time, he seemed not even to care, or to notice, that I was there. It was easy not to disturb him. Martine and I would sometimes spy on him as he sat in lotus position in his room, and when we rode our bikes outside, we would look up and see him on the flat roof, upside down. Usually he wore a ruglike wrap around his middle which, when he stood on his head, fell the other way and covered his chest. He didn't believe in underwear. When I started school, fourth grade, I never dared invite friends over to play.

"Look, Allegra. Come and see this."

Nana held up a magazine: *Vogue*. She flattened it open on the dining table. Underneath her strong, weathered fingers was a photo of a dark-haired girl with her hand to her cheek, gazing soulfully out at me.

"That's your sister. That's Anjelica."

I knew I had a sister and her name was Anjelica, but that was about all. I hadn't seen her since the turbulent, forgotten months after Mum died. She was, by now, nearly as lost to me as Mum was.

As I looked at her picture, a sense of recognition came to me, dimmed by strangeness. Was I really remembering Anjelica's own face? The dark coloring and arched eyebrows were Mum's.

In the three years I'd lived at St. Cleran's, Anjelica had never come there. Though I knew Daddy was her father, and though Tony came to visit, I didn't expect her to. She was the goddesslike creature who had inhabited St. Cleran's—and my room—before me, in the golden age when Mum was still alive, and who had left a mark so deep and lasting it would survive for all the decades of Angelica Healy's life. A visit from her would have been very nearly supernatural.

She was living in New York now, Nana told me, and working as a model. Soon she would come out to Miller Place to see me.

Anjelica was tall—taller than anyone else—and thin, with the bony angles of someone who was important in the world. Her clothes—I don't remember what they were—seemed dramatically casual, like nothing anyone in Miller Place would wear. We were either sloppy, or self-consciously dressed up like my teacher, Miss Burdi, a tiny woman whose long fingernails always matched her outfit, changing daily from green to blue to black to yellow. I was probably wearing my favorite outfit, which came from Kmart: a shocking-pink polyester T-shirt and matching stretchy pants.

Anjelica seemed distracted and distant, an exotic bird in a chicken run. My imagination strained to connect her to my earth. We were ordinary and suburban in Miller Place, despite half-naked Grampa on his head on the roof. I wasn't quite sure why she came to see me. What interest could I possibly hold for her? Neither of us knew what to say to the other. I showed off my bicycle-riding skills, waving with one hand. She didn't look impressed, which made me feel better about my half-cracked courage. I didn't think she'd have been any more impressed if I had let go with two hands, like Martine and Nancy did.

Because she was my sister, it made sense to me that she wanted to see me again, and brought me into the city to stay with her. Even so, I wouldn't have been surprised if she had disappeared without another word. Because, like Daddy, she existed on a more exalted plane, that would have made perfect sense too.

She took me with her on a modeling assignment. I watched her being dressed and made up, seemingly oblivious to the people fussing around her. Then she stretched out on the floor, on a giant sheet of white paper. The lights were so bright that I had to squint, but she seemed not to notice them. She knotted her fingers in her hair—which I'd watched being rolled and sprayed into the kind of curls my hair would never hold (my Irish ringlets had always fallen out by lunchtime). As the photographer jumped about, clicking his camera, she moved in slow motion, making constant tiny alterations to her pose, like a creature lifted and curled by the gentle swell of waves.

She looked comfortable, at rest in herself. This was, in my eyes, the real Anjelica; she'd been awkward in Miller Place because there she was in disguise, a goddess who'd had to put on human form. Here, in a secret studio suspended in the midst of a blindly bustling New York City, the handmaidens—who had seemed to be dressing her up—were actually removing the disguise. I was an outsider who had been allowed into this sacred space only because I was her sister: a sister with feet of clay, but her sister nonetheless. I felt favored. I realized that everyone I knew in Miller Place would live their whole lives without ever seeing anything like this.

When the seasons turned, Anjelica took me shopping for a coat. I knew what I wanted: one like a girl at school had, red with white fur trim. And there it was, in Bonwit Teller, hovering like an apparition. I think it even had a hood.

"There," I said timidly. "That's the one I want."

I saw the look cross Anjelica's face, and knew I should have expected it. My taste was small-town and childish: of course what appealed to me would be wrong. Still, she let me try it on.

"It looks like Santa Claus."

She picked out a coat of fawn-colored suede with fox-colored fur edging and embroidered swirls around the hem. I didn't like it at all, but she insisted I put it on. The color was dull, and the embroidery was exotic and hippie-ish. It was a New York coat, not a Miller Place one. I could imagine myself wearing it in the city, though I wouldn't actually like it, but in Miller Place it would be embarrassing. I sent one last, longing gaze over to the Santa Claus coat, now back on its hanger. I saw, through Anjelica's eyes, how tacky and garish it was. I still preferred it, though I knew I shouldn't.

I wore the hippie coat all winter, as I had to for warmth. Every time I put it on, I felt chic and fashionable—an alien. And, to a degree, a fraud: this fashionable person wasn't me. I felt torn, in a way I wouldn't have been able to describe: ordinary in myself, but made different by the accident of my birth. I understood that it was good to be attuned to art and beautiful things, to have high and exacting standards, to float above the ordinary as Anjelica and Daddy did. It was just that I doubted I could, and didn't know how.

That Christmas of 1972, Nurse and I went to California, where Daddy was living now, with Cici. Uncle Fraser drove us to the airport, late as always. It was, I guessed, his silent rebellion against doing Grampa's bidding. Just as we had done the previous summer, on our way back to Ireland, Nurse and I had to run to the gate.

Gladys met us at the airport. It was the first time I'd seen her since leaving St. Cleran's. She was wearing sandals with low heels; it seemed slightly indecent to see her in public in warm-weather clothes. The warm weather was odd in itself. This was Christmastime; I hadn't quite understood that it wasn't cold everywhere (except Australia, of course, where everything was the opposite of how it was supposed to be). Flowers didn't bloom in December—but suddenly, as we turned out of LAX, my eyes were dazzled by a cascade of blazing magenta: a waterfall whose element was transfigured into soft, flaming petals, with not a shred of green among them to crack the illusion.

I had loved the lilac at St. Cleran's—even more so because someone told me that Mum had planted it. There were three different colors: a pale, dawny mauve, a mid-purple which was my least favorite, and a darker purple the color of a summer sky just before night. I would watch the buds, waiting for them to burst out in little droplets; then the blossoms would blow about like skirts in the wind before they finally snowed to the ground. This bougainvillea seemed as indomitably permanent as the lilac was delicate: blooming bizarrely in midwinter, its color vivid and unearthly. It had no visible connection to the earth; it erupted from the stony innards of a high concrete wall. I couldn't take my eyes off it, and craned my neck as we drove past.

We left the flat streets lined with low, gap-faced buildings—not like any city I'd seen before—and began to climb a winding road. Around hairpin curves, along the side of sheer drops with only a flimsy guardrail, up a mountain so high and steep it didn't belong in a city. Here and there bougainvillea covered the guardrail, like padding; it comforted my fear.

"You'll be staying with Celeste's parents, Allegra."

When Gladys said Cici's name she pronounced it "sissy," as if she couldn't hear how everyone else said it. More often, she called her Celeste. It was her name—but from the way Gladys said it, with her lips tightening slightly like someone sucking a lemon, I knew she didn't like her.

"That is their house."

On the far side of a wide, deep canyon was a huge gingerbread house, with pointed gables and dark half-timbering. This mountain, unlike the cliff in Long Island, was not falling away. With its thick pelt of trees it made a vast pedestal for the house, which looked monumentally solid and phantasmagorical at the same time—being so English in this very un-English place.

"You may call me Aunt Dorothy," said Cici's mother when we arrived. She was a small woman in her sixties, strikingly beautiful, with perfectly painted nails and a large, dangerous-looking diamond on her right hand.

"And this is Uncle Myron." Cici's father shuffled forward and solemnly shook my hand. He was bent over at the neck, and his voice was hardly louder than a whisper. The glint in his eye made him look like a mischievous turtle.

I followed my blue suitcase—which, I noticed sadly, was starting to look a bit battered—as it was carried up the stairs by Aunt Dorothy's man-of-all-work, and deposited in a back bedroom. I was glad to see twin beds: one for Nurse, one for me. I would be fine here, I thought—and had no conception that I ought to be, or could have been, anywhere else. Nurse was with me, and I wouldn't have to sleep alone.

I was awed by the house, with its minstrels' gallery high above the vast living room, and an enormous plate-glass window looking out across Los Angeles to the glittering ocean beyond. Aunt Dorothy pointed out Catalina Island, rising in a long hump like the back of a whale. She took personal pride in the fact that the air was clear enough to see it. Even so, I could see the layer of brown below us, sunken as if it were heavier than the blue.

By the front door was a grandfather clock which Aunt Dorothy allowed me to wind, and the dining-room wallpaper showed the seven wonders of America. Aunt Dorothy told me that Mrs. Kennedy had chosen the same wallpaper for the Diplomatic Reception Room in the White House; I understood that Aunt Dorothy had found the wallpaper first. She told me that Greta Garbo had once lived in the house, and—she chuckled in her throat, as if it was something that shouldn't be said—that the servants from the houses nearby would hide in the woods to watch Garbo swim naked in the pool.

The next day Aunt Dorothy took me to visit Cici, who was in

the hospital for some minor operation. She lay in her bed doing needlepoint: a hunting scene of men in red coats on horseback. It was to be a belt, Daddy's Christmas present. In the lead was a miniature Daddy, top-hatted as master of the hunt, flourishing a riding crop. I was impressed not just by the tininess of the stitches but by the detail of the scene: dogs baying, stone walls being jumped, streaming manes, the rusty tail of the fox. She had drawn it herself, and transferred it to the canvas. But I was also silently, secretly upset, because this was a scene from the Irish life Daddy had left behind. I didn't know that Cici had even been to Ireland. Was she trying to take possession of that world, which she didn't have a right to? Or was it just that she was somehow—despite her beauty, her knowing drawl, and her sardonic smile—more naive than I was? I settled on the latter, and felt protective of her from that moment on.

I knew she was setting herself up for disappointment, pouring such meticulous work and loving anticipation into this belt. Daddy would never wear it—and why did I know him better than she did? It made me sad. I sensed the gulf between the two of them—maybe before they sensed it themselves. I wasn't present when Cici gave Daddy the belt, and I never saw it or heard it spoken of again.

I had worked hard on two Christmas presents that year: one for Anjelica and one for Daddy. I had already given Anjelica her macramé shoulder bag, and she had liked it as much as I'd hoped she would. I was eight years old: still young enough to make all my Christmas presents, but old enough to know that childish drawings weren't enough. I liked knitting and crocheting and hooking rugs; they always came with a pattern to follow. Macramé was hippie-ish, like the coat Anjelica had bought me, so I thought she would like it better. I was surprised and frustrated by how hard it was to get the tension of the knots and the distance between them just right; once I finished that bag, I never tried macramé again. I lined the bag—it was about eight inches by six—with pale purple material, the color of the lilacs at St. Cleran's.

But what would I do for Daddy? I'd knitted him a scarf the year before, so I couldn't do that again. He'd have no use for a rug. Crochet was too girly. Finally Nana suggested I make a picture out of beach glass.

I balked. My collection of beach glass was precious. Still, I couldn't think of anything else. But what kind of picture? I couldn't create one of my own. I wasn't an artist.

Nana showed me a book of paintings by Winslow Homer. They were seascapes, and their misty greens and grays had just the shimmery quality of the beach glass. I chose a picture of a lighthouse flying a small red flag—a showpiece for my rare, tiny piece of red. I wasn't thrilled about giving it up, and certainly I wouldn't have given it up for anyone other than Daddy, but it was the one thing I had that was worthy of him. Briefly I considered substituting a different color or choosing a different painting, but it was too late. I'd thought of using it, and I couldn't back out. What if my refusal to give up that prize red piece somehow got back to him, and he—rightly—held it against me?

Nana got me a small sheet of glass and we laid it over the page in the book. Carefully I made a mosaic. I had to give up most of my blue beach glass, too, the second rarest color; it was painful, but necessary. The beach glass wasn't flat, and sometimes the glue didn't hold, so I searched for flatter pieces, ones that fit into a tighter jigsaw, to make the picture as perfect a replica as I could. I was a bit disappointed with it all the same. I worried that it was childish and clumsy—maybe even silly. I'd never heard of a beach-glass picture before.

On Christmas Day, Aunt Dorothy drove us to Cici's house in Pacific Palisades, on the west side of Los Angeles near the ocean. Cici was back home, looking a bit pale because she'd had an allergic reaction to the hypoallergenic equipment they'd used on her. That impressed me: she, too, was special. I'd been a bit worried that, because she wasn't remote, she might be too ordinary to belong in Daddy's world.

Nervously I gave Daddy my present. His long, square-tipped fingers flipped open the card, and he read it out loud.

"With apologies to Winslow Homer." He looked at me quizzically, then slid a finger under the overlap of the wrapping paper and sliced it open.

Nana had suggested writing those words on the card, so I did, though it felt as if I were giving Winslow Homer some kind of credit for my piece of red beach glass while apologizing for making the picture at all.

"Aah-hah," said Daddy as he uncovered the picture, which, despite being wrapped in tissue paper and put in a box, had lost two of its pieces of beach glass. I longed to grab it from him and disappear with a tube of glue to fix it, but my limbs had frozen.

He started to chuckle. "You're a great admirer of Winslow Homer, I see. How well do you know his work, honey? And tell me why you feel apologies are in order."

I stumbled to answer him, unable to explain how special the red piece of beach glass was. I heard a contempt for Nana in his teasing, and I resented Nana for the waste of my treasure and the shattering of my feeling that it was treasure at all. I resented her fiercely, with every drop of resentment I had—so that none would be left over for him.

"Thank you, honey," he said finally. "It's a wonderful present." He put it aside, and I knew instantly that he would never pick it up or look at it again.

Why should he have liked it or wanted it, anyway? Beach glass wasn't paint, and when it was stuck to the glass it looked crude— like the trash it was. Winslow Homer had probably been the wrong choice, too: suburban, second-rate, not in the pantheon of artists Daddy admired. I realized I'd never seen that kind of painting at St. Cleran's—obviously Daddy didn't think it was worth having. I should have known better than to think a painter that Nana liked was good enough for Daddy. But what would have been? Even if I'd copied a Toulouse-Lautrec, it wouldn't have been a Toulouse-

Lautrec, just my copy of it. In beach glass. You were supposed to make up pictures yourself, not copy other people's.

I felt like a savage duped by worthless trinkets, an idiot who knew nothing about art. I wanted more than anything to please Daddy. At St. Cleran's I had felt able to, with my drawings, my gift for games, my Irish dancing. In the last six months, evidently, I had taken a wrong turn without knowing it, away from the person I was supposed to be if I was to be worthy of being Daddy's child, Anjelica's sister. In the absence of talent like they had, I'd relied on my intellect; but my intellect had let me down. It wasn't the execution of the beach-glass picture that was the problem; it was the very idea of making it at all.

7

~ ⤳

The car juddered down a cobbled street lined with plain, blank walls. I liked the colors of the walls—pinky-orange, pinky-brown, orangey-yellow—but their blankness was unsettling, like a row of faces with skin where eyes ought to be.

I sat in the back seat between Nurse and Gladys. A dark-skinned, dark-haired man drove. He had a round, flat face like the faces of Daddy's pre-Columbian idols, except that he wasn't scary like them, because his face seemed shaped for smiling. His name was Arturo and he always drove for Daddy in Mexico City. He had once been a boxer and had killed a man in the ring. Of course Daddy would have a driver with a story like that.

"*Gracias*, Arturo," said Gladys as we pulled up in front of an iron gate. A gardener unlocked it for us. As we went inside he locked it behind us. How odd, I thought—like a prison. This was a street lined with prisons that people had put themselves in.

The house was in Cuernavaca, a resort town about two hours from Mexico City, and belonged to Daddy's agent. He was borrowing it while he worked on the screenplay of *The Man Who Would Be King* with Gladys. Cici wasn't with them, and I didn't think that odd at all. I would have found it much stranger if Cici had been there and Gladys hadn't.

Though Gladys kept herself apart from Dad's social life—she'd never been part of the gang at the Big House, watching racing or the World Cup in the basement TV room, or following the hunt, or drinking cocktails in the study—it was impossible to imagine her without him. She was his moon, her orbit sometimes closer, sometimes farther, but always held by his gravity. She was ageless, as if she'd managed to keep the harshness of life at one remove, the way she'd kept the skin of her face untouched by the sun. Her severe hair and black-rimmed glasses were not designed to attract a man; she wore lipstick only because she would have been half dressed without it. There was something wraithlike about her paleness. She was neither heavy nor thin, but she moved silently, and sometimes you didn't realize she was there.

She and Daddy occupied the two bedrooms of the main house. Nurse and I were given the guesthouse. I was happy to be with Daddy again, but nervous too. I felt an intense pressure to be the kind of girl I ought to be—whatever that was. All I knew was that it was not the girl I was becoming as a Soma cousin in Miller Place. Trying not to be that girl made me mousy. Daddy didn't seem to notice. He was remote—traveling imaginatively in the fictional Himalayan kingdom of Kafiristan, or (I suspect now) wandering gloomily through the collapsing promises of a new marriage going bad. I watched him through the open garden doors as he sat in a leather bucket chair, the legs of his cotton trousers hiked up by his knees, his long bare ankles sinewy and brown like the leather of his loafers; or as he paced the room in long strides, arms hanging, while Gladys scribbled furiously on a yellow legal pad on her lap.

As the days wore into weeks, I felt more invisible than inspected. Daddy and I didn't play pelmanism anymore, and I'd lost any appetite for drawing after the Winslow Homer beach-glass debacle. As we didn't eat meals together, all conversations had to be initiated from across what suddenly seemed to be the vast gulf of the last year. We didn't talk about the lost paradise of St. Cleran's, or Nana and Grampa. Eventually Daddy hit on the idea of teaching me backgammon. It was like a rope flung across the abyss, and I quickly became good enough for him to enjoy playing with me.

Mostly I just splashed about aimlessly in the pool while Nurse watched from the side. One day Gladys showed me how to dive.

"You bring your hands together above your head," she said, "fingers pointing where you want to go. Then just fall forward." She demonstrated.

I couldn't follow her. Gladys climbed out of the pool and bent my knees for me.

"Like a frog," she said. I looked for a smile on her face, but she was completely serious.

Still I couldn't let myself fall, so she bent my knees farther, until I was squatting so low I was almost sitting.

"Try it from there."

She accepted my fearfulness as a matter of course, not worthy of notice, and that took away its sting. Her way of not treating me like a child made me think I could choose to be taught, just as she chose to teach me.

I longed to be physically competent. After a year in Miller Place, I had still never dared ride my bike with no hands. American schools gave a grade for PE, and it infuriated me when my straight A's were unfairly ruined. A mother—my mother, I fantasized—would have taught me to play tennis on the court at St. Cleran's, and would have kept at me until I learned to ride a horse.

I practiced diving for hours a day. There were no English-speaking kids to play with, no books I cared to read, and no bookstore to buy more, no beach or woods or river. Just this squared-off pool, a brutal burning sun, and packs of cards with which I played solitaire, recording my score on page after page in the cumulative Vegas style that Daddy showed me. I made endless lists of world nations and their capitals, and which ones I had currency from. Daddy gave me some, the leftovers from his travels—and so began a desultory, unexciting coin collection, which hung around me for years like a drizzly cloud. I feigned enthusiasm to please Daddy. He seemed to think a coin collection would distinguish me, give me an area of expertise. He liked people to be expert in something. I often heard him say things like "He's the finest mule breeder in the state of Jalisco," or "the cleverest plumber in the west of Ireland." Arturo was the finest driver in all Mexico.

On the morning of my ninth birthday, Daddy gave me three Mexican gold coins: tiny round slivers, each one showing an eagle wrestling a snake in its talons. I didn't want them, but saying so would have been heresy. I didn't like coins, and I didn't like Mexico. I got sick, I got sunburned, and I longed to be back in Miller Place, playing with my cousins. Martine—whom I might never see again— was probably finding blue beach glass, maybe even red. And here I was, in a prison.

A short-legged donkey covered with curlicued pink and white tissue paper was hung over the thick branch of a mango tree, and a gaggle of children turned up. I'd never seen them before, and they showed absolutely no interest in me, even though it was my birthday party. None of them spoke any English at all.

A blindfold was tied across my eyes and I was spun around three times. Dizzy, I felt a big stick being put in my hand.

"*Bataló!*" said a man in Spanish. He was probably the gardener.

"Hit it, honey," said Daddy.

I wasn't the kind of girl who liked to hit things, and the stick was heavy and hard to manage. I'd never seen a piñata before, and didn't understand what I was supposed to do.

I swung, and hit nothing. I could feel the excitement from the other kids, chattering in Spanish and laughing at me. I swung again and heard a rustle of tissue paper, and felt the ghost of something swinging away. Of course I would be useless at this. I didn't know that another man was stationed on the end of the rope, yanking the piñata out of reach.

I had gone first, since I was the birthday girl. Kids who grow up with piñatas know the drill, and people yell from the sidelines, "Now! Hit it now!" Dad and Gladys weren't the yelling sort. Nurse might have helped me, if she'd known what was going on—I know, after the England–Ireland rugby match, that she had it in her— but to her the piñata was probably as foreign as a penis gourd or a shrunken head. The gardener yelled in Spanish, which might as well have been Chinese.

I swung again and again, since it was expected of me. All I wanted was for this unfestive, barbaric, inexplicable birthday party to be over.

"Basta, hijita, muy bueno," I felt the man take the stick from my hand, then untie the blindfold. At least the humiliation was over.

"Well done, honey," said Daddy, sounding impatient and bored, as I went back to stand beside Nurse. I took it as disappointment in me, and it deepened my misery. I didn't know that the first child is never allowed to break the piñata; the men in charge yank it out of reach until everyone has had a turn.

Finally, the last and biggest boy stepped up to bat. The clay pot in the donkey's belly cracked, and candy showered down. The local kids rushed in, scrabbling for it on the bricks.

"Run in and get the candy, honey," said Daddy, irritated by my lack of initiative.

I found a few pieces that had skittered to the edge. I didn't like Mexican candy, and I was frightened by the melee, and the flailing stick, which the blindfolded boy was still swinging while the gardener tried to get it off him.

I wished I was anywhere else. I understood—without asking, and without being told—that I wasn't going back to Miller Place. I didn't know why. Maybe my long, miserable bout of chickenpox had sealed my fate, or maybe Grampa didn't like the way Martine and I used to creep up the slatted steps to his room and spy on him. But why couldn't Nana and Grampa at least have kept me for the summer? Why had I been spirited off the moment school ended and run into a siding in Mexico, as if there were no other roof on earth that could shelter me?

Cici told me later that Nana had written to Daddy to say that she and Grampa couldn't keep me anymore: they were too old, the responsibility of a child was too great. I doubt it was Nana's choice. Maybe all Grampa really wanted was more money from Daddy, as Cici contemptuously suspected. Whatever he said made Daddy determined to take me away from "the demented old dago" (as he called him in a letter to Cici) as soon as school was out. I imagine that Grampa took a bitter pleasure in forcing Daddy to take me back again. He hadn't treated Mum properly, and now that he had a new wife, Grampa was going to make it as awkward for him as he could.

I realized that this hated place wasn't permanent. It was just a holding pattern, as evidently no other place had yet been found for me. But the weeks were stretching toward their third month, and there was no sign that I was ever going to leave.

I sensed that plans were made up for me on the fly. I was an inconvenience—not unloved, but a problem that required constant solving. If I asked when I'd be going home—wherever that was—or whether I'd be staying where I was, I would be putting Daddy, or Gladys, on the spot. (Nurse, I figured, wouldn't know any more than I did.) I would be able to see the uncertainty on their faces as their brains churned through the possible answers that might keep me quiet, at least for another little while. That would only confirm how random my fate was. It was better just to wait and see.

⤙⤚

Euclid. I saw the word on a street sign, instead of the number thirteen. Fifteenth Street, Fourteenth Street, then Euclid.

Gladys's heavy Impala, a dirty gold color, swung left. After a few blocks of stop signs, it pulled up in front of the house that she, Nurse, and I were to share.

I did not want to live on Euclid Street. I despised the man who had named the streets for caving in to superstition and disguising Thirteenth Street—and despised the street itself for having a name that sounded like some nasty insect. No one would live on Euclid Street if they could possibly live somewhere else.

Still, at least I was back in Los Angeles, splotched with that seductively unnatural bougainvillea which seemed never to wilt or fade. The late-summer sun was softened by the haze of the Pacific thirteen blocks away, and kinder than the inland sun of Mexico. I would be going to a school where Cici's cousin was a teacher. That made me feel she was looking out for me.

The house had fake-wood plastic paneling and carpets the greeny-brown of cowpats. It was one in a long row of low houses, haphazardly mirrored across the asphalt, and duplicated on street after street between Ocean and Twenty-sixth, where the numbering ended. These were streets where families lived. I was the one who gave us the veneer of fitting in, a nine-year-old with blond pigtails and a bike with a bell and a white basket. It was my favorite part of the day: getting the bike out of the shed in the backyard, wheeling it over the maze of snail trails glistening in the morning sun, and riding alone and independent to school with both hands on the handlebars—in full control as I ought to be on a public road with cars on it. I felt securely placed in the world as I followed my route through the almost deserted streets—a route which was absolutely and entirely mine.

I could see the picture of myself, and I felt like an impostor in suburbia. I'd never lived on a street like this before, with front lawns studded with sprinklers and everyone mowing the grass strip between the sidewalk and the street like they were supposed to do. I doubted I ever would again. I resented the sameness, which depersonalized the people who lived there, but at the same time I yearned to share it. My nomadic life, with its high-drama story line and eccentric cast of characters, made me feel interesting and unusual—but also somehow fake, as if I hadn't done anything to earn my special status. I felt, in myself, bog-ordinary. My skin itself was tired by my chameleon life.

What I wanted more than any other impossible thing was to be called Nikki, with two *k*'s. Anjelica called me "Legs" for short, and though I didn't like the nickname, I loved the affection in it. But the TV commercials for L'Eggs panty hose made it unbearable. Women sashayed past building sites and workers wolf-whistled, "She's got LEGS!!!!" That same wolf whistle followed me, and it was worse because in my own eyes I was Fattypuff, pudgy and graceless, so very far from someone that men would whistle at—such as my mother, who'd been so beautiful she'd been put on the cover of *Life*, and my sister, who was always in *Vogue*.

Nikki: so close to Ricki, but I never realized it. The echo which must have pleased me subconsciously didn't extend to Vicki (or Vikki), which I used as a comparison and didn't like at all. I rarely thought about Ricki, my mother—I had no mementos of her, no photographs, nothing that had come with me from St. Cleran's or Maida Avenue. My most vivid memories of her were that silent car drive and her anger at my bouncing; and I'd started to feel that I was remembering remembering, not actually remembering the events themselves. It was a generation loss in the mental recording, and who knew what details had been fogged away, or what shadows or halos of color had sneaked into the picture? I was three worlds away from my lost mother—too far to ever find her again.

Nurse hated Euclid Street too, though she never said so—she wouldn't have thought it her place. But I could tell. She tiptoed around "Miss Hill," as she always called Gladys, and we would have taciturn dinners in the dining room, its windows barely penetrated by the dying rays of the sun, stagnant with the ghost smells of old food hanging in the curtains and trodden into the fibers of the carpet.

Since Nurse couldn't drive, she was virtually marooned. She had one afternoon off a week, on which she would walk a mile or so to an English tea shop to meet a friend. I wondered how she had found that friend, but she clammed up when I probed her. She was, I think now, clinically depressed. My teeth and hair were always brushed, cookies and milk awaited me when I got back from school, but Nurse was always too tired to play games with me and her patience was short.

On Saturdays, we would walk to the bookstore and she would buy me five Nancy Drew books—my new obsession. Nancy Drew was a teenage detective with titian hair, two sidekicks, and a sky-blue convertible car. I enjoyed the implausible mysteries, but what fascinated me most was that Nancy (like the Famous Five) could have such adventures while still being part of an intensely ordinary world—and that her world could be so ordinary, when her mother was dead too. When we got home, I would lock myself in the bathroom and read one from cover to cover. The rest I would finish during the week after school, lying on one of the twin four-poster beds that Aunt Dorothy had contributed to the house.

For someone who disapproved of Enid Blyton—as Daddy did, or at least as Gladys said he did—Nancy Drew would have been beneath contempt. I felt an unspoken collusion with Nurse as she bought me books that "Mr. Huston" wouldn't like. I don't think Nurse ever said the words "your father." I was starting to understand that people had taken sides when Mum and Daddy had split up. Nurse was—obviously—on Mum's, Gladys—obviously—on Daddy's. I wasn't sure where I was. It would be loathsomely disloyal to abandon my dead mother's memory, flimsy as it was; but then, how could I not be loyal to Daddy, since he was the center, and the puppet-master, of my world?

Gladys would never have directly defied Daddy's wishes, but she managed to seem blind to the blaze of yellow spines on my bookcase. Her gestures of friendship were so subtle it was easy to miss them. We were adopted by a Siamese cat, and Gladys suggested we call him Ignats, because she knew I'd find it funny. She gave me a type-writer and a book on teaching yourself to type, and when I had to write an essay for my history class at school, she suggested the subject of grottoes—someone had given me a book about them, which I could crib from—and helped me write it on the morning it was due, watching over me as I typed it. She drove me to school so that she could excuse my lateness herself.

Then Gladys's mother came on an extended visit, and our flickering understanding was snuffed out. It was winter, and the thermostat in the house was turned up to eighty. I didn't see why Mrs. Hill couldn't put on a sweater over the thin cotton housedresses she wore, instead of stifling us all in this claustrophobic re-creation of what I imagined must be the torrid heat of West Virginia, where she was from. The heat made the house smell even more strongly of old dust and carpet backing, and the air was as limp as the air in a tomb.

Nurse moved out of her room into mine so that Mrs. Hill could have hers. The low murmur of the radio came from behind the closed door, underscoring the absence of live human sound. Gladys and Nurse spoke to each other only when necessary, their exchanges polite but minimal. I rattled between them, trying to be as quiet as I could.

I kept the door of my room shut too—to block out the embalming heat of the furnace. I shut off the heating vents and opened all the windows, not caring how many sweaters I had to wear. Though I hated the house, I considered it primarily mine. I thought it wouldn't have been rented if not for me; without me it would, as far as the Huston family was concerned, not even exist. It didn't occur to me that Gladys would have had to live somewhere, that without me there would have been some rented house or apartment, that in fact I was sharing her digs rather than she sharing mine. She let me claim the master bedroom, with its own en suite bathroom, when we moved in. I saw the shock on Nurse's face, but Gladys let my arrogance pass. Now, as Mrs. Hill's visit wore on, I felt as if I was being isolated into a back corner while the rest of the house reverted to its true nature: smothering and lifeless.

Weekends were my release. I would go for the day, or sometimes overnight, to Cici's house. Or I would stay with my godmother Gina, the painter, whom I remembered clearly as Mum's closest friend. She was living in L.A. because her husband, a Bulgarian fencing master, wanted to be an actor. (After the fall of the Iron Curtain, he came second in the election for president of Bulgaria.) Best of all, Anjelica would pick me up and we'd drive along beautiful San Vicente Boulevard, its wide grassy median lined with gnarled, red-barked coral trees, toward Hollywood, where she was sharing a house with her old friend from London, Jeremy Railton. She had just got her driver's license, and she joked about how hard it had been for Jeremy, when he taught her to drive, to keep her under sixty miles an hour. The radio was always on. When Bob Dylan came on, singing "Knockin' on Heaven's Door," Anjel turned up the volume and sang along. That was how I wanted to be: carefree, knowledgeable about music, in control of the wheel, speeding ahead. I sang too, grateful to Dylan for writing a chorus that was the same line repeated four times over. The sameness of the boulevard, the sameness of the song: if only this sunlit cocoon of a drive could never end.

Anjel told me about the first time she had met Gladys. It was Christmastime, and Gladys came to St. Cleran's without any presents for Anjelica and Tony.

"I don't give presents to people I don't know," Gladys had told them. "I will give you presents when I know you better."

"Can you believe it!" said Anjel as we drove. She looked over at me, smiling. She didn't even need to keep her eyes on the road. "Outrageous! I hated her instantly." She was laughing at her greedy eight-year-old self, but some of the outrage had stuck.

"I would have too."

It was a lie. I didn't want to admit that I wouldn't have expected a present—or, if I had, I would have quickly and silently revised my incorrect views. I wished I had Anjelica's sense of entitlement. It seemed to sum up everything that made her more interesting, more confident, more truly special than I was.

In New York, being with Anjelica had been rather like being with Dad: stepping into a world where I didn't belong, unsure if I was measuring up. I didn't know then that the man she lived with there, a fashion photographer, was depressive and prone to rages, so she had been constantly on edge. Here she was full of enthusiasm and energy, and it flooded into me. She wanted me for her sister; that was all that mattered to me. We were allies: Mum's daughters, the Soma girls.

Jeremy had a truck, and we usually went to the garden center or the hardware store, me sandwiched between them on the bench seat, to buy supplies for his projects: cement to make ponds for turtles and frogs, jungly plants to attract wild birds, wood and wire to build cages for coveys of baby quail. Once, Anjel pulled an old dress out of a trunk, and they insisted I put it on. It was long and white, with tiny pleats and lace; it had belonged, she told me, to our grandmother Angelica. I hated all dresses—and worst of all was the frilly bonnet. Anjel had always loved dressing up, and couldn't accept that I didn't. The dress made me feel silly; it erased *me*. But I couldn't explain that, even to myself, and I didn't dare refuse outright in case they decided they didn't want me in their enchanted, artistic world. So I put it on, the bonnet too, and curled in the hammock like a surly hamster while they took a photograph of me.

I have memories of Anjel and Cici laughing together—and none of Anjel with Daddy. Anjel didn't spend Christmas Day with us, and I didn't think to wonder why not. My family was made up of individual people who shared an accident of circumstance; we weren't any kind of whole. Tony wrote to me, but I hadn't seen him since Ireland.

I doubted I'd ever see Danny again. Neither he nor Zoë wrote, and on the rare occasions when Cici mentioned Zoë's name, it was with such acid hostility that it was obvious that she and Danny couldn't be a part of Daddy's new life.

The circle of people who had loved Mum was more powerfully magnetic than this amoebic Huston family. Some mysterious force drew us together, seemingly coincidentally, in certain places at certain times: Anjelica and I and Gina and Jeremy and Anjel's friend, Joan Buck, in London and New York and Los Angeles, and later in New Mexico. They had known me since I was a baby, when Mum had been there. They were more important than family: they were the witnesses to the reality that my own memory couldn't prove was real.

One night Anjelica took me to Chinatown. It was my first visit to a film set, and the sense of occasion was exciting: a street blocked off to traffic, black vintage cars gleaming under the megawattage of huge round lights on high poles. But mostly it was boring. Lots of people stood around, muttering to one another with bent heads, while others ran about purposefully, making me afraid of getting in their way. When the camera rolled and everyone fell silent, I was too far away to hear what the actors were saying.

Daddy was on the set that night, though I barely saw him. Possibly, as he was playing an incestuous villain, he preferred not to see his daughters. Anyway, it was Anjelica's new boyfriend we had come to visit. We waited in his trailer for him to finish a scene. Finally, the door swung open.

"Hey, Toot!" Not as in *toot-toot*, the noise of a train. More like "tuht," the singular of "Toots." Sometimes he lengthened it to "Tootman."

"This is Jack," said Anjelica to me. At age nine, I hadn't heard of Jack Nicholson, or seen any of his movies. I'd seen very few movies, in fact. Nurse didn't take me, since there wasn't a cinema in walking distance of Euclid Street.

"Allegra. Pleased to meet you."

He shook my hand, then sat down in front of a big mirror surrounded by lights. A woman bent over his nose, where a line of black threads was sewn in knots, like a butchered centipede.

"It's just makeup, darling," Anjel reassured me. It made me queasy, especially when the woman's fingers fiddled with it. I could barely look at him.

A few weeks later, a fever suddenly hit me while I was at Anjelica and Jeremy's house. She put me in her bed, and sleepiness furred my senses. I heard footsteps on the stairs. A man appeared in the doorway. Jack.

"Leggsie!"

He drew out the name across seconds of time, like someone savoring toffee. I loved it suddenly: it was mine, it was me. The beam of Jack's attention made me feel like a minor deity evilly laid low.

"I brought Scatman to see you," he said. "The Scatman will make you feel better."

Beside him was a black man with a lined face like leather that cracked into a wide grin. He perched on my bed and started to sing, his voice gravelly, the tune wild and rollicking, every word balanced on the brink of laughter. It was the title song from *The Aristocats*, a Disney movie which Anjel had taken me to see. My fever made the room dreamy and fantastical, and misted Scatman into a sweet, gnomish Rumpelstiltskin. This was the L.A. I'd been seduced by: a place out of time, where flowers were permanent, where sickness didn't mean boredom and misery but instead brought Scat Cat himself to my bedside, singing just for me.

8

When summer came, my weekend visits to Cici and Daddy grew longer. Most days we'd head up the Pacific Coast Highway to the Malibu Colony, where they had rented a beach house. Cici's car was a Citroën Maserati—there weren't many of them, she said   and when she turned the key in the ignition, the back end rose up hydraulically, like a robotic baboon in heat. She called it the Brown Mound, or just the Mound. I sat in the front seat, a leather bucket tipped backward as if by g-forces. Her son, Collin, pretzeled himself into the stunted back seat, his double-jointed elbows and knees sticking out at odd angles, a sheepish grin on his face.

Cici rested her right hand on the gear stick as she drove, tapping it so that the underside of her ring pinged against the chrome. It was a long slab of jade, a green as soft as wool, the stone shaped across her index finger like a snippet of armor. Sometimes she also wore an emerald-cut diamond the size of my thumbnail, which she told me had been an engagement ring from a man she hadn't married. She'd tried to return it and he'd refused to take it back—but should she still be wearing it? I was a bit shocked, but I felt a thrill too. Cici didn't feel the obligation that I felt: to do what other people thought I should. She did exactly what she wanted.

She drove fast, changing lanes constantly to weave through the traffic. It was like an arcade game: the other cars were there only to make our journey more exciting. My job was to watch for cops. Cici showed me how to lower the visor and watch behind us in the makeup mirror—because, she said, a face looking out the back window would be suspicious. We didn't want to let the cops know we were onto them. When I yelled "Cop!" she'd slam on the brakes, smiling a fake-innocent smile to amuse Collin and me. "Nasty little piglets," she'd say with a kind of hiss as we drove past the cop car at exactly the speed limit, or as the cop whizzed past us on the tail of someone else.

I'd never swum in real surf before. Collin showed me how to get out past the breakers, jumping and diving through the incoming walls of water, and paddling to catch the wave. All I had to do was close my eyes and hold my breath, and let the wave pick me up and throw me onto the shore. The graze of sand on my skin was just this side of painful. It was the present scraping against me, letting me know I was there, part of the real world, as long as my breath held out.

Collin was two years younger than I, and I felt protective of him. Gladys had warned me that he had learning disabilities. It was true that he couldn't read or write well, though he was eight. But he was a very long way from "slow." He called Cici's brother David—a classic seventies swinging bachelor, with shoulder-length curly hair, shirt unbuttoned to the navel, and gold chains nestling in the chest hair—the Chicksweeper. I wished my brain was quick enough to come up with a name like that.

Collin was obsessive about his enthusiasms, and his sense of the border between reality and fantasy wasn't strong. But then, neither was mine—though mine was the mirror image of his. For him, fantasy was real; for me, reality was as unreliable as fantasy. He wasn't "normal"; he didn't operate on the ordinary wavelength. I wasn't "normal" either. A cloudy sense of foreignness enveloped me. I felt it like a veil between me and the girls at school, and it was hard to make friends. Collin took me on my own terms, and I took him on his. With him I was in the present, or in a fantasy; either way, future and past fell away. It was a relief.

Daddy always said the same thing to prove that Collin wasn't stupid: "He can name all the prehistoric reptiles." It was the tone you'd use to tell someone about a memory freak or a circus act: "Just imagine that," I could hear him saying. "He can juggle jellyfish." He said it with exaggerated seriousness, as if this feat of Collin's was so extraordinary that one could only gape in wonder. It drove me nuts. He sounded so pleased with himself for being able to appreciate Collin's particular intelligence—as if he felt the need to demonstrate that Collin wasn't an idiot, which only showed that he entertained the possibility. And why "prehistoric reptiles"? Was he afraid that if he said "dinosaurs" people would think he was ignorant?

Besides, what made Collin's intelligence remarkable was his sharp wit, which Daddy seemed unable to hear. Collin knew as much, and as little, about dinosaurs as any boy. I knew that, at least as far as dinosaurs were concerned, Collin was totally normal—and Daddy obviously didn't. It nagged at me too that the dinosaurs might not all have been reptiles. So many seemed to be between one thing and another, like the fishy ichthyosaurus or the feathered archaeopteryx. Because I actually talked with Collin, rather than making pronouncements about him, I soon knew more about "prehistoric reptiles" than Daddy knew—or, it occurred to me, pretended to know.

I'm not sure when it happened: that Daddy became fallible. Perhaps during that dreary summer in Cuernavaca. Perhaps when he parked me in the house on Euclid with Nurse and Gladys, and

I felt banished to the murky outskirts of his world. My heart had been readied to see faults in him—and that obnoxious, patronizing, pseudo-admiring evaluation of Collin was the first.

I didn't like the enclosed, sullen person I'd become in the dark house on Euclid, and I couldn't be that person in Cici's house. Almost every room had a door to the outside. I liked to lie in bed and count them in my head—there were eight. Some were huge sliding doors that stood open all day long.

The house was tucked away in a dead-end canyon off the rural, western end of Sunset Boulevard. Just to start with, that address was a huge improvement on Euclid. The house was perched on a ledge halfway up a steep hill, with a semicircle of lawn fringed with rosebushes, which Cici fed with the manure from her horses. They lived in corrals across the creek at the foot of the hill. She watered constantly, wearing a bikini and floaty chiffon tunics, barefoot on the paving stones. I loved how permeable the house was: the smells of wet flowers and distant horses drifting inside, the purring rumble of Teddy Pendergrass and Isaac Hayes drifting out.

Cici's feet had high curved insteps, with long second toes that, to me, looked exotically deformed. She'd tuck her feet up beside her on the sofa, or rest them against the coffee table, and when she talked she flexed them, like a cat arching its back in the sun. She even flexed them when she walked, as if each step gave her a jolt of physical pleasure. The tendons of her toes made ridges under her brown skin, and she put her feet down almost flat, as if she were stamping her footprint into the ground. I imagined the elegant shock waves cannoning through the wood and tile and concrete and imprinting her tracks in the earth's crust below. The sound made a mark on the air too, and set the paper-thin leaves of the Etruscan gold diadem on a table in the living room shivering.

The diadem had been on a table outside Daddy's bedroom at

St. Cleran's. In Cuernavaca, or during the year on Euclid, I was told that St. Cleran's had been sold.

In secret, I imitated Cici's walk, turning my toes in, pressing on the ball of my foot, holding the big toe taut so that the inner part of its crease touched the ground. I stretched my ankles, trying to get my insteps to curve as hers did, but they wouldn't rise above a frustratingly straight diagonal line. Within a minute, my feet got tired.

The house was filled with things from St. Cleran's. Collin slept in the brass bed that had been Betty's. The black table with playing cards painted on it, which had been in the Red Sitting Room upstairs, was the coffee table; and the living room was staked out by the Mexican tables from the study and the two giant mermaids from the inner hall. The three narwhal tusks from the dining room—unicorn horns of spiraling ivory—made a kind of triple axis at the heart of the house. The tallest had had to be sunk below floor level to fit under the ceiling, and Daddy had had a pond built around it, lined in black marble, with three low, Brancusi-shaped fountains gurgling in it. We all loved that pond; it was wonderfully ridiculous in the middle of a living room, and best of all visitors sometimes fell in.

I slept under the headboard from the Gray Room, where the Baroness Pauline de Rothschild had slept. It was knobbly and uncomfortable to lean against, if you wanted to sit up in bed and read a book, which gave me a sudden rush of sympathy for the Baroness Pauline, who had always seemed so grand and remote. (Her eyelids blinked constantly, and very fast. I used to stare at her in fascination across the dining table during lunch.) However beautiful the headboard was, I didn't think Daddy would ever have had it in his own room.

I felt at home among these familiar objects, though they were mixed up higgledy-piggledy. I slept in the bed that Daddy's most important friends had slept in; but looking down on me was the dark, sad-faced Madonna from the kitchen, her heart pierced with arrows and Latin words surrounding her like ribbons of ectoplasm. It threw my sense of order out of joint; it was a rearrangement of the cosmos. Everything—everyone—was equal here. There was no upstairs and downstairs, master's domain and servants'. I liked that.

I was so happy, day after day, not to be told that it was time to return to the house on Euclid that I almost forgot about it. Cici and Daddy seemed to have forgotten about it too. Finally, I asked when I'd be going back there.

"You won't," said Cici. "This is your home now." I could see how pleased she was to be saying it.

"What about Nurse? Where will she sleep?"

I didn't want to share a room with her again, and the only spare room was mine.

"She went back to Ireland a couple of weeks ago." Cici made it sound like it had been Nurse's idea.

My stomach shriveled up. I knew Nurse would never have left me unless she was told to go. If I protested, it would sound like I didn't want to stay with Cici; if I didn't protest, I would be faithless to Nurse. Instantly I chose the latter. The deed was done. I was here with Cici, and Nurse was gone.

I took it personally—not as an insult, but as my failing. Nurse, whose only role in life was to look after me, had been sent packing. And I hadn't even noticed. I had let *weeks* go by without asking after her, without caring that I hadn't even spoken to her. I had let her be bundled off in secret after twenty years with the Huston family, with no more than a thank-you and a plane ticket. How must she have felt, knowing that I'd moved on so quickly without even a backward glance? She had given me love my whole life, been there with me always, and all I had given her back was forgetting. She was being thrown out into a hostile world. With me, she'd been protected under the shelter of Daddy's influence. I would be fine without her, but what would she do without me?

The truth was that without her there, I felt freer and stronger. If she wasn't there to protect and look after me, that meant I didn't need to be looked after and protected. Anyway, she couldn't protect me from the things that made me feel really vulnerable—being tossed about from this house to that one, not knowing where I'd be when the next month came. All she could do was share them, and the farther we went from Ireland and London, the more miserable I knew she was. I figured they hadn't told me Nurse was leaving because they were afraid I'd protest or make a scene; if they waited until I asked, maybe I'd accept it more easily. And I did. Had they all been winking at one another, Cici and Gladys and Daddy, thinking how wonderful it was that Allegra *still* hadn't asked about Nurse? I couldn't blame them. It had been up to me to ask, to remember, and I hadn't. It showed what kind of person I was.

Once again, the pattern had been played on me: wait for the end of the school year, send me somewhere that seemed temporary and see how I liked it, then fix things behind my back and tell me it's permanent. I was happy with the outcome this time, but the technique wasn't hidden anymore. I resented being the subject of an experiment that nobody admitted was being conducted on me.

At the airport, while Dad walked up to the Mexicana desk, Collin and I stood to one side with Cici. She was wearing her usual summer outfit of bikini top—my favorite one, with a tropical sun setting on each breast, which I had encouraged her to buy—and jeans. Her stomach was bare and brown and her light-filled hair tumbled onto her shoulders.

It was just like an ordinary (though still rather special) family going on vacation—but it seemed all wrong to me. Daddy didn't deal with things like tickets and passports; it was Gladys's job to be his intermediary with the everyday world. Gladys wasn't here (that seemed right—it was a family vacation), so perhaps it should be Cici's job; but she seemed so calm and sure of her place, waiting while her husband took charge, that it didn't seem like it should be her job either. Her job was to be beautiful and patient, and hold the children's hands.

A slim, rectangular, zippered, chestnut-colored leather bag dangled on a thin strap from Daddy's right shoulder. Men like Uncle Nap and Uncle Fraser didn't carry bags; they had pockets. Daddy's safari shirt was covered in perfectly pressed pockets; I wished he'd use them. I hated that feminine bag. It diminished him. Fumbling in it, he looked incompetent and pretentious. As the father of a regular, two-plus-two family going on vacation, I realized, without quite knowing it, that he was miscast. It just wasn't us; it was a pretense, it couldn't last. From that day on, I noticed every sign that Daddy and Cici's relationship was coming apart. When it finally happened, I couldn't have been less surprised.

I wasn't thrilled about going back to Mexico, but at least I had Cici and Collin, and we weren't going to the low-security prison of the Kohners' house in Cuernavaca. We were going to Puerto Vallarta, where there was a beach.

This was a Cici kind of Mexico. We tooled around in a jeeplike Volkswagen Safari with plain metal sides and no windows, full of her friends, with me and Collin stuffed into the space behind the back seat. We were part of the gang. Her friends were loud and laughed a lot, and had romances, and smooched in the ocean. Dad was rarely with us. Often we'd meet him for lunch at the beachfront El Dorado—don't eat the tomatoes or the watermelon, Cici told me, they water the fields with sewage; always order drinks *sin hielo*, without ice. After lunch, Daddy and I would play backgammon. Under the table I dug my toes in and squelched them in the sand.

We stayed in the house Richard Burton had built after making *The Night of the Iguana* there with Daddy, ten years before. It was on the side of a hill, and the long wall of the living room was only half height, a balcony open to the hot, humid air. Collin and I were allowed to go out by ourselves after dinner and run down the stepped street to Bing's ice-cream parlor for hot-fudge sundaes. The fat pink and white stripes painted on its walls made it look exactly how an ice-cream parlor should look. It sat in the shadow of the cathedral, whose tower was topped by a filigree iron crown which—I loved this detail—had been donated by the Corona brewery. The Catholic icons everywhere reminded me of Ireland, but religion wasn't as glum and heavy here. It was candy-colored and lighthearted. It didn't wag a finger at people on Sundays and drive them to drink.

Every evening, as dark fell, the towering yellow-purple thunderheads that had been gathering all afternoon erupted into an apocalyptic storm: jagged lightning tearing through the sky, thick rain falling in sheets, thunder so loud my body shook. It was prehistoric—the way storms must have been in Collin's dinosaur world. I felt I was sharing it with him.

Ritually, as the thunder crashed through the living-room wall that wasn't there, Cici put the same record on the turntable: a mystery story called *The Shadow*. It began with creepy chords and a sepulchral voice intoning: "Only the Shadow knows what evil lurks in the hearts of . . ." Men, the line went. But Cici, Collin, and I were chanting along with it, and by the time we got to the end of the line—that is, if the electricity didn't fizzle out—we had drowned it out: ". . . what evil lurks in the heart of Henry Hyde!"

Henry Hyde was Daddy's lawyer in New York. I never asked Cici what he'd done to make her hate him so; it just seemed natural. The name fit: *Dr. Jekyll and Mr. Hyde* was one of Collin's favorite movies. I had met Henry Hyde once during the year I lived with Nana and Grampa, when he had given me a pile of books published by Random House, on whose board of directors he sat. Even though one of the books was a big, flat, illustrated *Just So Stories*, which I loved, the businesslike blandness of the gift rankled. I wasn't quite sure whether he was giving me the books, or Daddy was. Someone should have gone to the trouble of choosing books for me, but these were just freebies Henry Hyde had been given; so I took a dislike to him.

I'm not sure what Daddy was doing while we were gleefully

shouting about the evil heart of Henry Hyde, but he must have heard us, night after night. Cici was unapologetically vicious about people who crossed her—such as her neighbor Dr. Chainsaw, a psychiatrist she loathed because he was always cutting down trees—and devised all kinds of imaginary torments for them. I, who held my tongue about anything and everything, was awed by it. Plus, it was fun. We were a little cabal—and it didn't bother me that Daddy wasn't in it. I didn't understand that the chant was partly aimed at him.

Cici trusted animals more than she trusted people. Her favorite dog, Meece, had saved Collin's life when he was a baby and the house caught on fire, by howling at the maid until she rescued him. Cici loved to make Meece sing. Being a malamute, he couldn't bark, so they would howl "yow-yow-yowwwwww" together.

In her favorite photo of herself, which was taken a few years earlier on the set of Daddy's film *The Life and Times of Judge Roy Bean*, she is riding a lion. She's not smiling or even looking at the camera. This isn't a pose. All her attention is focused on the lion as it lopes forward. Her hair falls in soft curls like the lion's mane; her legs, in jeans and cowboy boots, hang strong and loose by its muscular sides. That was the image of her I internalized: powerfully beautiful, protective of her own, and able to turn in an instant fierce and unforgiving.

It was odd, and a little nerve-racking, to live in the same house as Daddy. The months in the Big House didn't quite count, for the Big House had been so big that our lives ran on separate tracks, and I saw about as much of him as I had when we'd slept under different roofs. Cici's house, though comfortable, wasn't very big; it was a family house, not a formal one. And family rhythms were foreign to us. I thought they might be foreign to Daddy entirely. I knew he hadn't been an approachable, domestic father with Anjelica and Tony, and I didn't expect it of him. But the terms of our lives now begged for it. We both had to learn how.

Cici went back into the hospital for an operation. And I got out of bed with a tangle in my hair.

Mum had let my hair grow long, and Nurse had brushed and combed it every morning and night. Anjelica kept talking about cutting bangs across my forehead, and the thought terrified me beyond reason. I wouldn't even let Cici trim off the split ends. My long hair was my past made visible—and proof that my past was really part of me. I had been a little girl with long blond hair when Mum died, a little girl with long blond hair running in the woods in Ireland and playing on the beach in Long Island. Without my hair, who would I be? Who would even know that I was me?

The tangle was in the sensitive hollow under the curve of my skull, at the top of my neck. It was there most days. Usually I could get it out by myself, with the help of Johnson & Johnson's No More Tangles—a discovery Nurse and I had made when we came to America. If I couldn't, Cici did it for me.

I struggled, wincing with pain. The tangle held solid. I couldn't just leave it; Nurse would never have allowed that.

The door to the hallway which led to Daddy and Cici's bedroom was open. Tentatively, I moved forward, comb in one hand, the bottle of No More Tangles in the other. The hallway was maybe fifteen feet long, with sliding-door closets on one side and an alcove with an always-closed bathroom door on the other. It was a passage between worlds: the kind of place where Orpheus turned to look back at Eurydice, or a horizontal version of Alice's rabbit hole.

"Dad?" It was around then that I stopped calling him Daddy.

"Yes, honey?"

It was okay, I could approach. There was no door at the far end. The hallway led straight into the bedroom.

Dad was sitting on the bed, about to put on his shoes. I knew he was going up to his studio on the hillside above the house. I loved to go up there and watch him paint, just as I had at St. Cleran's. But, now I was older, I was self-conscious about intruding on him. Quiet as I was, I knew I disturbed the air when he wanted to concentrate, alone. I didn't want to put him in the position of asking me to leave, so I didn't go up there often.

"I've got a tangle, and I can't get it out."

A look of confusion crossed his face, as if he didn't know what a tangle was. He glanced around to locate the person who could deal with it. But he and I were the only ones in the house.

"Well of course, honey." I could hear in his voice that he didn't know what to do.

I held out the comb and the bottle of No More Tangles. "You squirt this on it," I said, and settled myself on the floor at his feet. I wanted to make it as easy on him as possible. This way, he wouldn't even have to move.

We were facing mirrored closet doors. I saw him lean forward in his typical pose, bony elbows on bony knees, trousers riding up above his long ankles, elongated like a painting by El Greco. I could feel his fingers teasing out the tangle. They were gentle—gentler than Nurse or Cici would have been.

I closed my eyes and sank into the cushiony intimacy—and realized that it was as brittle as an eggshell. Dad was gentle because he was afraid of hurting me; at this rate, we'd be here for hours. I was afraid his patience would turn. I gritted my teeth and made sure I didn't flinch.

I was electrically aware of the enormity of what I'd asked of him. Dad was a great man, a famous film director, revered almost like a god—not someone who should be expected to comb a little girl's hair. I was transgressing the boundaries I'd set for myself: of being no trouble, of being able to look after myself.

"That's okay. That's good enough." I lost my nerve, and stopped him before the tangle was gone. "Thank you, Daddy."

I'm sure of that "Daddy." It sits like a shard of glass in my memory.

I kissed him, went back to my room, and attacked the tangle

again. I had to give up. All day I felt the stub of it, like a tuft of fur in the nape of my neck—or like the soft pressure of Dad's warm fingers.

I remember that morning alongside the night in the Bhutan Room when Dad passed his hand across my feverish forehead: ordinary moments, maybe, between most fathers and daughters. They are the only two I have. I feel certain that if there had been others, I would remember them.

9

The first time Cici met me, she wanted to mother me. I know
this because she wrote up a little memoir of it, and stored it
with her letters and Dad's in a box on the floor of the guest-room
closet in the house where she lives now, on her stud farm in Santa
Ynez.

She remembers meeting me the day before my memory of the
party at the Metropolitan Museum of Art. I was brought to Dad's
hotel room and told to do my party piece, the double jig that Karen
Creagh had taught me. Cici saw an uncertain eight-year-old girl
eager to please, with a steely-haired Irish nanny smoking grimly in
the shadows; a trick pony put on show for a roomful of old codgers
chewing cigars. She hated it. And even though she wasn't yet married
to Dad, she knew she was the only person in any position to change
things.

Cici felt a kinship to Mum, too. The day after she married Dad, he took her to Ireland, where she found Zoë and Danny in residence. Dad hadn't warned her, hadn't even told her that they existed (and hadn't warned Zoë, either, that he had a new wife in tow). She was appalled to discover that she was expected to stay in the Big House while her six-year-old son was put with his nanny in the Little House, a ten-minute walk away. Swords were drawn against the new Mrs. Huston. Betty O'Kelly, resentful at being supplanted as the mistress of St. Cleran's—and the mistress of its master—told the maids that Cici beat her servants. Knowing that Dad's finances were rocky, Cici set to work at the accounts with the exactness that Uncle Myron and Aunt Dorothy had instilled in her—which led to Betty's departure in a fury. Cici was not allowed the keys to a car, on the excuse that she might have an accident since the Irish drove on the other side of the road. Lonely and miserable, she longed to run away. She thought of Mum's departure for London, ten years earlier, as an escape from jail.

Back in Los Angeles, with St. Cleran's sold, Cici lobbied again to take me. Nurse was the sticking point: Cici couldn't see Nurse living in her house, and Nurse didn't want to live there either. "Oh, Miss Medcalf," my godmother Gina remembers Nurse sighing plaintively before she left, racked by worry over Cici's influence on me.

But the arrangement on Euclid was untenable: I was getting older, Nurse couldn't drive, Gladys would be going with Dad to Morocco to film *The Man Who Would Be King*. Plus, I loved Cici; she treated Collin and me equally, and I felt her love for me. In her letters from the time, Collin and I are always "the kids": no distinction between us.

I was given money for my birthday, or maybe it was Christmas. Cici took me to the bank to open a savings account. Since it was my account, she let me answer the questions that the woman on the other side of the counter asked.

"Name?"

"Address?"

"Phone number?"

The woman was filling in the form by hand. She held her fingers at a weird angle so that her long fingernails could slot together around the pen.

"Mother's maiden name?"

I wasn't sure what to say. I didn't call Cici "Mom," but in every other way she was my mother now. I didn't want to hurt her feelings. And Mum had dwindled to a rumor in my memory.

"Shane," I said.

It was close enough to the truth, I told myself. Still, I felt shifty. I wondered if Cici was pleased, or shocked by my disloyalty to Mum. I'd lost my moorings, and was steering by instinct. With one word, I'd given myself a live mother again.

I wanted Cici to think it was the most natural thing in the world for me to put her maiden name on the form. I wanted her to think that I didn't doubt myself and I didn't want her to doubt me, which she might if she saw me look to her for approval. So I kept my eyes fixed on the woman's nails as she wrote.

Cici said nothing either. But I felt a warmth emanate from her, as if a heater had been switched on.

I had the sense that Dad had married Cici without quite knowing what he was doing. She unsettled him; he didn't seem at all sure that she was the kind of woman he was supposed to be with. To start with, he was thirty-four years older than she was; exactly double her age, as I calculated it. She wasn't "a lady," as I'd been brought up to conceive of one: she walked around wearing very little, she swore, she cackled when she laughed with her friends. There was nothing proper about her. She wasn't particularly interested in art, didn't read books; she and Dad didn't have the kind of intellectual conversations he had with his friends or in watered-down versions with me. When he laughed at something Cici said, they weren't really laughing together. It wasn't that he was mocking her, but he laughed at her in the way you laugh at a thing that amuses you—which, at another time or place, might not. I sometimes doubted that he respected her—or himself for marrying her.

Cici loved horses. It was the one thing about her that fit in with Dad. The room by the garage door was a tack room, full of saddles and bridles and ringed with blue and red and yellow and green and white ribbons from horse shows. She rode almost every day, even though she always came back with her nose and eyes streaming with allergies. But Dad didn't ride with her. He seemed to have given it up. Her kind of riding wasn't his. Irish hunting was full of dress-up and ritual, with huge gleaming horses, red coats and hairnets, flimsy English saddles, crazy hounds, a galloping tear across fields and stone walls—an intensely social event. Cici rode western, in boots and jeans and, being her, bikini tops; usually alone, on trails up into the hills of Will Rogers State Park, which was across the canyon from her house. Her riding was meditative and private, quiet and slow.

She gave me one of her horses, an albino with blue eyes which we named Blanca. Because Blanca was a Connemara pony—from Ireland—Cici said it was right that she should be mine. I loved Blanca for being Irish, for being white, for being small and gentle. I liked combing her mane and brushing her tail, though the power of her back legs so close to me was frightening, but I dreaded having to get on her back. I'd retreated into books so completely during the year on Euclid that my physical ineptness had calcified. My body felt disconnected, out of my control.

I wanted to like riding, both because Dad prized good horsemanship and because it would give me something to share with Cici—especially since Collin didn't ride. She led me along trails on her gray Arabian stallion, Khedeer. The ground was sandy, rocky, unstable, and even at a slow walk sure-footed Blanca would stumble.

With each tiny catch in her gait, my muscles seized up, my heart pounded, and my skin tingled as if my nerve endings themselves were sweating. I grabbed the saddle horn or Blanca's mane until the panic passed, hoping that Cici wouldn't turn and see what a coward I was. I understood what riding was supposed to feel like—a sense of oneness with the horse, the hoofbeats like the heartbeat of the earth thudding through you, the rich oxygen flooding your lungs—but it was unreachably distant. If I stretched for it, I'd fall.

I felt Cici's disappointment. This was something she wanted to give me, and to give Dad by giving me. All I felt from Dad was obliviousness. Once he came out the front door and remarked that I had a natural seat—but Blanca wasn't moving at the time, she was still tied to the iron hitching post at the edge of the rose-fringed crescent of lawn. After a moment he went inside. He didn't wait to watch us ride away.

Dad praised accomplishment, not effort. That made sense to me. I wanted to do things right, and I didn't see anything to praise in doing them badly just for the sake of it. And her good at so many things, made them all seem effortless. I had little concept of learning, outside of academics; I thought you ought to be able to paint, or sing, or ride, the first time you did them—or at least, show obvious talent that required only honing and direction. So I avoided the things I couldn't do, and played to my strengths. I read classic novels that I could talk to Dad about, I did my Irish jig when asked, and I was always ready for backgammon.

I was good enough by now to play him on equal terms. He had given me books on backgammon when I was living on Euclid, and I'd studied them thoroughly. I knew the theory of doubling; I knew the odds of any particular roll of the dice; I knew the pros and cons of every possible opening move. If Dad made a weak play or an old-fashioned one, I would—sometimes—point it out. I felt a spark of energy pass between us, a give-and-take that signified the possibility that I might be earning his respect and admiration.

He had ordered a special backgammon table, with the board sunk into the top under a removable panel. It had square, splayed legs like an alien landing craft, and the whole thing, legs and all, was covered in split bamboo. I saw Dad's face cloud over when it arrived; he found it as graceless as I did. As I watched, his face lost that vague expression and hardened into a grim half smile, daring anyone— even himself—to challenge his necessary delight in what he had caused to be made.

Though it wasn't beautiful, the table was lovely to play on. The rim around the sunken board was wide, with plenty of space for a drink and a scorepad—we had to be careful not to roll our drinks instead of the dice cups. The leather board was padded underneath, and the points had been sewn in seams, not appliquéd, so that there were no rough edges to catch against the pieces. Dad slid them elegantly across the leather surface, the pads of his flat, manicured fingertips caressing them firmly into their new places. When he had to pick them up—to bear them off, or to move them across the central bar—he trapped them with the barest amount of pressure, his knuckles straight, as if the pieces held to his fingers by magnetic affinity, not the crude clutch of anatomical joints. He looked pained if his opponent picked up a piece unnecessarily, and almost ill if you turned a piece on end and tapped it along the points to count out a move. He never had to count, and neither did I. We read the points as we read writing.

Dad's movements at the backgammon board were as rhythmic as a weaver's. He shook the leather cup three quick times, thumb and two fingers holding it lightly, fourth and fifth finger folded into his palm, all movement coming from the wrist. He rarely delayed to think, and as he slid the pieces he spoke the numbers in an incantatory tone, rounded and rolling like the buff-cornered dice. We talked only in short snatches—no probing questions or challenging discussion. Sometimes we played for hours.

"It's not a real game unless you play for real money," said Dad one day. "If there's nothing at stake, the doubling dice means nothing, and the doubling dice is the most fascinating element of the game. We'll play for a dollar a point."

That was big money to me. Three doubles would bring a game to an eight-dollar stake, and we played at least ten games at a sitting. We settled up whenever Dad went out of town, and usually I'd be up about sixty dollars. Solemnly he counted out the notes and I stashed them away, to spend on books.

I knew he expected the same from me if I was down, but I thought it would never happen. Then it did. His departure date was approaching, and my nerves made me turn down more doubles than usual. The decline was inexorable. I started to resent it: I was only a kid, and twenty-three dollars meant much more to me than it did to Dad. But even though I longed to be indulged, I didn't think indulgence was on offer and I didn't dare test it with even the most offhand remark in case Dad lost respect for me. I was proud that Dad took me seriously as a backgammon player, so I avoided playing in the last few days, then on the day he left I dug into my hoard and ponied up.

When Dad's friends came over to play, men in their fifties and sixties, he would say to them, after a few games, "Why don't you play my ten-year-old daughter?" The friends always agreed. That was polite, of course, but I noticed a glint of subservience in many of his friendships. As I played—sliding the pieces decisively, never counting, making my move the second the dice stopped rolling—I would see a hunted look come into my opponent's eyes. He'd glance at Dad, who sat to the side like a tennis umpire, and Dad would blandly raise an eyebrow as if to say, You didn't think I would indulge a child, did you? The joke was on them, and I was the implement of it. I glowed inside.

"Well done, honey," he'd say as he took my seat. I'd played my part, the innocent demon, and I was dismissed.

One day, Billy Pearson, Dad's closest pal, offered to back me against the rube of the day at twenty dollars a point. Thrilled to be playing for real stakes, I started setting up my pieces.

"No, honey. Absolutely not."

I was surprised, and upset. Dad seemed angry at me, and I didn't know why. I so wanted to play; I was good enough to win; I couldn't put up those stakes myself; and I'd known Billy since St. Cleran's. I implored Dad silently, and uselessly. A veiled rebuke was issued to Billy, and I was told to go to my room.

"Never gamble with other people's money," he said to me the next day, as if I should have known it. "If you lose, you'll be in debt to them. If you win, you'll feel you're owed something, but it's their choice whether to share the winnings with you—and how much. It's a position no woman should put herself in."

It is, I think, the only piece of life advice he ever gave me.

In a velvet-lined case in Dad's closet sat a collection of brooches: modernist sculptures of bone set in irregular rectangles of hand-wrought gold. They were ancient Coptic artifacts, ridged and splintered, very bonelike, as if the meat had been gnawed or weathered off them and they'd been left to bleach in the sun. They reminded me of saints' relics. It had been Tony's idea to make them into brooches, and Dad was now occupied with finding suitable women to give them to. Cici and Anjelica were each given one, one went to Aunt Dorothy, one was dispatched to France to the Baroness Pauline, one was given to his old friend Cherokee MacNamara.

I wasn't at all sure that I liked them, but I desperately wanted one. It would put me in the company of women to whom Dad gave treasures. I wanted him to think of me as someone who could appreciate the things he thought were beautiful.

I didn't ask for one. It would have been embarrassing—but more importantly it would have erased the value of the gift. Occasionally I would hear him tell Cici the name of another woman to whom he was giving a brooch, and which one. Finally the case was empty.

When he came back from Morocco, Dad brought more treasures:

exotic objects, such as those that had filled St. Cleran's. An old Moroccan door became the new coffee table. Rolled up in ropes of tissue paper were heavy Berber necklaces, of coral and amber. Mine had thin strands of tubular coral, strung in groups of three, separated by coins.

The coins were the reason he'd bought that one for me: and I hated them with silent fury. My necklace was the smallest of all of them, the thinnest, the crudest. The coins were set into rings of dark gray metal, like pull tabs from 7-Up cans. The rough ends of the coral beads showed the fraying black thread that held the whole thing together.

Where my necklace had coins, the others had beautiful amber beads, the color of honey, round like dull suns. Those went to Anjelica. I felt that Dad had an idea of me, which was partly true but not entirely. I was the egghead, but an "expert" type rather than the kind of creative thinker that Dad really admired. Tony held that slot, though I was aware that he wasn't, in Dad's eyes, quite living up to it. Anjelica, of course, was the beauty, the princess, the jewel, the one who deserved to be given the really special things—the things that I wanted too.

I felt furtive and guilty, as if it was I who was hiding some aspect of my true self from Dad—which I was, because I never told him that I didn't want the coins, didn't like them, wasn't interested in them. Secretly I blamed him for not knowing it, for not being bothered or able to notice that I had other dimensions to me. I felt I'd been assigned a part, one that was important to the story but wasn't a leading role. And if that was my part, I ought to accept it, and corral my emotions inside its limits.

"He's not really your father," said a girl at school. I'd been talking about how my dad was going off to Morocco.

I had no idea what she was talking about.

"You're adopted."

"No I'm not!"

I'd never heard this, or thought it before, but I knew instantly it was possible. I felt a trapdoor fall open, and I was teetering on the edge.

"That's what it says in the *Palisades View*. That's what your step-mother said."

I'd watched Cici curl her hair in rollers for the photo in the local paper, thought how beautiful she was, barefoot and relaxed, lit by the sunlight shining unbroken through the plate-glass windows of the living room. Why would she have said something like that if it wasn't true?

I searched the house, but I couldn't find a copy of the paper. The shops of Pacific Palisades were literally miles away, out of reach. Days later—or maybe it was only hours, or a day at most—I found the paper lying on the dining table, took it to my room, and closed the door.

The journalist wrote that Cici lived with her husband, the film director John Huston, her son Collin from a previous marriage, and John's adopted daughter Allegra. I read the words over and over, wondering if the journalist could have confused the fact that I wasn't Cici's real daughter with my not being Dad's. Was I Cici's adopted daughter because I had given her maiden name at the bank? She usually referred to me simply as her daughter, without "step" or "adopted" or anything like that. Was "adopted" better than "step"? Was that what Cici had really said to this journalist, who was so stupid that she'd mixed it up? The explanation held water—sort of. Not wanting to tip it, I never asked Cici what she'd said.

It festered. I sensed there was some kind of truth in it: it explained that vivid memory of playing on a rug in a hotel room with the sharp corner of a coffee table near my cheek, and a voice saying, "This is your father." If he was really my father, surely I wouldn't have had to be told. But if he was Tony and Anjelica's father, which he obviously was—and I was sure they were really my brother and sister, and that Mum had been the mother of all three of us—why hadn't I already known he was mine?

Mum *was* really my mother. It had to have been my real mother who died; otherwise the loss of her—the emptiness I'd felt my whole conscious life—meant nothing. "Adopted" stripped me of Mum and Dad both. I wouldn't accept it; the journalist had obviously got it wrong. It was a local paper, after all, so any journalist who was any good wouldn't be working for it, they'd be working for the *Los Angeles Times*.

I took my passport out of the shoe box in my closet where it lived. Etched into the soft surface of my photograph was Dad's distinctive handwriting: a signature that read "John Huston (father)."

The letters canted forward with determination and certainty, the crosses of the "t"s fierce downstrokes that allowed no argument. It was a legal document. Dad couldn't have lied.

I'd got that passport during the year I'd lived on Euclid. We'd had a number of meetings with a lawyer, which culminated in a white building with the tall, lone, slablike monumentality of a tombstone. This was the Federal Building at 11000 Wilshire Boulevard. We were there to make me an American citizen.

I'd never seen Dad in a situation like this: supplicatory, uncertain, not in control. His knees and elbows seemed stiffer and more angular than usual, as if a giant hand had folded him up and wrapped him in a rubber band. A feeble half smile was fixed on his face, waiting to be switched off. I sat tensely beside him, dreading the questions I was sure would come at me. The federal man didn't know that Dad and I didn't live in the same house, and I figured he ought not to. He might say I couldn't stay, couldn't be American, and I'd have to go live somewhere else. Where? In London with Tony, whom I'd barely seen for years? St. Cleran's was gone.

But the questions didn't come. The federal man pulled a blank passport out of a drawer. Gladys handed him a black-and-white photo of me that we'd just had taken. He glued it in, pushed my new passport across the desk to Dad, and handed him a pen.

I watched the pen dig into the thick surface of the photograph, the bones of Dad's knuckles radiating out like the points of a star. Then the federal man stamped embossed letters into it with a tool that made the muscles in his hand bulge, as if a mole were tunneling under the skin.

My old passport had identified me as a two-foot-six-inch British subject, with no distinguishing characteristics. It was signed by my mother. My new one gave my address as that of Dad's business manager's office, and it didn't ask for distinguishing characteristics. It was signed—it said so, straight out—by my father.

10

Sometimes in the mornings, while I was brushing my teeth, I would hear Cici and Maricela, the maid, talking together in the kitchen about how they'd had to carry Dad to bed because he'd drunk himself unconscious. Their voices were low and giggly, like thieves who had pulled off a heist of Dad's dignity. It made me uncomfortable. He was my father, after all. Maybe I ought to take his side, I thought. But how could I? It was shameful to drink so much you passed out. Besides, it was Cici I felt close to, Cici who had given me a normal life.

Maricela was Mexican, from a large family in Tijuana, most of whom were now in Los Angeles. She insisted that she didn't know how old she was, which I found impossible to believe. Cici used to say that Maricela was like a daughter to her, since she'd been with her from the age of fourteen. That was six years before, putting her at about twenty.

She had long, almost Asian eyes and cropped hair like a boy's. She never wore makeup or anything girly, just T-shirts and jeans. She had a way of hiding from people, like a feral cat.

She didn't like me. I did my best to win her over—it scared me not to be liked—but it was no good. She told Cici that I hated Collin, which was so obviously untrue that Cici, fortunately, didn't believe it. She also told her that I buried my food in the garden like a dog, a story she worked up from the time I hid some cookies in my room, for later. She had an introverted sense of humor, and her sudden curt laughs left me mystified. With Collin she shared a sense of being different from the ordinary world, and she was kind to him. Me, she ignored as thoroughly as she could. I attributed her disdain for everyone and everything to an unsentimental practicality forced on her by her poverty-stricken childhood, so I didn't hold it against her. In fact, it fascinated me. I wished I could care as little as she did.

During one of Dad's trips to Morocco, Maricela went into a depression. She had, she said, had an affair with an airline pilot named Juan, and she was pining for him. I heard some rustle in the air that she was pregnant, but there was no baby on the way. I wondered how, or where, she could possibly have met an airline pilot. She wasn't the type to go to bars. It was weird to think of Maricela with any man at all.

Cici was worried about her, and decided she needed a vacation. She gave Maricela an airline ticket to wherever she wanted to go. That place turned out to be Morocco; Juan turned out to be John; the airline pilot was actually a film director. Tony, my brother, found Dad and Maricela entwined. After three years—one of which I'd shared with them—Dad and Cici's marriage was over.

I typed the forms that Cici had to fill out for the divorce. It seemed natural, since I was good at typing and she wasn't. I was proud that she trusted me, at age eleven, to do them correctly. I decided it wasn't disloyal to Dad, since he had left me with Cici; but I did think that it was better not to tell him about it.

If I was asked whether I wanted to stay with Cici, I would have answered that I did. I don't remember being asked. Where else would I have gone? Not with Dad and Maricela to Mexico. Cici wanted to keep me. Either Dad recognized that she was a good mother to me and wanted me to stay with her—though the divorce turned vicious fast—or he just took the easy way out.

Cici had lists of objects that ran for pages and pages, more objects than it seemed possible for one house to hold, things with strange names, such as an Egyptian jade pectoral and Etruscan burial glass. These were the inventories from St. Cleran's, annotated according to what had been kept, sold, stored, or given away. The remaining items were marked with initials to show which things would go with Dad and which would stay with Cici. Cici was furious that Dad took the silverware. I was sorry to see that the gold-embossed champagne glasses were going too.

Cici pointed to one item, *Night Image*, with "JH" next to it. "That's Cousin Itt," she said. "He should be yours."

An abstract sculpture covered in differently colored segments of string and thread, about four feet high, *Night Image* looked exactly like the character in *The Addams Family*, without the sunglasses. We all loved *The Addams Family*, and watched it most afternoons. Cici did a brilliant imitation of Thing, the hand in the box, and was always doing Lurch voices, sometimes in the character of Gladys. The sculpture had stood on the table in the upstairs hall of the Big House, looking alien and slightly forbidding. At Cici's house, renamed, he became my pet. I loved to groom him, untangling his threads with my fingers and brushing him with a soft, silver-backed brush that Aunt Dorothy gave me.

Nervously I wrote to ask Dad if I could keep him. I would never have dared ask for anything without Cici's urging, and I worried that I was letting her push me into a big mistake. What if it made Dad mad at me? Worse, what if he decided that Cici was a bad influence and took me away?

Dad wrote back to say that of course *Night Image* should be mine; it was only fitting, since the sculpture was the last thing my mother had given him. The formality of Dad's words—a sort of official presentation to me of this piece of art—seemed to be taking credit for his thoughtfulness in giving Itt to me. So why did I have to ask? I thought at once. If I hadn't asked, if Cici hadn't made me, Cousin Itt would have been swept off without a thought for me or Mum and who knows where he would have ended up. In storage, somewhere, in a box in a dark warehouse.

Also, why not call him by the name we always called him? The words *Night Image* had never passed our lips, at St. Cleran's or at Cici's house. The whole letter rubbed me the wrong way. Sides were being taken, and I knew whose side I was on.

When the moving van came, Cici and I were waiting. It was summer, so I wasn't in school. Collin was.

The moving men set up a packing station on the lawn. Cici didn't want them galumphing around the house, so she and I carried Dad's things outside.

It was impersonal, like cleaning up the ash after a fire. Dad was gone, I wasn't sure where he was. These things, if they had any meaning left for me after their years in Cici's house, meant St. Cleran's, the place, not Dad, the person; and St. Cleran's had been lost for years.

We picked up the life-size crucifix from the living room, Cici at the top, me at the foot. We had to swing around awkwardly so that we wouldn't fall into the pond in the middle of the floor, or hit Cousin Itt where he stood on his table, safe now with me.

"Onward Christian soldiers," Cici started singing. She gave the words a sarcastic twist. Though I could only see the back of her head, I knew the corners of her mouth were turning down.

I thought it was funny too.

"Marching off to war!" We belted it out—wrong. Then we got stuck. Neither of us knew the next line.

Cici started at the top again. "Onward Christian soldiers," we sang as we marched in step with the cross on our shoulders out the wide front door. "Onward Christian soldiers," over and over, as we collected up the various saints and Christs. Hypnotized, I started to feel like a Christian soldier myself—fighting the good fight. Ridding the house of Dad's relics felt more and more like ridding it of devils.

Cici had started the singing to cheer me up, because she was afraid that I'd mourn the loss of these things as a symbol of losing Dad. Now each object that left the house was an enemy slain. I was almost disappointed when we came to the last thing on the list: the dark Madonna that loomed over my room.

I used to stare at her before I fell asleep, with the arrows in her heart and her tender wrists extended. The Latin words floated around her like horseflies ready to sting her; yet her face was calm. I felt a kinship with her but I hated her too: hated her for being so serenely shameless in her anguish, so ready to be hurt even more, so proud of her throne of sorrow. She kept wounds open, for to her they were badges of honor. Mine were well scarred over, and I didn't like the thought of her probing them as I slept.

Cici and I lifted her up between us and carried her directly outside. Framing my door were beds of pansies, then the lawn with its ring of flowers. The Madonna lay on the grass, waiting for the men to pack her up: a node of darkness in the bright day. I was glad to see her out of my room. I hadn't realized how much she had oppressed me. Now that she was going, she pulled all the darkness out of my room with her. Liquid sunlight flowed in through the open door in her wake.

The next morning I came back up the hill from doing turds, as Cici called it—cleaning Blanca's corral—to find Cici on top of a ladder in the middle of my room, leaning over backward with a staple gun in her hand. Four wide streamers of cheesecloth in ice-cream colors—pink, yellow, blue, and green—trailed from a board on the ceiling to fat bolts on the floor.

"You like?" she said.

She'd already done one side of the room. The four colors draped in stripes across the ceiling like a circus tent and fell all the way down to the floor.

It was fantastic: girly and dramatic, but bohemian too, with light misting through the open weave of the cloth. Cici had been planning it for months, she told me, bringing back the fabric secretly on our trips to Puerto Vallarta. I knew she couldn't have done it if the Madonna were still there. It had been the Madonna's room and I a guest in it, as I had been in the Bhutan Room. But yesterday the Madonna, with all her masochistic sorrows, had been vanquished.

I helped Cici put up the rest of the fabric, holding it high above my head so she could reach out, her long toes curled over the edge of the ladder step, and staple it into the angle where wall met ceiling. She cut neat edges above the doors and closets, but let the fabric fall over the windows like curtains. I could push it back if I wanted and hook it behind nails.

In the center of the ceiling, over the board where the ends of fabric were stapled, she hung a little mirror rimmed in pink Venetian glass. It shot a thrill through me. I knew there was something shocking about a mirror on the ceiling, though I didn't quite know why. The Chicksweeper had a giant one, the kind you'd put on a closet, reflecting his king-size bed and white shag rug. Collin and I thought it was hilarious. Mine was beautiful.

It wasn't really me, this fantasy bedroom—it was more like the room Cici had had when she was a girl, but even more extreme, more amazing. But since I didn't know what was me, that didn't really matter. It was mine, and best of all Cici made it specifically for me. The amount of effort she put into it announced that I was staying put.

The billowing cloth covered every inch of wall, which meant there was no question of paintings, photographs, posters—no pressure to come up with a visible expression of who I was, or to make aesthetic choices that might be found wanting by Anjelica or Dad (even in his absence, I felt the shadow of his judgment). I was tired of things being serious and tasteful. The knobbly headboard that I couldn't lean against was gone, and I had the twin beds that Aunt Dorothy had contributed to the house on Euclid. Here, in my beautiful tent, I might actually invite a friend to sleep over in the other one.

In the meantime, our kittens loved to play with the loose ends of fabric that trailed on the floor under the beds. Mine was called Jinx, Collin's was D'Artagnan Porthos Athos Aramis Rochefort Richelieu Louis XIV Green. (Green was Collin's last name.) We'd brought them home from our neighbors' house in the pockets of our jackets when they were tiny—too young to have been separated from their mother. As a result, they sucked their tails. Cici wanted to put hydrogen peroxide or quinine on them to stop the sucking but I refused, even though the tails looked revoltingly nipply. I didn't feel guilty about having taken Jinx away from his mother, but I didn't want to punish him for missing her.

Anjelica had been living with Jack for as long as I'd been living with Cici. His daughter, Jennifer, was a year older than me, blond and pudgy like me, so that we could have been sisters. We found it funny that if Anjel and Jack married, I'd be Jen's aunt.

They took us to Aspen for two weeks, to ski. We made a perfect family: Jen and I sharing a bedroom, Anjelica cooking roast chicken and spaghetti Bolognese in the evenings, and Jack the ringmaster, the source of all excitement. Anjel mothered us, taking us shopping for ski clothes and putting sunscreen on our faces. Every day our ski instructor would bring us to a restaurant to meet them for lunch.

"She's a phenom!" Jack boasted to anyone who asked Jen how

she liked skiing. I was happy for her, shining in her father's eyes, even though I was far from being a phenom myself.

I loved Jack's voice. Like Daddy's, it had a way of soaking into all the air in a room. But Jack's voice was slangier than Daddy's and had a dangerous edge. Everything he said seemed to hold a hidden joke; a joke that you were in on if you heard the grin behind the words. Dad's voice made you his disciple; Jack's made you his accomplice.

I loved the way he called me Leggsington, and Jen Bimbooreen, and had nicknames for everybody: Curly and Whitey and Red Dog and Blackie and Beaner. Arthur Garfunkel was the G, or the Big G, or the New G. Warren Beatty was the Pro. When he called Anjel Toot, or Tootman, I felt I could actually see the bond between them. She *was* Toot, and he had christened her; she was singular and special, the way she was meant to be.

The first time Anjelica took me to Jack's house, she parked her little Mercedes in the open garage next to Jack's big maroon Mercedes—called Bing, because it was the color of a bing cherry—and we went into the house through the kitchen. Jack was sitting on a sofa, in an area off the kitchen that wasn't quite living room, leaning forward into the phone, as if telling a secret. He wore jeans and a white shirt, whiter than any shirt I'd ever seen. Near him was a hat rack covered in baseball caps—more than I'd ever imagined one person could own.

"Toot," Jack said as he hung up the phone, stringing out the word. He stood up to kiss her. It was the first time I noticed that Anjel was taller than he was.

I spent many weekends at Jack's house, with Jen. We had the living room to ourselves in the mornings, before Jack and Anjel got up. We'd do a heavy wooden jigsaw puzzle of a pig (Jack collected pigs, so there were pig-shaped things everywhere), or the strange silver robot figure that came apart into interlocking pieces, or we'd lie on the carpet out of the sun and play long games of Petropolis, which was a kind of special-edition Monopoly for millionaires. Some

French count had given Jack a set: the properties were countries, with embossed leather ownership cards; the houses were solid silver oil derricks; and the hotels were oil platforms plated in gold. Also, we designed our houses. We drew endless floor plans, usually with exercise rooms (though neither of us was sporty) and always with a slide from the master bedroom down into the pool.

Jack's bedroom, upstairs, had a little balcony overlooking the pool. Often Jen and I would be swimming when Jack made his first appearance of the morning—folding back the hinged balcony railing, taking a running leap, and cannonballing into the pool with a wild whoop. Bozo, his black Labrador, would leap in after him, crazy with excitement, his nails clawing as he dog-paddled close to us. I shrank away from him, fearing the red welts Bozo's nails raised on my arms.

"Grab 'em!" Jack urged me. "Dance with the Big Bo!"

Jack's ability to play awed me. He didn't play like a child; he played like an adult who knew how to have fun, like Jack: a bit wild, but always in control, abandoned to the moment, for just as long as the moment lasted and no more. He seemed to know exactly what he wanted to do, at any given second. He spent long hours upstairs in his room, reading—history and philosophy mostly, names like Hegel and Nietzsche that I'd heard of but hadn't imagined anyone actually reading. He collected paintings to the point of obsession; and he was as delighted at discovering a new painter he admired, or a lesser-known painter such as Alma-Tadema or Bouguereau, as he was at acquiring a new Picasso or a Dufy. I was there when a moving truck arrived with a giant canvas of a woman smoking a cigarette, by an artist I hadn't heard of named Tamara de Lempicka. There was only one wall big enough to hold it: the one opposite the stairs. Though the overall effect was cosmopolitan rather than mythical, I saw, in the woman's faceted face and angled body, echoes of Dad's Saint George.

Jack bought so many paintings that they soon overflowed the wall space and had to be stacked against the walls of the Garfunkel Suite, as the maid's room was known. Eventually, the room was so full of stored paintings that there was no room for Arthur Garfunkel to stay it in anymore.

Usually I slept on the sofa in the TV room, which was soft and deep and enveloping. The room was always dark, blocked off from the sunlight glancing off the pool by thick curtains, so that it felt as if it was deep in the bowels of the house. The sofa was set up on a little platform so you could see over the projector mechanism of the TV, which crouched in the middle of the floor, casting three eyes—red, blue, and green—onto a screen which virtually covered one wall. A couple of armchairs squeezed in beside the projector, and the walls were covered with paintings. It was hard to tell, but I thought some of them were of Anjelica.

Jack's pals came over to watch the Lakers' road games. I didn't really like basketball, but I liked watching it with Jack. On the screen, fuzzy, washed-out giants in yellow uniforms pounded up and down a court while Jack yelled at them, jumping up and down like them, cheering as loud as if he were in the stadium. His pals pounded the air and cheered too—a little less loudly, a little more decorously, like backup singers. It reminded me of Dad: another king, another court.

When Jack's friends gathered in the evenings, Harry Dean Stanton would sing Mexican songs. I watched intently for the moment when he moved to pick up the guitar. I couldn't understand the Spanish words, but they were full of torment. As Harry sang them, his voice seemed to catch on barbed hooks of heartbreak as it slid between one note and the next. I lost myself as I listened. The liquid of his voice picked me up and washed through me.

Harry Dean didn't laugh loud and crack jokes, like the others. When he spoke, his Kentucky drawl was slow, as if weighed down by the melancholy of centuries. I had to lean close to hear him. His narrow, drooping face reminded me of the farmer in the painting *American Gothic*. He wasn't part of the basketball crowd. He loved to play Scrabble, and so did I; and though I was a child, we started a regular game that lasted as long as I lived in L.A.

Anjel had her place in Jack's court, though she was not quite the queen. He was the only sun; she held the inner orbit. She was still in her early twenties, much younger than Jack. It seemed natural to me, as Dad's daughter, that she would defer to him. What happened was what Jack wanted, and everyone was there to service him. I loved the circus quality of his house, with people dropping in and out, and the coven in the kitchen—Anjelica, Jack's secretary Annie, and Helena, who lived next door—making grilled cheese and tomato in the toaster oven. It was familiar, though I didn't quite recognize it: a California version of St. Cleran's.

That Jack was somewhat remote felt right. Like Dad, he descended to have his needs met, then ascended again. I wasn't close to him in the sense that we did anything special together, or shared heartfelt emotion; but he treated me exactly as he treated Jen, and she was his daughter. I watched TV with him, swam, laughed at his jokes. That was all I wanted: to be included in the nucleus of his world.

Jen and I went together to Portland, Oregon, where he was filming *One Flew Over the Cuckoo's Nest*, and to Billings, Montana, where he was filming *The Missouri Breaks*. I knew Anjel was happy that Jen and I were such good friends, and I was doubly glad to be pleasing her. From Billings, we went on a day trip into Yellowstone. Jack drove. On the way back, Jack suddenly said, into the silence of the speeding, tired car, "Another day, another twenty-five thou!" I thought this was one of the wittiest things I'd ever heard and repeated it to everyone I knew. I was slightly baffled when nobody got the joke, but I didn't care; they were outsiders, and I was in. I'd even arrived on the set and found I already knew someone: Harry Dean Stanton, his face bumpy with mosquito bites and the mournful echo of the Mexican songs I loved to hear him sing shimmering around him.

The set rumbled with the unseen presence of the film's other star: Marlon Brando. Like thunder so distant that some sixth or seventh sense registers only an incalculable disturbance in the air,

Marlon's proximity made people jumpy—even Jack. He was, I knew, considered the greatest actor alive; he was certainly the most famous person ever to have visited St. Cleran's, and County Galway had still been talking about it a decade later. Though Marlon wasn't even on set the first few days I was in Montana, Jack seemed nervous, thrown a little off his axis. I was surprised, because I knew Marlon lived on the hill above Jack's house and shared a driveway off the main road, and they were friends. (The following year, Marlon would play an April Fool's joke on Jack, telling him he was selling his house to Sylvester Stallone unless Jack could come up with some huge sum of money to match it.)

In two years of visiting Jack's house, I hadn't met Marlon. In Montana, in 115-degree heat, with grasshoppers splashing up at every footstep, I did.

"Look at his eyes, Legs," Anjel whispered to me. "He has violet eyes."

I looked at them furtively, not quite daring to look into them when he was looking at me. They weren't violet; they were bluey-gray.

I'd failed a test. I didn't belong in this company. Living on the grand scale, like Dad and Anjelica, meant mythologizing the great people. I knew that Dad would have agreed that Brando had violet eyes. If you were special, you saw what was special in other people— and even if you weren't quite a god yourself, you could recognize a god when you saw one. That marked both of you out from the ordinary. I knew I wasn't playing the game; I couldn't play the game. It was a flaw in me that couldn't be fixed: I was prosaic. I wished I wasn't, but I was.

And then, a few months after Dad left, Cici's brother died.

Stephan was the baby of the family, her only younger brother. I had met him once, when Aunt Dorothy took me and Collin to San

Francisco for the weekend for Stephan's graduation from law school. He seemed sad and dutiful; I got the impression that law school was such a serious business that one should never laugh again. (Aunt Dorothy told me frequently that I should become a lawyer.) She kept Stephan's wedding photo on top of the TV in her bedroom—he was handsome and golden in a white suit with embroidered flowers— even though he and his wife were already divorced. She talked about his ex-wife often, as if pretending they were still married would make it so. Often she said of her two older sons, "I wish Bob [or David] would find a nice girl and settle down," even though it was obvious to both Collin and me that nice girls held no interest for the Chicksweeper, and girls of any kind held no interest for Bob at all.

Stephan had been flying a glider, and it crashed into a mountain. Cici's friend Dyke Debbie the tennis pro told me it was suicide. Aunt Dorothy insisted always that it was an accident. The day the phone call came, I stayed in my room with Collin, watching TV, on our side of the swinging kitchen door, while Cici's friends took charge. That night, we were sent to stay with her friend Joey.

I didn't like Joey, with his too-curly, too-long hair and gold chains. I felt him looking at me when Collin and I came back through the living room after taking our nightly Jacuzzi. (The Jacuzzi was off Cici's bedroom, sunk into the floor of its own glassed-in room, T-shaped with lots of levels and curved places to lie molded in concrete. After Anjelica brought Jack to see it, he ordered one exactly the same for himself.) I didn't want to go to Joey's house, but under the circumstances I didn't see how I could protest.

Joey set out a sheet and pillow for Collin on the sofa, and gave me his bed in a bachelor bedroom of dark gray sheets, black metal furniture, and a deep pile rug (though nothing as ludicrous as the Chicksweeper's). I woke up in the middle of the night to find him in bed beside me. His chest was bare. Was he naked? My breath started to come short and panting, my heart thumped so loud that I was afraid the noise of it, cannoning through the molecules of air, might wake him. I wondered if it was okay that he was in bed beside me and felt quite sure it wasn't, then decided I was being ridiculous. It was his bed. It was kind of him to let me sleep in it.

There was no way I could go back to sleep with him there beside me. Morning was a long way away. I worried about offending him if I got out of bed. Would it be tantamount to accusing him of molesting me? That wasn't fair. He hadn't so much as brushed against me by accident.

I got up and went into the living room. I lay down on the floor next to Collin's sofa, feeling like I was protecting him: his older sister, there beside him if he should wake upset because his uncle was dead. I was desperate to fall asleep quickly. If I was asleep when Joey woke and realized I wasn't in bed anymore, it would prove me innocent of fear and suspicion; a suspicious, frightened person wouldn't, obviously, be able to sleep. But my mind raced in circles around the picture of me sleeping, and vulnerable.

Joey came out of the bedroom. He was wearing pajama bottoms. I knew immediately that he'd been wearing them all along, and I felt my face flush hot. Of course he wouldn't have betrayed Cici's trust—especially at a time like this.

"What are you doing on the floor? You'll be more comfortable in the bed."

"I'm fine here," I stammered. "I want to be next to Collin."

"I'm not going to touch you," he said. There it was—he could read my mind. "There's nothing to be afraid of."

"I'm not," I said, backpedaling desperately. I didn't want him to tell Cici that I didn't trust him, because she would think that meant that I didn't trust her. "You know . . . Stephan. I just want to be with Collin."

Collin was waking up by this time, befuddled and sleepy. I shushed him in what I hoped was a concerned-looking, big-sisterly way. Joey shrugged and went back to bed.

I didn't tell Cici, of course. I didn't tell anyone, such as Aunt

Dorothy or Anjelica, because I didn't want Cici to look bad—or worse, give them the idea that I wasn't safe with her. I was supposed to be no trouble. No harm had come to me. I think Joey told her, though—because soon afterward he disappeared from our lives.

I was used to Cici drinking rather than eating. She'd stand at the open fridge door and swig fruit juice and liquid protein, which came in evil-looking plastic bottles covered with writing to give the stuff scientific credibility. After Stephan's death, the trips to the fridge were for grapefruit juice and vodka. I didn't think much of it; grapefruit juice was normal in the mornings, and every freezer I'd ever known was stocked with Stolichnaya. I never saw her drunk; she just wasn't really there.

In place of Maricela, we now had Ana Maria and Eduardo. They had an air of concealed malevolence which Cici, clouded by grief and desperate for help in looking after us, couldn't see. I guessed that they resented us for being spoiled American kids.

One day Collin and I were in my room playing with Snowflake, our dog, a Samoyed. She loved to ride in the back of the pickup truck with us, and her black mouth looked like it was always laughing. We had the lunging whip from the tack room, an eight-foot-long snake of leather, and we were wiggling it across the floor. Snowflake yelped as she tried to trap it between her paws. The door was closed, probably because we always closed it against Ana Maria and Eduardo, since they had a way of staring in at us as if we were doing something wrong.

Suddenly the door slammed open and Cici stormed in, grabbed the whip from my hand, and slashed it across our legs.

"Don't you ever whip an animal!"

"We weren't—" I started.

"Ana Maria said you were whipping Snowflake. She could hear her crying." I could see Ana Maria in the hallway outside, looking pleased with herself.

"We would never whip Snowflake!" I was furious through my

tears. I couldn't understand how Cici could believe we'd do that, even if Ana Maria had told her so. Didn't she know us any better than that? But she wouldn't listen, and disappeared back into her isolation at the other end of the house.

We were forbidden TV for a week and kicked out of the house for the afternoon. Cici did that sometimes, chastising us for not getting enough exercise or fresh air. Nurse had rarely told me what to do with my time, and I resented being made to do something because Cici decided on the spur of the moment that I should. Still, it was better than indifference; it proved she cared about us.

We climbed up past the last house in the canyon to the caves. I trod gingerly on the sandy trail. The mountainside was steep, and there were prickly plants; though I probably wouldn't have fallen far, my fear seemed more legitimate than my old terror of jumping across the little chasm in the woods at St. Cleran's. I was proud that at least I wasn't afraid of rattlesnakes. Saint Patrick had driven the snakes out of Ireland, and I was certain they'd never come near me.

The caves were shallow dents in the mountainside, barely caves at all, not deep enough for bobcats or bats. The sandstone was bare around them, glowing golden even at midday. We sat in the snug shadow of the overhang, tossing stones down the mountain as we talked. As usual, Collin led the conversation to dinosaurs and superheroes. I didn't care about dinosaurs or superheroes except in that they were the coin of my communication with him. I could discuss them as long as he wanted.

The sandstone was nubbly and gritty under my fingers as I crumbled it into little stones. We didn't hear them land when we threw them; they disappeared into the soundless air. The tang of scrub oak and dry dust stung the membranes of my nose. The heat and the ocean haze fuzzed the outlines of things, making the world filmy and vague. I felt disconnected—from the earth and from my place on it, wherever that was. Irish rock had been cool and damp on the warmest summer day, velvety with moss and lichen, so solid nothing could break it apart. This sun-heated sandstone was more like dead skin: satisfying to pull off, and only a few steps up from dirt. The roiling towers of white cumulus that built in the sky were nothing like the low, fast-scudding clouds of Ireland.

With Dad gone and Cici adrift in a parallel world, there was something unreal about the progression of days. They ought, I felt, to pass solidly, one by one, like bricks, forming a solid mass of past that I could stand on to look out at the future. Instead they were undifferentiated, all blending into one—like the sandstone, which looked like rock but crumbled to dust in my hand.

11

There were three lanes in the drop-off zone at the Beverly Hills Hotel, separated by thin strips of curb. The red Datsun pickup truck was out of place among the Mercedes and Porsches, and usually whoever was driving it—whoever was working for Cici at the time, as maid-cum-nanny headed for the slot farthest from the door.

I picked my way through the limos and fancy cars and walked up the green carpet to the door, which Ennis opened for me. I think he recognized me as Dad's daughter, though his professional smile of welcome could have been for anybody. Gladys told me that it was Ennis who had tended to Dad's father, Walter, as he died from an aortic aneurysm that burst there in the lobby.

I knew where the house phones were, and asked for Dad's room.

"Come on up, honey," he'd say, and give me the number of his suite.

The corridors were lined, the top half, with wallpaper of dark green palm fronds on a background creamy with age. I loved that wallpaper; it seemed to contain everything good about California, and best of all was how well I knew it.

Inside the rooms, the hotel uniform of dark green and baby pink gave way to a warm yellow. Dad was always installed on a sofa, knees pointing up, long shins narrowing down to his perfect shoes. Gladys was usually with him—it was she who always called Cici's house and asked to speak to me. "Your father would like to see you," she'd say each time, like an incantation.

Maricela was not in evidence. She was either hiding in the bedroom, or had been left behind in Mexico.

This was Dad's world more than Cici's house ever was, even with all his treasures in it. Are hotel sofas always set facing the window, against the wall where the entry door is, with a painting above and a coffee table in front—in Claridge's as well as in the Beverly Hills Hotel? In my memory, I always approach him from an angle somewhere over his right shoulder.

He quizzed me about school, asked after Collin and Aunt Dorothy. We played backgammon. He never mentioned Cici's name.

Their only direct communication consisted of curt notes informing her of his plans to be in L.A. and his desire to see me. Cici showed them to me, trying to conceal her fury and failing completely. She had been betrayed, and now she was being made the villain. I didn't know—still don't know—what made Dad hate her so. In his autobiography he referred to her only as a crocodile.

I felt the injustice, and the inconsistency. If he really hated her that much, what did it say that he left me with her? That newspaper story, the word "adopted," nagged at the edges of my thoughts. Was this proof that the story was true? An adopted child could be left anywhere; all it needed was a home, any home. Would Dad have left his real daughter with a woman whom he now obviously despised?

When Cici and I played backgammon on the specially made

bamboo table—which Dad had left behind—she'd snarl made-up
words when she got bad rolls: "Glurm" or "skrungle," with a twist of
her double-jointed fingers into witchy talons. When she got a good
roll she'd snort and cackle. She chanted a rhyme every time I won:

> "Nasty little rat-slime,
> Icky picky poo
> Horrible little rotten child
> I hate you!"

The ease with which she said that told me how much she loved
and trusted me. And I made myself her champion in the lists of the
Beverly Hills Hotel. I took every chance to speak her name, tell Dad
the good things she'd done for me, the fun we had. "Ah-hah," he'd say.
"Very good." Noncommittal. Patient. A warm stone wall.

In one letter, he asked for me to be sent to Mexico for a visit.
I didn't want to go. I feared that he'd try to turn me against Cici. I
feared that Maricela would take out her various insufferable resentments on me. And Mexico as I'd known it without Cici and Collin
consisted of germs, sickness, goopy food like beans and guacamole,
and boredom. I couldn't just refuse, so I said, at Cici's suggestion,
that I wanted Cici or Aunt Dorothy to go with me. The subject
wasn't broached again.

"Do you like Chinese food, honey?"

For once Dad was staying not at the Beverly Hills Hotel but at
the Shangri-La in Santa Monica, and it was dinnertime, which it
usually wasn't when I visited, and there was a Chinese restaurant
downstairs.

"Yes," I said. "I love it." Cici often took us to Madame Wu's. An
enormous tree in the lobby grew up through a hole in the ceiling. We
had sweet-and-sour pork, and fortune cookies.

"It's one of the three great cuisines of the world," Dad said. "French, Arabic, and Chinese."

I knew French food was supposed to be the best in the world. I'd never heard of Arabic food. I was a bit surprised to hear him put Chinese in this company, since the Chinese restaurants I knew didn't have that kind of reputation, but I never questioned Dad's pronouncements. They often elevated an unexpected opinion to ultimate truth, and seemed calculated to throw people off balance.

"What about Italian?" I said. I hated to advance opinions except on the subject of backgammon theory, but Dad expected me to converse, so I offered myself up again and again. At the Beverly Hills Hotel, I had listened to him order prosciutto and melon from room service. When I protested at the combination of meat and fruit, he'd said, "Anyone who knows food will eat melon only with prosciutto."

"Italian food can be good, if prepared well," said Dad. "But it's not a *great* cuisine."

I was learning the ways of the sophisticated world, and that was a good thing; and certainly I preferred that he wanted to see me, even if it meant that I felt, often, inadequate or in the wrong. But I was always tired when I left.

Dad didn't like eating in public. He said it was revolting to watch people stuff food in their mouths; eating ought to be done in private, like going to the bathroom. But civilization dictated that meals were a social activity, and so—if they had to be public—they were, with Dad, as civilized as possible. I was always hyperaware of eating properly around him. At the Big House, I had struggled to cut the lettuce on my side plate with the blunt edge of my fork, because Nurse had told me it was bad manners to take too big a mouthful, and Betty O'Kelly said it was improper to cut salad with a knife.

We were seated across from each other in the middle of the restaurant, near a column. Madame Wu's had booths; so did Grampa's restaurant in New York, and so did the Hamburger Hamlet that Gladys took me to near Dad's agent's office in Hollywood. This table felt formal and exposed.

The waiter set my chicken with pea pods in front of me, and spooned rice onto my plate. I picked up my fork.

"Put that down, honey," said Dad immediately. "Chinese food must be eaten with chopsticks."

"But I don't know how to use chopsticks."

"Then you'll learn, right now." He gestured to the waiter to remove our forks.

I picked up the two sticks. They looked like wood but they were shiny and hard-surfaced, more like plastic, or some other substance that I couldn't identify. The square ends seemed like they'd be better at picking up food, and the round ones fit better in my fist.

"No, no. Like this." He reversed the chopsticks in my hand, and demonstrated how to hold them, the upper chopstick protruding a precise distance beyond the lower one. They lay against his long fingers like stiffer extremities of the same insect.

"I'm surprised you don't know how to use chopsticks, Allegra. You say you love Chinese food, but you've never really eaten Chinese food if you haven't used chopsticks."

I took this as criticism of Cici. I didn't feel that chopsticks were as important a gauge of cultural refinement and mothering skills as Dad obviously did.

I went for a piece of chicken. Its irregular shape looked easier to grasp than the slippery pea pods. The chopsticks scissored in my hand. The chicken bounced off the column onto the floor. Dad winced and pretended not to notice.

I managed to spear another piece of chicken and maneuver it to my mouth. It was too big. Two awful choices: stuff it in and make my cheek bulge, or bite off a chunk and put the rest back on my plate. I risked a furtive glance at Dad. His eyes were on the waiters moving silently around, on the potted plants, on the piece of chicken

I'd Frisbeed onto the floor—anywhere but on my face and clumsy fingers.

He waited until I'd dealt with that bite, then rested his eyes on me again.

"What are you reading, Allegra?"

I didn't own up to the bookcase full of Agatha Christies. *"Gulliver's Travels,"* I said, truthfully.

"Very good." He nodded approvingly. "The horses are far superior to the humans."

At night, Cici and I would creep outside like criminals under cover of dark, drop a hose into the septic tank that lay underneath the lawn, and siphon the sewage over the side of the hill. "The nighttime drools," she called them. The toilets had taken to backing up and she couldn't afford the constant visits from Walt, the Reddi-Rooter man. Soon we had to stop, though, because of the smell, and Walt came back. In a new truck.

"Walt!" As usual, she was wearing a floaty top and a bikini bottom. Her legs were long and lean from riding, polished by the sun. "What happened to Old Red?"

Walt's face was weathered, as if it was carved out of wood. "Well, Miz Huston, I done cut some holes in her an' my wife 'n I're usin' her for an RV."

Cici let out a screech. "Walt! You're not!" Her toes scrunched up the grass as if she couldn't bear the delight. She looked at me to see if I believed him.

I didn't, and I didn't think she did either. But she held the possibility, like some exotic feathered creature that she didn't want to let go of just yet. Sturdy, rational me: I wanted to feel the pleasure of the forbidden like that.

Walt held it too. I wondered if that was just how long it took for his features to crack apart and rearrange themselves into a smile.

"Naw, Miz Huston," he said at last. "I jes' wanted to make you laugh."

The dark days of winter and the February rains and Cici's sunken grief were over. She sacked Ana Maria and Eduardo—I hoped, because she realized they'd lied to her about Collin and me—and Lisa moved in. She'd just broken up with the Chicksweeper, and she needed somewhere to live.

I nursed prim reservations about having blond, breathy-voiced, big-haired Lisa as a nanny, but they didn't last long. Lisa tore down the invisible wall that the dark machinations of Ana Maria and Eduardo had built between our end of the house and Cici's. Collin and I adored her, and best of all Cici was happy again.

"How is everything with Lisa?" Aunt Dorothy asked me when Collin and I were spending the day in her pool.

"She's great," I said. "Only she had to go to the doctor because she had gonorrhea."

Aunt Dorothy's head jerked back as if I'd poked her in the throat. She took a deep breath, arranged her face, and moved her fingers around like she was conducting an orchestra on the sly.

"I'm sure it was diarrhea," she said in her most carefully modulated voice.

It wasn't diarrhea. I knew perfectly well what that was, and even though I didn't know what gonorrhea was, I knew the two weren't the same. I'd never heard of anyone going to the doctor for diarrhea. Lisa did have a habit of mixing up her words, saying "bugular" for "burglar" and having to concentrate really hard not to say "pasghetti." But that wasn't it; I'd heard her and Cici in the kitchen laughing as if it were a huge joke, and I'd just wanted to share it with Aunt Dorothy. Inwardly I cursed my big mouth. That's why they'd been laughing—there was something secret about gonorrhea, and I shouldn't have repeated it.

Aunt Dorothy was staring gimlets at me. Her lipstick-pink lips were pressed together.

"It must have been diarrhea," I said.

She looked satisfied; she'd heard what she wanted to hear. How could she not know, or care, that I was lying? I was weirdly impressed that she didn't. She'd altered reality by the force of her will.

"We loved having a little girl in the house again," Aunt Dorothy had said to me when I left after that first Christmastime visit. The longer I was there, the more I felt some unreachable residue of misery from the time when Cici and her brothers were young. I knew Cici had escaped it as quickly as she could, by getting married at age seventeen to Gene Shacove, the hairdresser who was the model for Warren Beatty's character in *Shampoo*; it lasted a year. Her older brothers, in their different ways, had rejected family life; her younger brother had killed himself. Something was wrong, but I didn't know what it was.

Cici called Aunt Dorothy "Mother" to her face. A note of exasperation echoed in it, trapped in the syllables. Sometimes I thought I even heard a lilt of sarcasm. Behind her back, she called her mother Gloom Lady, and Uncle Myron Gloom Man, and their house Gloom Castle.

Still, they seemed comfortable with their spiky relationship, and obviously it was better than nothing. I didn't exactly envy Cici having a mother, but I tried on different feelings about it, the way I tried on her shoes. Sometimes I was almost glad Mum had died when I was so little—before I was old enough to know her. Not that I feared we might have had the kind of relationship Cici and Aunt Dorothy had—Mum was always "Mum," not that formal "Mother"—but how much worse would it be if I had been six, say, when Mum died, or ten or twelve? I would have known her as Joan Buck, Anjel's best friend, had known her: her beauty, her wisdom, her way of treating children as if they were just as important and interesting as adults. I felt the injustice of Mum having been more a mother to Joan than to me—but I felt a kind of gratitude too in not truly having known what I had lost. As it was, I'd lost only a promise, not the thing itself.

I look worried because I'm afraid of Tony's hawk.
(*Photo Richard Avedon*)

I'm only a few days old. On her
wedding-ring finger, Mum is wearing
the gold panther ring that Anjel gave
me for my twenty-first birthday.

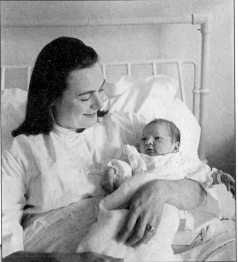

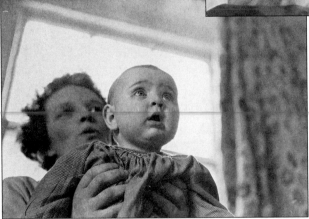

Nurse with me. In the few photographs
I have of her, she is in the shadows.

Mum in the courtyard at St. Cleran's.
This is my favorite photograph of her.

Mum and Dad.
(*Photo Lillian Ross*)

John Julius around the time
that he and Mum fell in love.

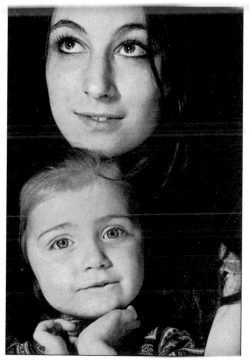

Me and Anjel.
(*Photo Norman Parkinson/Condé Nast*)

The back of the Little House, taken from the garden. The upstairs window is Mum's room. She sent this photo to John Julius the first Christmas they were apart.

The Big House. It looked even bigger approached from behind, with the basement story visible.

With Danny and the Lynch girls and one of the hunt hounds. I'm using Danny as my shield.

At the beach in Connemara.

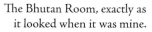

The Bhutan Room, exactly as it looked when it was mine.

The day of Caroline Lynch's first Communion. Standing behind is Karen Creagh. I was quite envious of Caroline's dress but thought Daddy would laugh at me if I asked to make my first Communion too. (*Photo Mary Lynch*)

Daddy in his studio, sketching one of Tony's hawks.

Through the knowledge of me, I wish to share my happiness with you.
TONY YOGI

One of Grampa's mad Christmas cards.

In lotus position at
the Beach Club.

Nana.

Mum and Grampa on the roof of the restaurant.

Philippe Halsman, *The Act of Creation*. The man holding the paintbrush is the artist Jean Cocteau. (*Magnum Photos*)

In the drawing room of the house on Maida Avenue.
Mum loved to dress us up in antique clothes.
(*Photo from the author's collection*)

With Cici and Collin on the
beach in Malibu.

With Dad at Cici's house
in L.A., on the day of the
Winslow Homer Christmas.

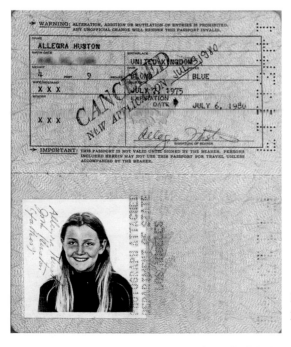

My first American
passport.

With Aunt Dorothy.

Gloom Castle.

In the back of Anjel's
rental truck in Montana.
(*Photo Joan Buck*)

With Jack and Jennifer (left) during the filming of *The Missouri Breaks* in 1975. This photo was part of a *People* magazine cover story.
(*Photo Harry Benson*)

With Anjel and Joan Buck during the expedition to Yellowstone.

With Dad and Danny, one Christmas at Las Caletas. (*Photo Joan Blake*)

Dad swimming at Las Caletas.

With Marisol. (*Photo Joan Blake*)

My favorite photo of
Dad and me, taken
on the set of *Escape to
Victory*. I was fifteen.

L to R: Harry Dean Stanton,
Miguele Norwood, Jeremy
Railton, Helena, Charles
Valentino, me. We're all wearing
roller skates. I'm probably fifteen.

With Helena on Valentine's Day
at the roller rink.

With Helena, when I was about seventeen.

With Artemis, the day Eleanor Allegra Lucy Beevor— my goddaughter Nella—was born.

With Jason in Sri Lanka.

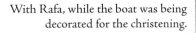

With Rafa, while the boat was being decorated for the christening.

Rafa's christening: Anjel welcomes the boat to shore.

My favorite photo of Cisco and me. We stayed in the boat while the ceremony took place.

L to R: Tony, Anjel, Steve Harris, Jeremy (looking up at the banner), Tara holding Rafa, Joan Buck, Cisco's niece Ana. You can see the descanso on the far shore.

The Norwich family in 2004.
L to R: Artemis, her son
Adam, her husband Antony
Beevor, John Julius, me and
Rafa, Jason, Mollie, Nella.
(*Photo Jill Robertson*)

The Huston family in 1992,
at Anjel's wedding.

On the back of this photo, my
mother wrote "January 1969."
It may be the last photo taken
of her before she died.

And if I had been old enough to know Mum's perfection for myself, before she died, my own inadequacy would have been even harder to bear.

Once a month, I sat with Cici on her bed while she did her accounts. Every penny of expenditure was entered in columns, every check she'd written ticked off. She let me fill in the numbers and I started to write them like hers, the sevens with a dip in the roof and a cross-bar. I felt privileged and helpful. And I could see that no matter how tight a hold she kept on her expenses, the income and the outgo didn't add up.

Dad's studio was empty now, so Cici decided to rent it out. The tenant was Anjelica. I was impressed by how she was able to walk up the pebbly stepping-stones in spiky high heels, her feet balancing on them in a very deliberate way, like those toys that wobble and don't fall down. She and Cici went out after dark in the pickup truck and stole flowers from people's gardens, made fabulous arrangements back home, and called it the Palisades Florist. Cici learned that one from Aunt Dorothy, who used to go by chauffeur-driven Rolls-Royce to get her tulips from Lucille Ball's garden.

I assumed that Anjel had moved out of Jack's house because they'd broken up. I'd seen her in tears often, and somehow I had gotten the idea that she had her own room at Jack's house so that she would have somewhere to cry.

The room was at the top of the stairs, at the gateway to Jack's private realm. The first time I went into it, my head swam. For an instant I didn't know where I was. The room was filled with her things. How I knew they were all hers from years before, down to the tiniest glass and silver vial, I don't know—I didn't remember them from the house she'd shared with Jeremy. Where had they all come from? Paintings and drawings and photographs covered the walls, many of her, many by her friends or Mum's friends. There were framed letters from Mum's friends too. And there, in the crowd, I saw the oyster shells and pearls sunk in cotton wool, surrounded by a rectangle of mother-of-pearl, that had hung in my room in the Little House at St. Cleran's.

I had thought it was mine. I realized now that of course it was Anjel's. Everything that I thought was mine had once been hers. It was mine only if she didn't want it anymore, if she had forgotten it. If she claimed it, my right to it was lost.

She saw the wonder on my face as I stared around at this trove, the visible accumulation of days and loves and houses and experiences, the proof that life had been lived. I traveled through life so lightly loaded—not much more than my clothes and my suitcase went with me from house to house, clothes which I grew out of within months—that I was sometimes waylaid by a sense that my own existence wasn't quite real. In Anjelica's room, each thing anchored her further to her place in the world; and each thing that I lost, by seeing that it was hers, unanchored me from mine.

"That's Mum's bed, Legs."

She said it fondly. For her, I guessed, it brought only warmth. She had many memories of Mum, and in them Mum was alive.

I was almost afraid to look at it, as if it would turn me to stone. It had faces on it, carved into the high finials at the head and foot. It was painted gray, the color of low cloud.

Was that the bed I had sat on, between Anjelica and Tony, when Leslie told me my mother was dead? It gave no clues: no scratches in the paint that could have been made by my fingernails, no splotches that could have been the watermarks of my tears. Not that I expected to find them: I knew I hadn't clawed and screamed, and Anjel had told me that I hadn't cried. But how could it be so impassive, so cold, so *gray*? It was Mum's bed; it had been heated by her body, it had held her as she slept and dreamed. Suddenly it was in the same room as me; she was in the same room as me. How could it show no marks at all?

Anjel didn't bring the bed with her to Cici's. I figured it must still be at Jack's house. To me, that meant she hadn't really left him. And among the photographs she hung on the wall of her dressing area was one of a teenage boy with that same dazzling grin: Jack's high-school-graduation photo.

"He was cute, wasn't he, Legs?"

She loved him still. I could hear it in her voice, and it made me happy. I was sure she'd be back with him soon—where, I felt, she belonged.

One day we went down to the basement, to get a bottle of wine maybe, or to store one of Anjel's fur coats in the temperature-controlled room where Cici kept hers.

"Oh, my suitcase!" cried Anjel. At first I wasn't sure what she meant—if she had brought a suitcase and stored it down there, why would she be surprised to see it? Then I realized that she was look-ing at the square-cornered, dark blue canvas suitcase that had gone with me everywhere, from Maida Avenue to St. Cleran's to Grampa's house to Euclid Street and now finally to Cici's house. My suit-case—the one with "A.H." stenciled on it in white below the clasp.

"You have it," said Anjel, delight in her voice. "How wonderful!"

No, I wanted to scream, that's *my* suitcase! Those are my initials. I am A.H.! But I wasn't *that* A.H., *the* A.H. She was.

I'd been so proud that I had my own suitcase, with my initials on it, and that I still had it even after Nurse was gone. I knew I'd had it my whole life, which meant that Mum had put the initials there.

She had—but for Anjelica. My whole self crashed away.

The big gold A on my bedroom door in the house on Maida Avenue: that was for "Anjelica," not "Allegra." I already knew that everything that had been mine at St. Cleran's was actually Anjel's. Everything that had been Mum's was now hers, it seemed. Had anything ever been mine—even Mum? I didn't look like her, with my pale skin and blond hair, not the way Anjelica did, with her arched eyebrows and dark Italian beauty. I had almost no memories of Mum; and the ones I had weren't about her, they were about me. Anjel had the ownership rights. All I had was an abstract fact.

One day in February 1977, Cici sat me down on the rust-colored suede sofa in the living room. Water gurgled out of the stone fountains in what I still thought of as Dad's pond. The narwhal tusks were gone.

"I have something to tell you," she said. She'd chosen a time when Collin wasn't there. I didn't know what was coming, but I dreaded moments like this. I felt like my world was about to split apart.

"John isn't really your father."

Once I heard the words, I knew I'd been expecting to hear them. Everyone I'd ever lived with was temporary, and Cici might well be the same. Losing them, I could deal with. Even though he was gone from the house, Dad was all I really had left to lose.

I couldn't stop myself crying. It all made sense: meeting Dad when I was too old to meet a father; the word "adopted" in the newspaper; the constant uncertainty about where I belonged.

"Your real father is an English lord. I told him he should come and visit you. He's coming tomorrow."

I saw dark spots on the suede where my tears had wet it. I hoped they wouldn't leave a stain; then I realized I hoped they would.

"Your mother went out and found love," Cici went on. "John was furious, because she was supposed to be his slave and put up with the Zoë thing and Danny and so on. But she wouldn't do it. She went out and got a life."

I could hear how Cici admired Mum for that, the kinship she felt with her. When I finally lifted my face and looked at her, she held my eyes. She smiled—not her usual square smile but something soft and almost invisible. Her voice asked me to believe her.

"You were a child of love."

It wasn't what I wanted to hear. It seemed to be important to

Cici. I heard—in her words, or maybe only in the pleading gentleness of her voice—that somehow it was better to be me, the child of this love that was suddenly being sprung on me, than Anjelica and Tony, the children of the right mother and father, whose love hadn't lasted and maybe, if I believed Cici, had never been there at all.

She wanted it to be important to me, but I was just tired. I wished my life was rounded off and simple, like the basketball hoops above the driveways of normal families. I felt bombarded. This new father wasn't—couldn't be—the last piece of the puzzle. He was just one more shudder in my precarious sense of self.

The next day, a biblical rain pelted from the low sky. Sheets of water tumbled down the steep driveway and turned the grass and trees beyond the big plate-glass windows into distorted swirls of green. I sat with Cici, silent, waiting for the knock on the door.

When he came inside, he was dripping rain. Cici shook his hand.

"I'm Celeste," she said. And, with her hand on my shoulder, "This is Allegra."

I think he thanked her. His manners were elegant and easy, as if he met his secret children every day of his life. That threw me. Then I saw the unease underneath, and felt better. I didn't see why this should be any more comfortable for him than it was for me.

He came toward me, and dutifully I approached him. I let him embrace me.

"I'm very happy to meet you, Allegra. I loved your mother very much."

Did he say that then, or later? Did he say, in so many words, that he was my father, that I was his daughter? I don't know.

I wasn't happy to meet him. I wondered if that meant I was unhappy to meet him, but that wasn't it either. I just felt blank. Somebody else would have to turn a key and rev up my emotions, if they wanted to.

I wasn't sure if this gray-haired man with glasses and a square face and his initials embroidered on his shirt did want to. He could hardly expect me to leap into his arms—could he? The alternative would be floods of tears and hysterics. I wondered if he'd been afraid that I would go that route. Maybe he was relieved that I was so flat. Or was I disappointing him by acting like the walking dead?

I was disappointing Cici. I knew she felt that he was, in a way, her gift to me. Everyone had lied to me, my whole life; she was giving me the truth. She wanted the knowledge that I wasn't really Dad's daughter to make me happy.

He and Cici did most of the talking, though they kept trying to pull me in. We sat on the other sofa, the one I thought of as more formal, farther from the swinging kitchen door, away from the fountain in the floor. The fractured light through the rain-smeared windows behind him dissolved the outlines of my father's face.

His voice and Cici's seemed to come from some far distance, beyond the pounding of the rain. The wish jumped into my head that he and Cici would fall in love and get married. That would round things off beautifully. But that mayfly died when he said he had a wife, and I had a brother and sister in London.

Words came easily to him. They didn't come to me. He wanted to know who I was, but—even with Cici's promptings—how could I tell him? This was a random hour flung like a boulder into the river of my days. He was leaving for London the next day, and I had no idea—or even any curiosity—if I would ever see him again.

I felt them struggling. The visit had to last a certain length of time—the taxi was coming back in an hour. An hour—just one hour—seemed almost insultingly short for something as big as meeting one's father. But that hour, on that sofa, was an impossibly long time.

"Why don't you play the piano for your father?" said Cici brightly, grabbing the thought like a passing trapeze.

"Yes, please do," said my father, clutching on. "I'd so love to hear you play."

I knew Cici hated the way I used to dance my double jig for Dad's friends, and I didn't like performing either. But playing the piano meant we wouldn't have to talk.

"Okay."

Cici had persuaded Collin's father, the screenwriter Walon Green, to rent the piano for me. I never understood why he agreed to—or quite believed that he really was paying for it. In Dad's absence, Cici had fostered a relationship between Wally and me; I went with Collin to stay with him for weekends, and on a camping trip to Washington state. And she wanted Dad to know that.

I'd had piano lessons during my year in Long Island and my year on Euclid. The teacher Cici hired worked differently, writing out the chords like guitar music. It was easier than the conventional system, but the drawback was that I could only play pieces that he had transcribed.

I started with "Danse Macabre," my favorite. I was conscious of the fact that I wasn't playing from proper music, that I had some kind of hippie L. A. way of playing that my new English father must look down on. Of course he was disappointed in me. Still, I had to play on. It was better than the alternative.

When I started the next piece, my father sat beside me on the bench and improvised above my careful chords. Cici beamed. I plodded on, aware of how comfortable he was at the keys, aware that this couldn't exactly be fun for him either. When I visited Dad at the Beverly Hills Hotel, we had a kind of script that we followed. I had no script for meeting a new father—and, evidently, neither did he for meeting a new daughter. I wondered if he was as keen as I was for this difficult hour to end.

12

On a spring day in 2007, I sat waiting on a tastefully upholstered sofa in a bank in Trafalgar Square. Huge chandeliers
dropped flat sheets of light, brighter than the London day outside,
unnaturally intense, like a stage. At intervals—as if propelled by an
assistant director filling the scene—people walked past, heads down,
the way people intent on business are supposed to walk.

I heard the footfalls of the well-suited young man I was waiting
for before I saw him reappear: walking a little slower than the others
to underscore the importance of his task. He had the confident look
of someone performing a duty well.

He handed me two large, lumpy manila envelopes tied into a
single parcel. The ends of the string that quartered them were fixed
to the paper by a ragged circle of muddy red sealing wax.

A smaller envelope was tucked into the cross of the string,

marked, in small, elegant handwriting, "Disposal Instructions." The letter inside was signed simply "Norwich." No "John Julius" before it: with a title, a first name isn't necessary. In the event of his death, it said, the letters were to be sent by the bank to his solicitors, who were to deliver them to me, his "natural" daughter.

That event hadn't happened. When I told him I was writing this book, he told me that he had kept the letters my mother had written to him, and arranged for me to collect them. Seeing two envelopes, my heart leaped: perhaps the second contained the letters he had written to her. Had she returned them to him when their affair ended?

I had already sorted through every letter in the tin trunk, and none were from him. His handwriting is unmistakable. The letters I knew he had written weren't there.

I found myself reluctant to break the seal and open those manila envelopes. "You were a child of love," Cici had told me. But, in reading the letters Mum had kept and her scraps of diary, I'd seen her in love with other men—and not Dad: the struggling young man, the Argentinian diplomat, the writer/adventurer Patrick Leigh Fermor. I knew by now that she hadn't left Dad because of Zoë, as Cici had suggested. She was already living in a rented flat in London. I was glad that she had found happiness in those romances, until they curdled. But I wanted my father to be different: to be the man she loved above all others. I thought he was—because of all those men that she fell in love with as an adult, he was the one whose child she had kept, had felt kicking her as she looked out her bedroom window to the house where he lived with his wife and children, across the canal.

Reading her letters to him was the promise of pain. I dreaded it. I tried to put them into date order without opening them, according to the postmarks on the envelopes. Many were missing or too smudged to read. I could order them roughly by the address on the

envelope: only one to his house, the others care of the Foreign Office, where he worked, or to his club, or to a hotel in Geneva: these
last with her handwriting disguised so that it wouldn't be obvious
that a member of the British delegation to the nuclear disarmament
conference was being deluged with love letters. But to reconstruct
properly the shape of the love that created me, I would have to un-
fold each one.

The first letter was dated October 1961, nearly three years before
I was born. The last was written in January 1969, the month Mum
died. I corralled my eyes within the top inch of the top page of each
letter, but always words leaped up from below, like fish rising: "dearest," again and again. Most of the letters were six, eight, ten pages
long. Some were written only a day apart. Some, only hours.

Heartbreak lapped at me. The movements of my hands became
detached, robotic, as I folded each letter again and put it back in its
envelope, marked the date on the outside, and slotted it into place in
the torrent. On my own sofa, surrounded by the physical manifesta-
tion of the love that brought me to life, I was surrounded also by
Mum's death. I would not be reading these letters, now, if she had
lived to see me grow up and bounce her grandson on her knee. And
I knew so much more than she did: I knew how this overwhelming,
mind-consuming passion—with so much absence in it, that demanded letters—would end.

All the letters were from Mum to John Julius; there were none
from him to her. What happened to his letters? Was she so angry, so
hurt, that she burned the record of a devotion that proved hollow? It
seems unlikely. She kept everything: good-luck telegrams, cards from
florists, paper coasters and straw mats from forgotten evenings. She
was good at transforming a finished love affair into a tender friendship. More likely she kept them apart from those other letters, and
when her belongings were disposed of, they weren't found.

But where would she have kept them? In the drawer of some
piece of furniture that was sold? Surely everything was emptied. In

some chilly, secret safekeeping where no accidental eyes would see them? These are the two possibilities: that my father's letters to my mother came into the hands of someone who thought them trash and tossed them; or that they lie entombed in some vault in London, where they will outlast us all for decades, maybe centuries, until the vault itself ceases to exist.

Mum met John Julius at a house party in the early autumn of 1961. By the time of the first letter, October, passion has flooded her. She yearns for his body, his mind, his generous self. She loses herself in the blue crystals of his eyes.

I am happy for her: for her delirium of passion, and for the fact that the person who aroused it in her was my father. But my emotions are wrenched by the intensity of the life force flooding through the ink of her pen. A life force that only a few years later will be extinguished in the split second of a car jouncing into a pothole and up into the path of an oncoming truck.

I put the letters down, unable to bear it; and the second I stop reading, I have to start again—as if the sorrow of reading them were heroin. She is electrically attuned to the currents of the weather: the tiniest fluctuations of the light, the breaths of wind that stir leaves and grass and brush her skin, the shadings of the clouds, the scents of flowers and rain. I can follow the wave lines of her moods: the joy of John Julius's love soaking into her pores and shimmering from her; the sadness she attempted to conceal and overcome; the shadow of iron circumstances from which she bravely turns her face away.

Mum had, by 1961, resigned herself to being John Huston's wife. They had worked out a modus vivendi: she oversaw the smooth running of St. Cleran's, designing and decorating and arranging for repairs, and creating the illusion of family life on Dad's sporadic visits home. She had "succeeded so well," she wrote, "that it really is John's place now." The rest of the time—most of the time—she was a single woman living alone in a house that Dad had never slept in. She kept her love affairs discreet so as not to cause scandal or confuse Tony and Anjelica.

She loved her little house—she always called it the Steward's House—and had no qualms about bringing the men she loved there. She sent John Julius photographs of it the first Christmas they were apart. Later she would bring him there too.

Growing in confidence, she began to push the bounds of what life as Mrs. Huston might allow. She thought of taking an apartment in Paris, then decided to rent one in London. Tony and Anjelica were getting too old for the local Irish schools. They, and she, needed to feel part of the larger world.

Even so, she felt deeply wounded by Danny's birth in May 1962. She knew, during the filming of *Freud* in Munich, that Zoë was pregnant; she makes forced, spiky jokes about it in her letters to John Julius. Obviously the insult wasn't in Dad's unfaithfulness; it was in his total disregard for her, and how it might affect her. He never spoke to her about the situation himself, but left her to guess; he betrayed not a twinge of concern that this child might subject her to gossip, humiliation, or those pitying glances that she would have dreaded more than anything. His silence suggested that it was none of her business, that it was irrelevant to the life they led together—which, to her, meant that he was careless of the impact it would have on Anjelica and Tony. That infuriated her. She struggled to understand, to accept, to banish hate and anger.

Still, she seems not to have considered divorce. John Julius was not free to marry—and I sense that after the first desire to possess him utterly, she saw advantages in that. Her life suits her: she has independence in London, the ongoing project of St. Cleran's, and stability for her children, who are the center of her world. She can toy with the idea of working, but there is enough money that she doesn't really have to. She had been with Dad since she was nineteen, married to him since she was twenty. Cutting those ties—changing her identity—would be an upheaval.

To my surprise, she writes fondly of Dad. The anger at his callousness over Danny's arrival wears off quickly; she understands him well and knows that he won't change. She doesn't call him "the Monster," as she did during her love affair with Lucio. Emotional distance has brought her closer to him. She writes of him as a wayward, exasperating, childish genius: her charge. She worries about his health. She finds his films remarkable, and recommends them proudly. She writes a screenplay and works on it with him, with the understanding that he will direct it. She is delighted when she finds the perfect Christmas present for him: *Night Image*, my own Cousin Itt.

He was, in his limited way, supportive of her. He encouraged her move to London, and seems to have been genuinely excited about the purchase of the house on Maida Avenue, and the renovations it required. In their shared enthusiasm for doing up houses, they seem almost not to have cared that they would not live in them together. Still, his desires always came first. Money suddenly became tight, and Dad insisted that what they had be spent on a new heating system for the Japanese bath at St. Cleran's, instead of on necessary repairs to Maida Avenue. Mum was forced to borrow from her father—Grampa.

She had been brought up to please a demanding, eccentric, irrational, charming, selfish, domineering man. The man had changed, but the pattern was the same. Grampa and Dad were the twin poles of her existence. Accepting that, and understanding her role in it, gave her freedom.

I find it hard to understand how Mum could have written, to her lover, so admiringly of her husband. The balancing act comes naturally to her. What really throws me is how sweetly she writes about Anne, John Julius's wife. How can she not be jealous or resentful? How can she not wish Anne at the bottom of the ocean?

But she doesn't. She writes with generous understanding of Anne's artistic struggle as a painter. She tells John Julius, who is leading a tour group in Turkey, what Anne was wearing and how beautiful she looked at a party at his mother's house.

Mum had become friendly with John Julius's mother, Lady Diana Cooper, with whom she shared a garden wall. When she was young, Diana was considered the most beautiful girl in England. Her husband, Duff Cooper, had many affairs; Diana dealt with them by becoming the best of friends with the women her husband fell in love with. She welcomed Mum in, I guess, the same spirit, and saw no reason not to invite Mum and Anne to the same party. I feel sorry for Anne (who, in the future, would be warm and welcoming to me); she was the one who wasn't in on the secret.

When she saw Anne at that party at Diana's house, Mum was pregnant. She first knew it during the Christmas holidays at St. Cleran's in 1963. She's cagey even in her letters to John Julius, hugging the secret—me—to her like a hot-water bottle. She is filled with joy. Literally. The English equivalent of my name is Joy.

I had always thought of my name as a sort of prayer. A wish for how I'd become, not a statement of who I already was. I'd imagined Mum torn by the fact of me: the marriages, the timing, all wrong. I didn't know whether she would ever have considered an abortion, but I'd thought that, at best, this seed growing inside her was somewhat of a problem. Happiness rushes in through my eyes and my fingers as I realize I was wrong. There is no tension about my name. I made my mother purely, completely happy by putting in that bid for existence. There was not the tiniest shadow in her mind that she might not want me.

When I read about that abortion with the Argentinian diplomat, I felt something of myself fly away from my fingertips. Instantly I knew how heart-tearing it was for her to snuff out the child of a man she loved. I knew it because I am the evidence that she wouldn't do it again.

Now I read something else, and it twists my guts: "All those children I stopped." There were others.

How many? When? With whom? I don't know, and I probably never will.

"Ephemeral regrets," Mum wrote to John Julius. "But even ephemera have substance." Is she being brave? She's contradicting herself. If they were ephemeral, the regrets have gone. If they have substance for her years later, how ephemeral can they have been?

Eight years earlier, she wrote about how she longed, too quickly after falling in love with a man, to have his child, and chastised herself for it. Birth control before the pill was patchy. But I know, from reading that scrap of diary, of her longing; and pragmatic as she must have been each time, I sense what the stopped child cost her. Each one stopped romance, stopped hope, stopped a possible future for all three of them. After that, the love affair could only be a death walk to the end.

What was different this time? It must have made things easier that she was living a sea apart from Dad, not just ten minutes' walk away. She didn't want to pretend that Dad was my father. At St. Cleran's, she would have had to if the routine of their lives was to continue. In London, she could brazen it out.

She never betrayed to John Julius any hope that my appearance would change things between them. It's impossible that she didn't feel it. But she could master her emotions. Grampa had been drilling her to do that, her whole life.

She dreaded only one thing: the scene that would take place when she told Dad. She wrote to him in March, as soon as she'd passed the three-month milestone. He summoned her to Ireland.

Cici tells a great story of the scene. She got it mostly—though obviously not all—from Dad.

Dad is in the study in the Big House, entertaining the local priest to after-lunch drinks. (First unlikely event.) Mr. Creagh comes in and announces that Mrs. Huston has arrived.

"Mrs. Huston," says Dad to the priest. "How wonderful. I haven't seen my wife in more than a year." (Not true. She was there for Christmas.)

Mum walks in, wearing a cloak. When she takes it off, the bump is only too evident. Dad is scarlet with embarrassment. Later, in his bedroom, he breaks her wrist with the poker from the fireplace.

He didn't break Mum's wrist. But Cici believes he was capable of it. She describes him in a fury as the Red Devil—the most terrifying creature she'd ever faced. And this, from a woman who rode a lion.

Mum had hoped for reason and understanding, but she knew it was unlikely. She had done nothing that Dad hadn't done two years previously. She felt she was due some generosity of spirit, some recognition of the partnership they had developed, some recompense for her own understanding. Even simple kindness. Instead, she was hauled over the coals.

Mum stayed silent as Dad flung vicious remarks at her, asking nothing of him, avoiding blame and all mention of Danny. He asked her if she wanted him to pretend to be the child's father. No, she said; all she wanted was silence, the space of a few years, until Tony and Anjelica were old enough to understand the truth. Until then, she thought they would accept simply that the child was hers. It would, she reassured him, be racially no different from them.

If she had said yes, she told John Julius, she thought that Dad would have "figuratively, at least, kicked my face in."

So ended the first scene. But Dad brooded on that one sentence. He decided to take it as a slight to Danny and his multiracial mother.

For the first time in years—and not jokingly—Mum calls him a monster. Did he hit her? I can't tell. He didn't the first day— though, as Mum tells John Julius, he had in the past. I'm pretty sure he called her a whore, and probably worse. She is deeply wounded that Dad would think her capable of a racial insult against Danny or his mother, when all she had tried to do was reassure him about Tony and Anjelica. He is, she thinks, willfully misunderstanding her to fan his own fury. "Why," she writes, "is it only he has pride to be hurt, feelings to be considered, good nature to be taken advantage of, patience to be taxed? Don't I as well? Why is all equality out of the question?"

Without excusing him, she questions herself. Was it her own tongue-tied silence, her lack of confidence, that provoked him to be so cruel? She is sure she could have handled it better—but how? She feels hate rising in her, and she begs John Julius to help her understand Dad so that she will not hate him. She hopes never to see him again.

He wanted, she wrote, for her to throw herself on his mercy, to come to him saying, "John, I'm in a fix," so that he could say something to the effect of "Well, honey, let me help you." She wouldn't do that. "My dear John Julius," she wrote, "I am not in a fix, am I?" Her contentment—which surprised me so, and makes me so happy—was what drove Dad crazy.

The day after these scenes, Mum wrote John Julius a second letter, this one on canary-yellow paper—which she apologizes for, it being so inelegant. But it's appropriate. Dad has left St. Cleran's; the storms are over. The sun shines through the balsam poplars outside the window of Mum's bedroom, and the viburnum is coming into bloom. Though she still loves her little house, and her blue room, she feels as if she is getting out of jail.

"My blue room." The room at the top of the stairs, whose door was closed. The room I barely dared enter until Danny came to stay. Its walls and bedspread were beige.

When Mum was gone, Dad erased her from the Little House. Anjelica's room was left alone, and the guest room, the garden room, the kitchen. He turned his anger on two rooms: her bedroom and her sitting room. That sitting room was, says Tony, the coziest room he'd ever known, with music playing and sweet-scented flowers and oversize art books which they'd pore over in the dark evenings. Its walls, as Mum described them, were the color of tomato soup. Dad had the walls repainted dark green, and ordered the furniture packed up and sent to Zoë and Danny in Rome.

It became the Yeats Room, a little museum of Jack Yeats paintings in frames with lights on top. There was no sofa; maybe not even a chair. Just tables against the walls. No one ever went inside. It was a dead room.

Mum was beyond insult. It was Tony and Anjelica who felt the cruelty, as—without comment, or any indication that they might be hurt by it—Dad dispatched the last vestiges of her warmth to his other family. I felt the chill that was left.

John Julius was away, leading a tour group through the eastern Mediterranean, during much of Mum's late pregnancy. She missed him terribly, of course, in the way any woman would miss a man away on business. She was distracted with longing for him, but—as at the start—filled with joy. She felt me kicking inside her. She thought I was a boy.

He returned a few weeks before I was born, at the end of August, so the letters stop. They start up again when I am less than ten days old. Now John Julius is in France, having a family holiday with his wife and children. The letters fly almost daily to a poste restante address in a country village. They don't show the serenity of the summer letters. There is a cold anger in Mum's longing that wasn't there before. The intense love she feels for him torments her now.

He excuses his absence with good reasons: his family has missed him too during his long absence, and this is their last chance for a holiday together before school starts. I know Mum was generous-hearted enough to see justice in this. She says she does not blame him. But she will not let him flit away from the consequences. "I don't want to embark on myself," she writes, "but I do want you to digest something: Allegra is an entity in herself, for all the joy and pleasure, and they are enormous, inherent in her presence, the wonderful new richness and dimension she adds to my life. She is not your understudy, a substitute for your presence. Thank heavens for her, these days, my endless gratitude for the mainstaying love of these last three years that have led to her, but never forget about these days, that I needed *you*." She ends with no sign-off: just "R."

She has never sounded so brutal, so dully certain. The words on the page, in her half print, half script, thud on my eyes like blows: like the blows of each hour of his absence. I feel a blast of loneliness freezing her in the spaces between her bones.

I spent most of my life believing that I am strong, that Nietzsche was right: whatever doesn't kill you makes you stronger. Not long ago, I decided that Nietzsche was wrong. An arm that has broken and knit is not as strong as one that never broke. Some hurts never heal.

Mum accepted a great deal: secrecy, other commitments, sporadic and stolen time together. She called them "the impossible facts." It was the bargain she made for love. But that week, a steely truth sliced through it: when it came to the crux, she was alone.

In October, when I was nearly two months old, Mum went to the Marylebone registry office to register my birth. Probably she left me at home with Nurse; documents from the hospital would have been enough.

I imagine her standing at the counter in one of those musty, pen-pushing rooms that still dot London. The varnish on the wood is worn through and peeling. In the corners, the linoleum tiles are curling up. The chairs that line the walls, for waiting on, are hard and scratched and randomly set about. The strip lighting hanging from the ceiling flickers in a futile effort to dispel the gloom of the autumn day outside.

"Christian name?" says the registrar.

"Allegra," says my mother.

"Any middle name?"

"No."

Mother's name is next. Then father's.

It had been agreed between Mum and John Julius that she would not name him. She hated the thought of scandal as much as he did; it was what had infuriated her about Zoë's pregnancy and Danny's birth. John Julius was well known as a writer and television personality, and he had a title, Viscount Norwich, so the gossip columnists would have seized on it. Many people in their circle must have known that John Julius was my father, but in fine English fashion it could remain unsaid.

In that last, awful scene between them, Dad gave Mum permission to name him as my father. He also banished her from St. Cleran's and insulted her by cautioning her not to intrigue with the servants. Worst of all, he made out that she was the one who had insulted him; that she was intolerant, prejudiced, unreasonable, unkind.

I doubt she paused for a moment. She had had weeks to make up her mind. Her armor was on.

None, she said. Unknown.

I imagine the registrar staring up at her: a remarkably beautiful, well-dressed, self-possessed woman with an American accent and the bearing of a ballerina. Not the kind you'd think didn't know who was the father of her child.

And I imagine Mum staring her down.

The registrar typed two dashes in that column. Father: unknown.

13

"My other children call me Papa, pronounced roughly to rhyme with 'supper,'" John Julius wrote to me not long after our strange, disconnected meeting. That flummoxed me for a bit. The way I said "supper" didn't sound like any pronunciation of "Papa" I could come up with. I was an American now.

I had avoided calling him anything that day. It was impossible to think of calling him "Papa." It sounded so intimate and easygoing, as if everything were normal father/daughter stuff between us. He didn't sound too sure of it either: something behind his words made me feel that he was trying it on. This whole relationship was so new as to be experimental. I wasn't at all sure that the experiment would succeed, or whether I wanted it to.

I didn't need a new father. I already had one. True, he wasn't around on a daily basis, but I was used to that. Sharing a house with him had been unusual: when he left for Mexico, he took on his true kingliness again. He was more himself when he wasn't living with Cici; I must have felt his unhappiness without understanding what it was.

I saw Dad every month or so when he came to L.A. It never occurred to me that he might not be "Dad" anymore; John Julius's arrival in my life didn't change my image of Dad in the slightest. Our relationship had never been based on the primal bond: its pillars were respect and gratitude on my side, generosity and affection on his. The love between us had grown from those. It didn't depend on biology or habit.

Dad never mentioned John Julius, though Cici must have told him that we'd met. He continued as if nothing had changed between us. So nothing did.

What could this new father give me? Not much that I wanted. He sent me books about his family—my family, in theory only—which I didn't read. I had enough people in my life who were family but nowhere near: Dad, Tony, Nurse, Nana and Grampa, my cousin Martine—and Danny, my lost brother whom I found again in the Beverly Hills Hotel, where I saw him with Dad for the first time since I'd left St. Cleran's. He gave me a ring of gold and turquoise, which sent Cici off on a fantasy about how he and I would marry, which we could since we weren't blood relations. It was a similar fantasy to the one I'd had, for a moment, when John Julius and Cici sat together on the sofa: that the far-flung ends of my family might come together and close the circle.

For as long as I could remember, I'd spent time with someone and behaved as I thought a daughter or a sister or a granddaughter should; then I'd been whirled away. I couldn't just abandon those daughterly, sisterly, granddaughterly feelings; so I was stretched thin, holding on to them all so many thousands of miles apart. My family bonds were like wires stretched around the curved surface of the earth, pulled so very tight they were liable to snap at any moment—and me with them. John Julius was yet another claim on me, someone else I had to write to, another hook in my flesh.

He'd disappeared from my life once before. Maybe after this first flush of rather lukewarm enthusiasm, he would again.

I was solitary; I had little emotional strength left for friendships. I had friends at school that I ate lunch with, but I rarely invited them home with me, and I rarely went home with them. All I wanted to do was read and play backgammon. Much of it was the vagueness of being twelve. The rest was exhaustion of spirit.

Cici got the idea of sending me to boarding school at Ojai Valley, where she had gone. Kids could have their own horses there, she told me; there were all kinds of great things to do. I think she hoped it would energize me, help me find a focus, some kind of passion for life.

I didn't want to go. Half of my favorite Enid Blyton books were set in boarding schools, but I knew they were fantasy—and besides, they were English. Nothing about Ojai appealed to me. And one thing terrified me: that if I was sent to boarding school, I'd get marooned there. When the next upheaval came, I'd be forgotten about. I'd have no home left.

I was sent to an educational psychologist, who had me do logic puzzles and asked me if I felt academically challenged at Paul Revere Junior High public school. Earnestly I lied and told him I did. When his report came through, Cici let me read it. I took pride in having pulled the wool over his eyes. Reading it later, I see that he was smarter than I thought he was. Partly disguising his reasons, he delivered the verdict that he knew I needed: he recommended that I stay where I was.

By this time Collin and I had Sue, from New Zealand, to look after us. I liked her at once, with her uneven teeth and unglamorous body: she seemed steadier, more reliable, than Lisa and tall, gay, handsome Rock. Cici's friends had made good companions for Collin and me, and they'd let us have Tuna Helper and Kraft macaroni and cheese for dinner as much as we wanted, but when something went wrong, I felt put on the spot. Rock had once taken a corner too fast when Collin was riding in the back of the pickup truck (usually we both did, sitting up on the wheel arches like Mexican gardeners): the truck went up on two wheels, and the road swam in front of my eyes. I was sure that Collin must have fallen out. Rock drove on as if nothing had happened. I'd have to stop him, I thought, and we'd go back to find Collin with his head smashed open on the asphalt. When I looked back, I saw only empty wheel arches—until I spotted Collin up close to the cab in a heap, eyes wide, his tanned face gone the dead color of sand. He gave me a crooked smile through the glass.

I didn't tell Cici. I didn't know what would happen if I did. Maybe it would destroy her friendship with Rock, put an end to the mad laughter of our evenings. Or she might just think I was exaggerating—after all, Rock hadn't acted as if anything awful had happened. Which was worse, to be the wet blanket tattletale, or to be disbelieved again? Best to say nothing, and take care of it myself. Make Collin ride in the cab, or ride in the back with him and demand that he sit down low and hold on tight.

Sue took me bowling with her English friends. I felt we shared some kind of Commonwealth bond. Even though I tried not to think about my new English father, something crept into my spirit beneath my consciousness: a rootedness derived from that long line of aristocratic ancestry. My father wasn't a random someone I met in a hotel room. He was someone who had truly loved my mother; who had been there when I was little; who was separated from me by social convention and by tragedy. This was the kind of story I read in books. I was the only person in the world with this history: arrows of circumstance had flown on a converging trajectory to produce nobody other than me. That sense of difference I'd felt for as long as I could remember: on bad days it still left me feeling fraudulent and alien, but now, on good days, it became a sense of specialness.

When Cici and Collin went out of town, Sue's English friends came over for dinner and Scrabble. Suddenly she keeled over backward, as if an invisible force had grabbed her chair and flung it flat. Scrabble tiles erupted off the table. Sue thrashed in spasms on the floor, her eyes rolling like a crazed horse. I screamed, and the only sound was the banging of her head on the floor. I wanted to run, but my muscles wouldn't move.

Her friends jammed a spoon between her teeth and cradled her head till the fit passed. They told me it was epilepsy. I'd heard of it; I knew it was a normal, maybe even common disease. I knew people used to think epileptics were possessed by the devil, and that "those who knew," as Dad would say, could look down on their ignorance.

"Please don't tell Cici." It was the first thing she said—lying on the floor still, looking up at me.

I felt a power seep into me, and I didn't like it. I knew Sue should have told Cici she had epilepsy before she got the job; and I knew that meant she probably wouldn't have got it. This time I knew well I should tell. But I wanted someone to look after me—Sue, the way she had been before this happened. I wanted her to tell me what to do. I didn't want the choice to be mine.

"I'll lose my job." Her eyes were wet and pleading.

I hated this. She was Sue again, but my heart was still pounding. I didn't want to go near her. I'd never imagined epilepsy could be as terrifying as this.

I felt the easy way out unrolling in front of me, like a carpet. I inched down it. Sue hadn't had a fit before now, I told myself. Maybe she wouldn't have one again.

"But what if you're driving?"

The words crept out of my mouth. I hated her to see that I was afraid. I didn't want her to think I was ignorant, or prejudiced against her for having a disease that wasn't her fault. I felt it was wrong to sound like I didn't trust her.

"I feel it coming on, and I can pull over," she insisted. "It doesn't happen very often. Please, Allegra. She'll send me away."

I tried not to think it: Hadn't she felt it coming on just then? Couldn't she have done something to stop it, or at least have run to her room and had the fit in private? If that was all the warning she got, it wouldn't be much use on the freeway.

We had already got Cici's permission to go on a road trip once school let out for summer, to the Grand Canyon, the Petrified Forest, and Yosemite. If I told Cici about the fit, Sue would probably be told to pack her bags at once.

"I won't tell," I said. I could watch Sue extra closely when she was driving. Now that I understood, I could grab the wheel if I had to.

"Do you want to go to the beach?" Anjel asked me. She was still living in Dad's studio on the hillside above Cici's house.

"Sure." She was my sister; I would have gone anywhere with her.

We headed up the Pacific Coast Highway toward Malibu: past Patrick's hamburger stand and the beach where Cici went; past Lou Adler's house with its rock-studded wall, where I'd been with Anjel and Jack. The beach was hidden by shoulder-to-shoulder houses, which parted only when a rocky outcrop, that couldn't be built on, broke into the waves.

We pulled out of the streaming traffic into the center lane. On the far side, a garage door swung up. We pulled into the cavern beside a burgundy, new-model Rolls-Royce Corniche.

Aunt Dorothy drove a vintage Rolls-Royce: 1964, the year I was born. Beside it in the triple garage at Gloom Castle was a James Young touring Rolls-Royce limousine, 1966, one of only two ever made. Both were a blue so dark they were nearly black. Those Rolls-Royces were elegant and streamlined. Corniches, on the other hand, looked fat to me, like the blood-gorged ticks Cici and I burned off the dogs with cigarettes. I looked down my nose at people who drove Corniches. They were showing off how rich they were.

This one even had a personalized license plate: PRO 3. But I was with Anjelica, at her new boyfriend's house, so I said nothing.

She led me along a tiled hallway, nondescript, with a door on either side, into a room whose huge windows were filled with beach and ocean and sky—nothing else, nothing between. The room itself seemed to disappear, irrelevant in the face of this vista. The wide beach was like golden suede: beautifully, serenely empty of people. The gray ocean rolled onto it in a rhythm so close to perfect, so minutely irregular, that it stroked smooth the knotty ridges of my mind.

I was prepared to dislike the owner of the Corniche, especially since he wasn't Jack. But I thought I could never dislike someone who lived in the embrace of these waves.

We changed into bathing suits and went out onto the small wooden deck that perched above the dry upper reaches of the sand.

The beach wasn't deserted, after all. Near the ocean, where the sand was hard with water but not soggy with too much, were three men, so far apart that I had seen, through the windows, only the space between them. There were two to my right, one to my left. Frisbees flew between them, flat and straight like precision missiles. Not one Frisbee, but lots: a bombardment fired back and forth, sometimes two together coming apart in midflight, a capsule birthing out of a mothership. A dog chased any Frisbees that landed in the water. I'd never seen Frisbee played like this. I'd thought it was a kids' game.

Anjel ran to the lone man and kissed him. I followed.

"This is Ryan," she said to me. O'Neal: I knew. He was big and broad-chested, with wavy blond hair and lips the same color as his skin. He'd starred in *Love Story*. When I was in fourth grade in Long Island, a boy in class was reading the book, and the rest of us were shocked.

The men at the other end were, I found out later, his brother and his coke dealer. They sloped off northward up the beach—playmates on call, no longer required—when they saw Anjel and me arrive.

We took up position closer to Ryan than where they had been, and the incoming fire started. I wasn't any better at Frisbee—even Frisbee as I knew it—than I was at any other physical activity. I could catch them if they didn't hit my hand too hard—which most of Ryan's did, except the baby of the mother-and-baby pairs. My dives after low-flying shots were almost always too late. When I threw, the Frisbee either went flinging off wildly or ran out of steam no more than halfway to where Ryan stood.

He loped up the beach. "Let's see you throw."

I wound up my wrist. Before I could let go, Ryan took my hand and flipped it over. My fingertips were flat against the underside, the way you'd carry a plate.

Ryan put his fingers over mine and curled them into a fist with the rim of the Frisbee inside. My fingernails were too long to get a grip, even though most of them were already broken. I bit off the ragged points.

With his arm still around me, holding the Frisbee with his fingers over mine, he moved me so that I stood with my back to the ocean, sideways on to where I wanted the Frisbee to go. He curled his arm, and mine, across my body, and tucked our wrists into the space beside my waist. Without letting go, he demonstrated a few times: the whip of the wrist that launched it into flight.

He didn't say much, and he didn't criticize. He took the attitude that nobody except him knew how to throw a Frisbee, and it was his mission to teach the underprivileged. So he was patient and precise. This one movement was the axis on which he turned. It was the secret of strength, grace, power—if only I could get it right.

"Let's try it." He moved his arm with mine, whipping it forward so hard that the momentum sent me after it. The second time, I planted my foot firmly. My back leg slammed forward into it, straight, like the snap of a scissors. I hadn't planned that, but it felt good: strong, balanced, controlled. Anjel smiled at me. I smiled back.

I ran and leaped for the Frisbees and flung them back again, my legs scissoring like Anjel's. It didn't surprise me that Anjel was good at it; she was good at everything. I traded with her for the lighter ones, which were easier to throw—and some actually made it to Ryan. He gave me a nod of approval whenever I threw one well. I felt sporty, coordinated, capable, for the first time in my life. I was with Anjel in her world—and I belonged there.

The next day I woke up and couldn't move. My brain sent messages to my legs, but they were as immobile as felled logs. I didn't know what was the matter with me. I was frightened.

"I can't get up," I said to Cici. She started laughing. I was hurt. She could often be curt and practical when I was in difficulty, but I'd never felt a lack of sympathy before.

"It only shows that you don't get enough exercise," she said, and left me to force my legs, seized up with pain, to move.

I knew that she felt both Collin and I were too indoorsy. She didn't like weakness, and I didn't blame her for that. But this was something different. She was angry about when I'd been ill

The previous Christmas, when Anjelica gave me an outfit of bell-sleeved blouse and bell-bottomed trousers in silky white rayon, and a pair of sandals like cat's cradles fixed into shiny wooden platforms, Cici had contemptuously pronounced them "Tatum O'Neal clothes." Tatum was only a year older than me, but Ryan bought her slinky dresses and took her to parties. Cici didn't approve at all.

I didn't dislike the Tatum O'Neal clothes: they just had nothing to do with me. I didn't even feel right hanging them up with my other clothes. Had Anjel given them to me because she wanted me to be like Tatum, whom I still hadn't met? I didn't have a tenth of the confidence to carry them off. They stayed in their box on the floor of my closet.

Now I was sleeping in Tatum's bed—actually, beds. Ryan had two houses: the Malibu house and another in Beverly Hills, on top of a mountain across the canyon from Gloom Castle. We'd spend a few days at one, then a few days at the other, according to his moods. Tatum was in England, making *International Velvet*, but her closets were bursting with the clothes she'd left behind, all scented with Saint-Laurent Rive Gauche, which—I discovered when she came home—she sprayed directly onto them and poured into the rinse water of the washing machine.

She and her brother Griffin lived with Ryan because, I was told, their mother was crazy. Griffin was a year younger than me and small for his age, with leaf-green eyes and a freckled face like a street urchin out of Dickens. Instantly he became like another little brother to me. I felt tender toward him, protective of him. He seemed lonely.

He tried on my high-platform shoes once at the beach house, acting the clown. Anjel was fixing a Coke and lemon in the kitchen, and I saw her glance nervously at the stairs, I realized that she didn't want Ryan to see this: his son wearing girl's shoes, even for fun. I made my laughter less loud, and tried to get my shoes back. But Griffin kept clomping around in them, stretching out the joke, as if daring his father to come down and see him.

Ryan was filming *The Driver* that summer, and it was mostly night shoots. He'd wake up around two or three in the afternoon and head out onto the beach, Anjel and I following, for a session of Frisbee. Griffin rarely played—he liked to surf, but mostly he just stayed in his room, smoking dope. Ryan's next-door neighbor, a white-haired man we always called Lee's Bars Stools and Dinettes—his commercials were all over the TV—plowed through the waves some way out, parallel to us, as the sun started to sink behind the ocean.

Then we'd all have a sauna together. Soon I stopped being self-conscious about my nakedness, or about Ryan's. I did start shaving my legs.

Once it was dark, we'd drive in the Corniche down to the dock neighborhood of San Pedro. Usually I sat on the armrest between the two front seats, while Griffin burrowed like a little animal in the back. Ryan draped his right arm across me to rest his hand on Anjel's thigh as he drove.

In an alleyway near the set I found a tiny cat, barely bigger than my hand, with long gray-brown fur and a perfectly triangular face. She seemed completely alone. She let me pick her up and carry her back to Ryan's Winnebago.

"She's probably hungry," said Anjel. We had bacon, lettuce, and tomato sandwiches—Ryan's favorite food, aside from tomato soup. Her tiny teeth seemed too small to deal with bacon, so I held a tomato slice out to her. She reared up on her hind legs and batted at it with her front paws.

"She's a boxer," said Ryan, delighted. He loved boxing. He had a heavy bag and a speed bag hanging in his bedroom at the beach house. He'd given Anjelica boxing gloves too and taught her to punch.

We called the kitten Sugar, after Sugar Ray Leonard. Anjel said the name was street tough, which fit her. We went back to the Beverly Hills house that morning, and Sugar lived in Tatum's white-carpeted suite with me. It was a separate building only a few feet from the master bedroom—I thought of it as sitting at the right hand of God. Griffin's bedroom was on the far horn of the U-shaped house: a room the architect had intended for the maid.

When I got out of bed Sugar attacked my ankles—scratching and biting me, drawing tiny pricks of blood—until she realized it was me. She made a run for the door whenever I opened it, but I didn't want to let her out in case a coyote got her, or she ran away. I felt like her jailer. Soon she did escape, and I never saw her again.

On our last night in San Pedro, a big stunt was planned. The location was a vast parking garage with a row of concrete posts down the center, and a wide trench in the floor alongside them; a car would run up a ramp on two wheels, flip over, and slide along the trench. The stuntman, Billy Burton, was a friend of Cici's: a cowboy with a drawl, tight jeans, and a slow smile. I'd met him once before that night, so I felt I knew him.

Even though Ryan wasn't in the shot, we all gathered, in the small hours of the morning, to watch the stunt. Billy, wearing a padded suit, walked casually to the car.

"Roll it. Action." The car hit the ramp and flipped over—and then, sideways, smashed into the concrete pillars, bounced off the sharp edge of the trench, and came to a dead stop. That wasn't the plan: crushed metal, jagged thuds, a pinballing car smashing to pieces. My heart stopped. The trench in which it came to rest made the car look like it had been pounded flat by a crusher.

The last clangs echoed away into the silence. Nobody called "cut." The cavernous space, and everyone in it, was frozen in shock. I expected people to run to the car, but nobody did. It seemed like minutes passed. Probably it was only seconds.

A hand emerged from the car window. Billy's hand. Now people ran to pull him out. I heard them ask why he hadn't let them know he was okay.

"Didn't want to ruin the shot," he said. His voice was as soft and slow as ever. "Never heard nobody say 'cut.'"

I was shaking, and trying to hide it. Once the relief had sunk in, the set went back to normal—people hurrying this way and that with equipment, clipboards, cases. As Ryan, Anjel, Griffin, and I went back to the trailer, I caught sight of Billy, still in his padded suit, heading over to the craft-services table to get a cup of coffee. I didn't dare look at him, fearing that somehow the pressure of my eyes would make him vanish; I still couldn't believe he was really there. I'd seen him get smashed to pieces in a car wreck. I'd seen him come back from the dead.

Marymount High School, and its associated convent, of the order of the Sacred Heart of Mary, was in an old Spanish mission-style building on Sunset Boulevard. Dad had filmed a commercial there. He loved nuns, and they loved him—especially Irish ones. He flirted with them in a gentlemanly sort of way. Few men, probably, treated them like ladies.

"I think I'll send my daughter here next year." I could hear his voice rolling the words like bonbons to be wrapped up in tissue paper and given to the nuns.

They weren't proper nuns, in black habits and wimples, as the nuns in Loughrea had been. They wore murky pink and green polyester outfits, and you could see their legs, which were smothered in thick flesh-colored stockings. I thought that was very improper. Their only nun-mark was the big silver cross on a long chain that hung around each nun's neck. The principal's name was Sister Colette—unsuitable, I felt, for a nun.

Sister Charles was the Irish one. She taught sewing, and she was a big fan of Dad's. "Such a wonderful artist, your father," she'd say almost every time she saw me. "That fillum of his, *Ryan's Daughter*, sure it's the most beautiful fillum I've ever seen, the love of Ireland that's in every inch of it . . ."

I was confused. I didn't think Dad had made a film called *Ryan's Daughter*, though I wasn't a hundred percent sure; could she, somehow, mean Tatum? Ryan had made a film in Ireland recently, *Barry Lyndon*, but I didn't think Tatum was in it. I didn't want to correct Sister Charles, she was in such raptures over the film, and that meant she liked me. When I did finally discover that a film called *Ryan's Daughter* existed, and that David Lean had directed it, I didn't dare tell her in case she lost interest in Dad and me—or, worse, in case she thought I'd bamboozled her, out of a tawdry and hypocritical desire to be liked, into thinking the film was Dad's.

I wanted the girls at school to know of my connection with Ryan, so I dropped his name whenever I could. When one of the older girls mentioned that some girls had boyfriends at Loyola, the boys' school twinned with ours, I said, "I've already got someone. Ryan. My sister's boyfriend. Who drove me to school. Ryan O'Neal."

She looked at me weirdly, and stopped talking to me. I knew it had come out wrong. I'd made it sound like I was sleeping with him too. I felt ridiculous. Why did I have to be a name-dropper, and then make a hash of it? Still, I was glad I'd said it. My movie-star connections made me interesting—I'd never been a popular girl, or good at sports—and if I hadn't said it, maybe no one would notice who was at the wheel of the magenta Corniche that sometimes dropped me off or picked me up in the curving school driveway.

When I was alone with him in the car, Ryan rested his right hand on my thigh, the same way he rested it on Anjel's when she was in the passenger seat.

"You don't mind, do you?" he asked me once.

"No," I said casually, though I wasn't sure it was okay. For one thing, it didn't seem safe for him to drive with only his left hand.

"I can't drive any other way," he said, and held the silence until he was sure I understood that he was telling the truth.

The Pacific Coast Highway was solid with traffic in the mornings, and Ryan would pull onto the hard shoulder and put his foot down on the gas. I watched the needle climb—50, 60, 70, 80—terrified that another driver would have the same idea and pull out in front of us, and we'd have no time to stop and no way not to crash into them. I didn't wear my seat belt; I don't think I'd ever seen anyone wear one. I wanted to put it on, but I was afraid Ryan would take it as an insult to his driving. I tried to relax my thigh so that tense muscles under his hand wouldn't give me away.

Before long, I was spending most of my time with Anjelica and Ryan. I knew Cici wasn't happy about it, but I put that down to things like no proper bedtime and the fact that Griffin was allowed to smoke dope and snort coke and maybe she thought I was doing that too, which I wasn't.

The whole idea of taking smoke into my lungs revolted me. I didn't make much distinction between cigarettes and joints: Anjel seemed to smoke them pretty much interchangeably. I liked the smell of grass better than the smell of tobacco. Beyond that, I didn't see any difference. People smoked to relax, or just because they smoked. I knew marijuana was illegal, but then so was speeding and everybody did that.

Cocaine was different. That obviously was a drug—and Anjelica had been arrested for possession of it during the Roman Polanski scandal, when the cops searched Jack's house after Polanski took a thirteen-year-old girl there. I was twelve, but the whole thing seemed remote from anything that might happen to me. I'd seen people snorting coke: bent over a mirror with a rolled-up twenty-dollar bill or a fat silver straw stuck up their noses, their heads wobbling and their eyes crossed as they followed the white powder line. Then they sat around leaning their heads back and occasionally saying "oohhhh." The whole thing looked idiotic. I had no interest in trying it.

After a while, Anjelica asked me if I wanted to live with her. Of course I said yes: Anjel was my sister, my goddess, everything I wanted to be. And I was, basically, living with her already. On the phone, Dad asked me formally to confirm it, and whether I agreed to have my half of the rent for a house paid out of the trust fund he'd set up for me. Anjel had found a house in Hollywood, in the shadow of the Chateau Marmont. She ordered a hazelnut-colored sofa, upholstered in fat rolls like the Michelin man. I bagged the room with the bookshelves.

Cici, in a fury, put all my stuff out on the driveway. It ended up at Gloom Castle, since Anjel wasn't yet ready to move into the Hollywood house. In the end, she never was. We spent one night there, camping, for fun. Six months later the lease expired.

Cici and Anjelica were battling over me, and I didn't know it. None of us can remember exactly what happened.

I've read Cici's letters to Dad, and John Julius's replies to the ones she wrote to him. She described me, more than once, as "a creature of love and purity." She said, again and again, how important it was to protect my innocence. She urged John Julius to take me, step in, do something. John Julius said he couldn't do anything just then; his own family life was in upheaval. He asked whether she believed I was truly in "moral danger." He offered her his backing—whatever that was worth—if she wanted to legally adopt me.

I imagine she felt taken for a patsy. Of all the people around me, she seemed to be the only one who was putting my interests first—she who wasn't related to me, who had met me only a few years before, who was being vilified by Dad—and she was powerless. She was being accused, I think, of lax morals; but her home was stable and Collin and I knew our place in it. She gave us rules and responsibilities and made sure we felt loved. She may have had many lovers and minimal clothes, but she had an iron sense of right and wrong where children were concerned.

By her standards, Dad had virtually abandoned me—and though he had left me with her, he would back anyone against her. My real father (who had after all only met me once since Mum's death) was unwilling to accept commitment, even in the emergency circumstances that Cici laid out for him. And my sister, heedless and headstrong, was insisting on taking me into a circle where, Cici knew, there were no rules for children at all.

I dimly understood Cici's qualms, but I didn't care. If Anjel wanted me, I would be there. I sensed that she felt a chance of making us all a family: her and Ryan, his children and me. I hadn't had a place at Jack's house, except on weekends, but at Ryan's—especially with Tatum away—I fitted in. I knew how much Anjel wanted to fill the loss of Mum for me, though she never said it in so many words. But every casual mention of Mum added another filament to the cord that united us, and nobody else: the Soma girls. We'd both lost our mother, but we had each other. What was broken for me was broken for her too. I was coming to realize that it had broken long before Mum died.

14

I was sitting on Tatum's bed in the beach house with Griffin, talking. In her absence, it was my room—and like Griffin's it was big enough for a king-size bed and nothing else. No bookshelf, no desk. Suddenly Anjel ran in and slid open the closet door.

"Don't tell him I'm in here," she whispered to us. She looked really afraid. She was shaking. "If he asks, don't tell him, please."

She squeezed in behind Tatum's Rive Gauche–scented clothes. I could barely see her bare feet behind the ranks of Maud Frizon shoes. My heart started to race. I didn't know how close behind her Ryan might be. I couldn't hear footsteps; but maybe he was being quiet, to surprise us all. From inside, Anjel slid the door closed.

Griffin and I made an instant, silent pact not to even look at the closet. I hoped we'd be brave enough to keep Anjel safe if Ryan came in looking for her. How could we stand up to him, if she couldn't?

I hadn't heard any arguing or fighting from upstairs. I wanted to know what had happened, but I didn't dare talk to Anjel through the closet door in case Ryan was listening outside, waiting for me to give her away.

Five minutes passed. Griffin and I forced out casual words, waiting for the crash of the door slamming open. I imagined Ryan, as big as a bear in that small room, tearing open the closet door . . . And then? I wasn't sure. I tried to keep my breathing slow and steady so that whatever happened, I'd be prepared for it.

I knew he didn't have any reason to be so angry. Anjel couldn't have given him one: both because she was too good to have done anything bad enough to deserve this, and because she knew him well enough to be afraid of his temper. I also knew he didn't need a reason. He enjoyed the power.

I heard a grating creak. The closet door was sliding open, catching in its runners. My eyes caromed from the closet to the door and back again as Anjel pushed Tatum's clothes aside and came out.

Her eyes were swollen and red. From crying, I thought—not from being hit. She was still shaking.

"Are you okay?" I asked her.

She didn't answer. I hugged her. She hugged me back, tight. I felt I was the only person she had to rely on—and I wished I was stronger, that I could go upstairs to Ryan and face him down, scold him and shame him for scaring my sister like that.

I never thought for a second that she was overreacting. I was afraid of him too. He had a way of coming up behind me and placing his hands on either side of my head, over my ears. I had to relax into it, because the next thing would be a sharp twist as he cracked my neck. It was supposed to be affectionate, and he did it to everybody; but however good it felt afterward, to me it was a reminder that he was strong enough to break my neck if he chose to.

One day when I got back from school (a friend of Tatum's had been hired to drive me), Anjel wasn't there. Griffin was in his room watching TV, looking hunted.

"Allegra!" A barking shout from above.

I went to the foot of the stairs. "Yes, Ryan?"

"Bring me some soup. And a Coke."

Soup was always Campbell's tomato. Coke was always on ice, with half a lemon squeezed into it.

I heated the soup, poured it into a bowl, put the tall glass of Coke beside it, carried the tray upstairs, and set it on the bed in front of Ryan. He took a spoonful.

"Where's the pepper." It wasn't really a question.

"Sorry. I'll go get it . . ."

He stood up. He seemed bigger than usual. I took a step back. His hands were clenched into half fists.

"Get down those stairs before I throw you down."

I sensed, without thought, that the sight of fear in me might make him snap, as if I were accusing him of something. So I went with calm, mute obedience. The stairs were wood slats, and I tried not to let my feet make too much noise. I didn't look back. With each step down, I supposed to feel the blow of a china bowl on the back of my head, and hot soup scalding me.

I made it to the corner where the stairs doglegged. I heard Ryan leave the upstairs landing and go back into his room. Then I ran.

I didn't know where to go. I was too scared to get the pepper and go back upstairs. I didn't think he'd come downstairs after me, but if he did, I didn't want him to find me in Griffin's room. I wasn't sure if he'd dare hit me, but he might well hit Griffin instead. I didn't want to stay in the living room, right underneath him, where the stairs came down; he'd think I was spying on him, or maybe I'd make some noise that would set him off again. I could go outside onto the beach, but that felt exposed, with nowhere to hide or run to, and the ocean was stormy. Anjel would be back soon, and she'd worry if I wasn't there.

So I sat on Tatum's bed, nervously doing my homework. The window was a slit high up on the wall, like a jail cell, too small to climb out of. If I heard Ryan's footsteps coming downstairs, I decided, I'd run for the back door and just stay on the edge of the Pacific Coast Highway until Anjel got back. Cars could see me; I'd be protected there.

I heard the garage open, and Anjel's footsteps. I caught her eye through the open bedroom door.

"How is he?" She sounded wary. He must have been in a bad mood when she left.

"He wanted soup and I forgot the pepper. He threatened to throw me down the stairs."

She nodded. Her face was gray and cloudy. She looked like someone going to execution as she headed on down the hallway.

The important thing was that he hadn't thrown me down the stairs. He would come out of this bad mood, and everything could carry on as before.

Ryan used to boast that his birthday was the same day as Hitler's. It was in mid-April, on the cusp of Aries and Taurus, which seemed significant to me. If you were neither one thing nor the other, you could be anything—or both. The cosmic tides acting on the fluids in his brain meant that he and Hitler shared something. That explained his dark side—even that he seemed to be proud of it.

His moods alternated: a few days wonderful, a few days demonic. When he was in a good mood, he was the nicest person in the world, and it was hard to hold the bad side against him. He picked me up from school and took me shopping: to Maxfield Bleu, to a boutique on Sunset Plaza—where he bought me a beautiful off-the-shoulder chiffon dress, brown-speckled like a bird's egg—and to Maud Frizon for shoes. Other days, we would all go to his favorite car wash, on the gay part of Santa Monica Boulevard opposite the store Ah! Men! (I loved that name), and get burgers from the burger stand and buy handpainted hairbrushes and glittery things from Oray's Salon across the road.

Or we'd all sit on his bed and watch TV. I was working on flirting and I practiced my look on him: not turning my head, but swiveling my eyes ninety degrees to the side. It hurt.

"One day you'll drive men crazy with that look," he said. Exactly the response I wanted.

One night we went out to dinner, and then drove up to the front of the Whisky nightclub. Ryan got out, spoke to someone, then came back and drove around the corner. We went in through a side door near the kitchen, and straight up to the balcony. We were given a table at the edge, with a good view of the stage—and Griffin and I were placed at the back, where we couldn't be seen from below. Toots and the Maytals were playing. Anjel and Ryan danced in place at the table, so I did too. She rolled her hands around each other the way John Travolta did in *Saturday Night Fever*, so I did too. It was harder than it looked; the beat tripped me up and my arms wouldn't do what I wanted them to. So I gave that up and just stepped from one foot to the other. Ryan grinned at me. He pulled a little vial from his pocket and took a toot of coke with the tiny spoon that was chained to the lid. He didn't bother to hide it. He was untouchable.

Even at the Santa Monica Civic Auditorium, when we went to see Joan Armatrading in concert, he hardly hid it. Just leaned down a little for the toot. We were sitting at one end of a row of seats, with real people—not in some special place reserved for movie stars, where the law didn't apply. I was afraid he'd be seen; but I didn't want to look around since that would make us look guilty.

The little vial was with him always: when he was driving, when we went to the movies, or when we were just sitting around on his bed watching TV. He bent down to it as casually as Cici would put a stick of gum in her mouth.

I didn't always know who would be picking me up from school: sometimes Ryan, sometimes Tatum's friend Esme, sometimes Roberto, who worked for Aunt Dorothy, to take me to Gloom Castle for a few days. Sometimes Anjelica.

I was happiest when I saw her little gray Mercedes waiting for me, the car that Jack had given her for her twenty-third birthday. The fact that she still drove it meant to me that she still loved him, that somehow, behind it all, he was the permanent one.

"Dad's in hospital, Legs," she said as I got in. "He couldn't breathe."

When they examined him they found an aneurysm in his aorta: a bulge in the artery wall like a balloon. If it burst, he would die, as his father had in the Beverly Hills Hotel.

Anjel and I talked only a little on the way to the hospital. She told me they'd made him quit smoking, cold turkey, to give his lungs a chance to strengthen before the operation. He'd had emphysema for nearly twenty years by then, and sometime in the 1960s he'd been given five years to live. Anjel told me how she remembered meeting him at Victoria Station in London after Mum died, nearly nine years before. He'd taken the train from Rome because his lungs were too weak for him to fly.

He was on the eighth floor of Cedars-Sinai, the VIP floor, holding court as usual. Aside from the hospital bed and the high-mounted TV, the atmosphere was just like the hotel rooms that I was used to seeing him in: a sofa of people discussing his next project, a pile of scripts and books, Gladys in a straight chair taking notes. Except for the bland curtains and furniture and waiting-room art on the walls, it could have been a French king's levee. When the nurses came in to check something, Dad tolerated them graciously. When someone lit up a cigarette, he leaned over defiantly to inhale the smoke.

Maricela was there. She disappeared as soon as we arrived.

It was a balancing act between aneurysm and anesthesia: the longer they waited for Dad's lungs to strengthen, the higher the risk the aneurysm might burst and kill him instantly. They waited a week. I spent the day of the operation wondering whether, if Dad died, they would call me immediately or wait till school was over. The sight of Anjel's little car in the driveway at three o'clock reassured me. If Dad was dead, she wouldn't have been able to drive, or if she had she'd be standing outside the car to embrace me.

Dad was in intensive care. I'd never seen anyone look so ill. His skin was blue and dirty-looking. The bags under his eyes hung to the sides of his face.

"Hello, girls." His smile was weak. And then, to the nurses: "My daughters." A formal introduction to assert his control of the situation, or a boast? I wasn't sure which.

Every day Anjel picked me up at school and drove us down Sunset, to Beverly Glen, along Santa Monica Boulevard, and into the parking lot entrance between the twin towers of Cedars-Sinai. I began to dream about that drive, like a scene from a movie with the sound turned off, Anjel and I side by side framed by the windscreen and the top arc of the steering wheel under her hands, a rear projection of green lawns and trees and nondescript corner stores rolling past the windows on an endless loop. We never arrived. We were both anxious in those dreams, as if we'd be driving for our whole lives and Dad would die just before we got there.

We took Dad for walks down the corridor of the VIP floor, Anjel supporting one arm, me supporting the other. It was carpeted, wide and silent; the nurses' station reminded me of the reception desk at Dad's business manager's office. Spaced out along the walls, a little too far apart, were small, ugly paintings by famous artists: the ones that nobody wanted to look at, I figured, so that's why they'd been donated for tax deductions. There was something grotesque about these million-dollar paintings in a hospital. I wondered if the VIPs felt better knowing they were dying within twenty feet of a Picasso.

Dad was very grumpy; I guessed the bad-paintings-by-the-best-painters thing annoyed him. All they gave him to eat was baby food, like Jell-O and squelchy lasagna, and 7-Up with the bubbles stirred out. Anjel solved this problem by getting takeout from Chasen's. When Dad was discharged, she convinced Ryan to lend him the beach house to recuperate in. It was November. We'd have Thanksgiving there.

Anjel cooked a turkey, stuffing, mashed potatoes, green beans. I hoped desperately that it would go well, for her sake, but I knew from the start that it wouldn't. Dad was in a foul mood: he didn't like Ryan, especially in comparison to Jack, and hated being beholden to him for the loan of the house. He also, of course, disliked holidays that were centered around eating. Maricela was her usual silent, inscrutable self. Ryan sulked—because, I figured, he resented being a guest in his own house. The sky outside—which was inside too, thanks to those huge windows—was suffocatingly overcast. Lee's Bars Stools and Dinettes pounded south, as usual, through a malevolently still ocean.

I hated the meanness. Anjel had tried so hard, and Griffin and I were the only ones who appreciated the work she'd put in, or valued what she was trying to create: goodwill, warmth, togetherness. Dad was sick, so I cut him a bit of slack, but Ryan had no excuse. Anjel wanted a family as much as I did, and she was doing all she could to make us one. And they were spitting it back in her face.

It rained hard that winter: apocalyptic rain. The sandstone cliffs above the Pacific Coast Highway started to crumble. Huge clods tumbled down, threatening to cut off Malibu from the city. Houses slid down the hillside as the earth collapsed away. The templelike Getty Museum, with its Roman balustrades, hung on the edge. I wondered if I'd see it fall, on the way to school or back again: the museum breaking into its separate blocks of marble, paintings and sculptures skidding across the highway, a Greek arm here, a Cubist canvas there, and people screeching to a halt and diving through the traffic to grab a fragment of mosaic or Vermeer.

It seemed like the coastline was dissolving—and we were in the middle, on the front line. I stood at the huge windows, watching the hungry waves eat up the beach. At high tide, they smashed and sucked beneath the house. Up the coast, Linda Ronstadt had students from Pepperdine University helping her sandbag her house; I pictured her in her Boy Scout hot pants and the students in regular Scout uniforms heaving away. Floating tree trunks and telephone poles thudded against the pilings. I'd lie in bed imagining one splintering and a corner of the house breaking off like a piece of cookie— the deck probably, and some of the kitchen with it.

I was sharing Griffin's room now, as Tatum had come back. He had a king-size water bed, and we'd try hard not to move in our sleep so as not to send waves to wake the other. In my dreams, if I wasn't driving endlessly to where Dad lay dying, I was adrift on an endless ocean, emotionlessly alone.

I got into Anjel's car one morning, ready for school. I loathed my uniform, but it set me apart at Ryan's house. I was a schoolgirl—not a thirteen-year-old glamour-puss; not a neglected, stoned surfer-child. Griffin and Tatum didn't go to school. I did: I was normal. Plus, I was good at school.

Anjel swung her door closed and put the key in the ignition. She didn't turn it. We sat there in the half-light of the garage, in the cocoon of the car, suspended between the house and the highway. The traffic roared outside the closed door behind us.

"What am I going to do, Legs?"

I looked at her face, expecting tears. I didn't see any. She'd cried them all.

"Leave him."

The answer was so obvious. But Anjel looked at me like I'd said something amazing.

"You don't have to stay with someone who treats you like that."

I didn't want to stare at her, so I looked through the windscreen at the washing machine and dryer against the wall of the house, and the door into the hallway. I was half afraid that Ryan would come through it and see us sitting there talking. And he'd know what I'd said. Actually, I hoped he would know, but that we'd be out of there first.

"I love you, Legs." It seemed like the first time I'd seen her smile in months.

"I love you too, Jel." She put her hand on the gear stick, as if she wanted to take some action and that was all she could manage in the small space of the car. I put my hand on hers. I couldn't understand why she'd never thought of leaving Ryan before, and I didn't know whether she'd do it, but at least I'd put the possibility in her mind. I felt like I'd given her a gift.

Gradually I seemed to be moving into Gloom Castle, because Griffin's room at the Beverly Hills house was too small to share, and there was no question of Tatum—now that she was back—sharing hers. I missed Anjelica, and our expeditions to visit Jeremy in a bohemian section of Hollywood, with fancy old stucco buildings and a bookstore-café with swirly flyers on a pinboard, phone numbers everywhere. People seemed connected there, part of a web of things going on: not like the isolated compounds on the mountaintops of Beverly Hills. Jeremy's paintings covered the walls of his one-room studio, colorful jungly African scenes, memories of his childhood in Rhodesia. One end was curtained off for his friend Tim.

"Tim can levitate," Anjel told me almost in a whisper, the first time I met him. "He's a master of TM. He can fly."

I longed to see him fly, but it seemed rude to ask. I guessed it was something he did in private, behind the curtain. He was gentle, like a deer that you didn't want to spook.

At the pharmacy in Beverly Hills, where Aunt Dorothy would take me to buy what I needed with the ten dollars a week she gave me, I saw the *National Enquirer* at the checkout. In the middle was a photo of Anjelica, with photos of Jack and Ryan on either side. Anjel's head was lowered, her hair falling lank over her face as she hurried into a doorway. The headline said she was back with Jack: and the photo arrangement had her skulking in his direction, with Ryan glowering behind her.

Anjel used to like taking me to Schwab's drugstore and buying every trashy magazine, fashion magazine, and gossip rag on the racks. We'd get back to the beach house with twenty or thirty of them: the *National Enquirer*, the *Globe*, the *Star*, *Cosmo*, *People*, *Us*, *Playboy*, *Playgirl*, *Redbook*, *Harper's Bazaar*. She'd dump them all on the bed in Ryan's room upstairs, and we'd make our way through them, laughing at the gossip and comparing the horoscopes. I thought this was so chic and cool: it was sad to buy one magazine and take it seriously, but fun to buy them all.

Now that she was on the cover of the worst of them, it wasn't funny or chic at all. I wanted to know what the *National Enquirer* was saying about her; I knew how vicious they were. But I couldn't pick it up, couldn't touch it, couldn't buy it. I felt ashamed: because she was my sister, and they were making her out to be a slut; and also because I didn't know she'd left Ryan and gone back to Jack; and I didn't want Aunt Dorothy to know I'd found it out from a checkout-line rag.

The whole thing wasn't fair. I knew what she'd put up with from Ryan, how patient and forgiving she'd been, how hard she'd tried to make it work. She was right to go back to Jack; I knew how kind and fun he was. (Conveniently, I forgot about her crying.) I prayed Aunt Dorothy wouldn't see the *National Enquirer*. And of course she didn't want to see it, because she didn't want to talk about it with me. So she didn't see it. It didn't exist.

I wondered if I'd ever see Griffin again. I missed him: my comrade, my ally. I worried that I'd been his last hope, and I'd abandoned him.

15

I'm in the back seat of a car, driving down a narrow street that turns a sharp corner to the left. The reddish brown buildings are high and solid, squaring off the right angle. I'm little, maybe four. It must be before Mum died. Is that her sitting next to me in the back seat? I'm not sure, but I'm not alone. And it's not a taxi: the seat is low, and I'm craning my neck to see the tops of the buildings, which are crenellated with pointy arches and dormer windows. It's silent: no talking, not even any engine noise from the car. I'm not sure how I know there is a corner—it looks like a dead-end street. Perhaps because we're driving so fast we won't be able to stop, and the road must go somewhere.

I know it's London. That's part of the memory.

When school finished for the summer of 1978, Anjelica took me to London. It was the first time I'd been back since moving to Ireland.

Everywhere we went I looked for that street. It was so vivid in my mind that I could have drawn it—but no street matched it exactly. I figured out, from the height and design of the buildings, that it must be in the West End. Stratton Street, off Piccadilly, was close, but it was one-way the wrong way; it bent right, not left. Could the traffic planners have changed it, or had my brain recorded a mirror image? It haunted me, that memory street. I was driven down it again and again, never turning the blind corner, never discovering the secret of what was on the far side.

I didn't tell Anjel about the memory, or even ask in a roundabout way where that street might be. I didn't know what its significance was, or if it really had any. Maybe it was just some random image that had stuck to a sticky spot in my brain. We didn't go to Maida Avenue either. If she had wanted to take me, I would have gone with her—but I was relieved that she never mentioned it. That was the past, and the past was gone.

I had learned not to want what wasn't there. I tried not to ask, or expect, of people what they didn't have—or want—to give. Really, I tried not to ask or expect anything; that way I wouldn't be disappointed, and whatever came to me would be a bonus, a treat. I wasn't by nature a doormat, but I tried to look at things from the other person's point of view. Circumstances were difficult. Everyone was doing the best they could.

We were in London because Jack was filming *The Shining* there. It was a six-month shooting schedule, so Anjel had to go. I felt it was especially important to her that she took me.

The *National Enquirer* had been right: Anjel did go back to Jack. But then she suddenly disappeared to Aspen, without him. I was at Jack's house, with Jennifer, when I spoke to her on the phone and discovered she wouldn't be back in time to help me with some bit of homework she'd said she would do with me.

I hung up the phone, in tears. Helena promised to help me with my assignment, whatever it was. That was when I stopped being afraid of her.

Soon after I'd first met Helena, I saw her in *Kansas City Bomber* on the little TV in my room at Cici's house. Collin was a big Raquel Welch fan on account of *One Million Years BC*, and we both loved *Rollerball*, the sci-fi movie based on roller derby. *Kansas City Bomber* was the original roller-derby movie, and Helena was the villain who threw nasty fouls at Raquel Welch. Her viciousness in the movie fit so well with her wild black hair and tough Boston accent that for years I thought that was who she really was.

She had a tattoo on her left shoulder, its blue ink gone fuzzy with time, of a square cross, with the letters M–O–M above it. I'd never known anyone with a tattoo before; it looked fierce on her olive skin, even with the spaghetti strap of her nightgown falling over it. But gradually, I came to see it as a badge. She had no children of her own, but she looked after people.

I'd see Helena described in magazine articles about Jack as his housekeeper, but that was wrong: she was his rock, his anchor, his go-between with the real world. She used to say she didn't know how old she was, because her parents, when they came to America, put different dates on different forms. I hadn't believed Maricela when she said the same thing, but I believed Helena. As a little girl in occupied Greece, Helena had been a pet of the Nazi officers who had occupied her house, running messages for them. She told me how she'd been mesmerized by the blazing shine of their boots. In Boston after the war, when her family didn't have a home, Helena danced at a Greek picnic and made enough for the down payment—and later made thousands of dollars a night belly dancing in Las Vegas. She'd met Jack at a coffee house in Hollywood in the early sixties, when he was still making B movies for Roger Corman. Years later, when she left her husband and needed a place to stay, he gave her the downstairs bedroom in his house, and later the house next door.

Helena distracted me from Anjel's absence, and I began to hang out with her, helping her with whatever she was doing. Even when Anjel came back, the foursome that she and Jack, Jen and I had once made was gone. Jen would move to Hawaii with her mother within a year—but our spontaneous little family didn't survive the interlude with Ryan. I sensed, without ever quite formulating the thought, that Anjel had been defeated.

She didn't come back in time for the Academy Awards either. Jack was presenting the award for Best Picture, and he took Jen and me instead. Aunt Dorothy's handyman Roberto picked me up from school early and drove me to Jack's house, where I changed into a silk outfit patterned with tiny rosebuds that had been my Christmas present from Anjel. As I dabbed makeup that Anjel had given me onto the acne on my forehead and chin, I could hear him getting ready above me: water turning on and off, bare feet padding from bedroom to bathroom and back again, then the heavier tread of the pointed shoes he liked so much. The limo picked us up at two and, after we collected Jennifer, dropped us disappointingly at the back door of the Dorothy Chandler Pavilion. Jack shepherded us to the two seats reserved for him, and disappeared off to spend the entire ceremony backstage.

Our seats were next to Pat Boone, whose daughter Debby was singing "You Light Up My Life." I felt completely cheated. How could the Academy seat Jack Nicholson next to Pat Boone? Mrs. Boone looked pretty pissed off too, when Jack deposited two spotty teenage girls and headed off backstage. I didn't have any sympathy for her. She should have been someone exciting, like Warren Beatty or John Travolta. Plus, I loathed that syrupy song, and it was even worse to have to listen to it with Debby Boone's parents beside me. They left during the next commercial break, and two men in tuxedos filled their places.

In 1975, just after I'd met Jack, I'd watched the Oscars in the house on Euclid. "Come on, Jack!" I'd said silently to myself, willing him to win Best Actor for *The Last Detail*. Jack Lemmon won, for

Save the Tiger. I blamed myself for not being specific enough so that God, or fate, would know which Jack should win. This time, as far as he was concerned, I would get the Oscars right: I would repay his trust—as he left us, by ourselves, with cameras on us—by behaving perfectly. If I'd been Tatum, I knew, I would have gone to the after-show parties—but Jack put us in the limo and said good night, and I didn't mind.

When I told one of the girls at school how generous he had been to give us his seats and stand for the whole four hours backstage, she laughed at me. Backstage, she said, was where all the fun was. I hadn't thought of that—that there were rooms, and sofas, and a bar. For some reason I'd thought there was nothing beyond the wings of the stage. Still, it didn't diminish the gift—and he had given it to me even when Anjel wasn't there, and so very soon after we'd come back from Ryan's house. I worried sometimes that he might feel I'd been a traitor, in accepting Ryan. But he never showed any sign of it, never mentioned Ryan at all.

A week after Anjel and I arrived in London, Bob Dylan played Hyde Park. Anjel was excited; it was a Sunday and Jack wasn't working, so he could go too. I knew we'd get VIP treatment. We'd go backstage, maybe spend the whole concert backstage; we'd meet Dylan. I had the impression that Jack and Anjel knew him already.

That morning, when Anjel came upstairs to get me, I wasn't dressed. I clutched my stomach. "I feel sick," I said. "I can't go."

I made believe I was very upset to be missing it. "I'm sorry," I said, seeing her disappointment and confusion. She knew I loved Dylan's music. I was pretty sure she saw through my sickness, though she didn't accuse me of faking it.

I couldn't explain why I couldn't face it. I didn't want to be the invisible little sister that I'd been when we met the Lakers after a basketball game and I'd felt like a speck among those famous giants. Not with Dylan, who had become a kind of totem of my closeness with Anjel ever since that day when we drove along San Vicente Boulevard singing along to "Knockin' on Heaven's Door." If Dylan looked through me, I truly would disappear.

I spent the day in the room at the top of the house the production had rented for Jack. It had purple carpet, and fake gilt chairs upholstered in purple velvet, like the cast-off furniture from a sheik's newly redecorated diplomatic reception room. Flat sunlight poured in through the windows that lined one side, curdling the purple dyes into hallucinogenic shades. There was a little portable TV on the floor, and a stack of classic movies on video that I watched one after another, all day long. Even though I was alone in the house, I clutched my stomach from time to time, as if to convince myself that I really was sick and couldn't have gone.

Anjel brought me back a program. I kept it, and looked at it every day. On the cover, Dylan ringed his eyes with thumb and forefinger. His thumbnails were almost an inch long, thick and yellow like a bird's talons. Behind them, his eyes were shadowed and dark. I stared into them, imagining I'd been there, imagining those eyes looking at me. Would they have seen me? They weren't a normal person's eyes; I knew from his songs that they saw things normal people didn't see. I hated my cowardice for staying behind.

"Come on, Legs," said Anjel one day soon after that. "We're going jogging."

I'd never known her to go jogging before, or do any kind of exercise just for the sake of it. Once, when we were cruising along Mulholland Drive with the top down, Anjel had yelled out at a fat jogger laboring along, "Keep going, sucker, it's not gonna do you any good!" I thought that was hilarious. It confirmed—as if I needed confirmation—how glamorous and special she was.

I made a face. But I knew she was trying to look after me, make me get outside, which was good for me, like Cici had. Left to myself, I'd just read all day. We had tried going to Hyde Park to play Frisbee, but that invoked the shade of Ryan, so we hadn't done it again.

"We need to get healthy! It's so great to be in London again, where the air is clean."

The house we were living in was on Cheyne Walk, overlooking the river Thames—but with four lanes of heavy traffic in between. Trucks pounded along it twenty-four hours a day, belching diesel fumes. Every outside window ledge was black with the residue. It wasn't possible that Anjel hadn't noticed. I realized she didn't want to, didn't want to give it any importance. She meant the famous L.A. smog. London was for her, even more than for me, a special place, which had to be, in every way, better than L.A.—and which she wanted me to love.

I did what I was told, though with a bad grace. Truck drivers honked at us in our shorts. I felt ridiculous, jogging in place on the pavement as we waited for the light to turn green. Nobody jogged in London—especially not on the streets, especially not on that smoke-choked arterial road. I was conscious of how American we looked. I hated it: hated standing out, hated looking different. Fortunately, jogging was never mentioned again.

Mostly we went shopping, browsing the stalls in Antiquarius, a vast antiques market on the King's Road. Anjel told me that Mum had loved poking around in antiques shops. When we walked past the Chelsea Cobbler, she told me that Mum had had shoes made there. She pointed out these spots more in the manner of a tour guide at a holy site than as incidents from her own life with Mum. She didn't want to tell stories of what they had done together, and I didn't want to hear them. It would have made me feel even more insignificant, since they weren't mine.

This was 1978, and the King's Road was punk central. Mohicans glued into foot-long spikes, dyed black and blue and green; ripped jeans and leather and fishnets; chains and safety pins through the skin. I'd never seen anything so extreme. I stared at them, trying not to let them catch me staring in case it made them mad at me. I envied them. They seemed so sure of who they were: punks. And where they belonged: right there on the King's Road.

They were angry. That awed me: I'd wrung my anger out of me, and I didn't know what it felt like anymore. I felt disembodied compared to them. And I felt that the genteel streets of Chelsea, where Jack and Anjel's friends lived, were unreal compared to this. So was Los Angeles, where everyone went about in little personal shells with a wheel on each corner, insulated from the real world.

I'd also never seen so much physical deformity: bad teeth, gammy legs, people with growths on their faces or blind, thalidomide victims with stunted arms. They were on the buses, walking the streets. I decided it was one of the things I liked about London: people didn't have to be perfect, they didn't have to hide or all look the same. Or sound the same either: I loved the different accents, the chummy way people called me "luv," the laughter and arguments spilling out of pubs, the cheering coming from behind the streamer curtains in the doorways of betting shops. Life wasn't sanitized and wrapped in cellophane the way it was in L.A.

I loved that I could walk out the door of the house and go somewhere. At Cici's house I'd had a canyon, with a mountainside and a creek, to wander; but since then I'd been marooned either on a beach or on a mountaintop, unable to go anywhere without someone to drive me. If where I wanted to go was farther than I wanted to walk, in London I could just stick out my arm for a taxi.

There was still BRITS OUT graffiti on the railway bridges, and bombed-out buildings left over from the Blitz. They fascinated me: buildings with their sides sliced away to expose zigzagging staircases, faded wallpaper, plumbing with nowhere to go. I loved walking the streets and looking into people's windows: lots of round paper lampshades hanging from the ceilings, and beneath them people cooking, working, playing, or just moving around.

Joan Buck was back in London now, living in a book-crammed top-floor flat in Earls Court Square with her new husband. She showed me her wedding dress, ruched and pleated in a deep smoky purple, her signature color. She told me what a bitchy columnist had written: "The bride looked purple in a radiant dress." It was the kind of witticism I wished I could come up with, and I admired Joan for being able to laugh about it even though it was cruel and aimed at her. She took me to the offices of *Vogue*, where she worked, and introduced me to people as her little sister. She didn't have a sister of her own, and I was thrilled to be that for her. She had known me since I was born.

We'd walk down the street playing general-knowledge games like Botticelli, or a category game where you had to guess a person by asking questions like "What kind of kitchen implement is he?" Joan was clever and read lots of books, but she wasn't bookish and boring—which meant that I didn't have to be either. She was fun and glamorous and knew famous and interesting people; and she actually wanted to spend time with me. Our minds seemed to work the same way—which was a new experience for me. Usually I had to try hard to get it right, to be the kind of girl I thought the person I was with wanted me to be. When I was with Joan, I seemed to get it right without thinking about it.

Knowing of my crush on John Travolta, she gave me her ticket to a press screening of *Grease* at the Fox offices on Soho Square. The journalists howled with laughter, and I did too—and felt my crush thin, like paint mixed with turpentine. When I came out of the screening room at ten o'clock, there was still light in the sky: an otherworldly, luminous gray-blue, as if every atom of air and solid matter glowed from within. In L.A., so much farther south, the space between day and night was short, and the light was never like that. Somewhere in the blind passages of my memory, maybe, summer evenings at St. Cleran's or in London glowed with that same magical light. I drank in its energy through my eyes; I wanted to swim in it, as if it was the elixir of joy.

～✕～

The house we lived in was strange, with the gilt-and-purple sunroom on top (next to my bedroom, which had a wallpaper of green trellis that made it feel like a birdcage, and me the bird), and a windowless dining room furnished like a monastery on the ground floor, with a long table and hard, narrow pews to sit on. Every room was ringed with cast-iron heating vents, which tripped you up if you were wearing high heels, and the only way out was down a tightly spiraling cast-iron staircase, which you had to take on tiptoe in order not to sink through the holes.

Jack and Anjel's room was on the middle floor, off the living room, which was rarely used. I thought of that as a movie-star thing: they hung out in their bedrooms, and living rooms were more like transit zones. The only time I ever saw anyone sit in the living room of Ryan's Beverly Hills house was when he was meeting with a producer about *The Champ*, which he hoped to star in with Griffin. When I visited Marlon Brando's house, the living room had that same deserted air. That lifeless room separated us, so that we seemed to be living in the house separately, not together.

In the mornings, after Jack left for the studio, I'd go downstairs and sit with Anjel on her bed, watching her put on her makeup. She kept it in a pouch in her enormous handbag, and she'd apply coat after coat of mascara, twirling the brush into her eyelashes, which grew longer and longer in curved arcs, in perfectly parallel lines. I wished my own short eyelashes would do that, but they just stuck together in tarry clumps. The whites of Anjel's eyes glittered like quartz, and the greeny-brown irises shimmered like sunlight on a tree-shaded pond.

When she finished, she'd open a baggie and put a generous pinch of grass into the lid of a shoe box. Then she opened a packet of rolling papers and used the flap to winnow out the seeds. I thought of this as Anjel's job, since she always did it, not Jack. A sweet smell rose up, and the seeds rattled dully against the cardboard. Her wrist, cocked just so, was bony and elegant, the stroking of cardboard against cardboard rhythmic and soothing.

"Can I do it?" I asked one day.

"Sure."

She handed over the shoe box lid and the Rizla packet. It was harder than I thought; either the clumps of seedy grass just got pushed up the box, or the whole lot fell to the lower edge. But soon I got the hang of it: I learned to look for the black-green spots in the densest clumps, and tease them free. It was work I could do for hours—a service for Anjel, a meditation. Maybe it chimed with some strand of our Italian peasant DNA: the satisfaction of a good harvest.

She showed me how to roll the grass into a joint: stick two Rizlas together, spread the pinch of grass so that the sausage was a little fatter at the ends than in the middle, then fold over the edge of the paper and tuck it in, pressing down the outside edges of my index fingers while my thumbs rolled it tight. Then a quick, businesslike lick from left to right to seal it, slide it under the elastic strap of an enameled Art Deco cigarette case, and start on the next.

I never wanted to smoke one, and she never offered one to me. Fiction was my drug of choice. I could lose myself in a story for hours, but snap back to reality in a millisecond. My emotions were so exhausted that I felt very little, and I liked it that way. The thought of getting stoned, of losing control of my thoughts or my body, terrified me.

Anjel's birthday came in early July, and not knowing what to give her, I gave her the thing I valued most in the world: a print of the photo of Mum that had been on the cover of *Life*. It had been in a portfolio of Halsman photos of her, which was among the things that had arrived at Gloom Castle one day: a trunkload of my stuff from St. Cleran's. I didn't know where the trunk had been during those years that I'd lived at Cici's house, but seemingly Dad had decided, as soon as I'd been parked at Gloom Castle, that my situation was now permanent enough to have it delivered to me.

Aunt Dorothy had put the photograph—Mum posed as the *Mona Lisa*—in a pale green-and-gold frame. I'd brought it with me to London—a guardian angel.

Thrilled with myself, I wrapped it and gave it to Anjel. When she opened it, tears came to her eyes.

"Thank you, Legs." Her voice broke as she said it. I knew I'd given her something no one else could have given her, something far more valuable than the diamonds and rubies she got from Jack.

My fourteenth birthday was six weeks later. We went to stay at someone's country house for the weekend, and I was put at the children's table for dinner. I felt that Anjel had betrayed me, so I sulked. When everyone went for a walk the next day, I refused to go. The woman whose house it was didn't go either, but sat on the step in the sunshine, shelling peas. They dropped with ghostly pings into a metal bowl, making little whispers as they skittered around and came to rest. I stopped reading, and watched. She was so serene, warmed by the sun, green pearls falling from her fingers. That was who I wanted to be.

We'd been in London for a month or more before John Julius called and asked to see me. I had made no effort to get in touch with him. Probably Cici told him I was there, and gave him the number. I didn't particularly want to see him, but I accepted the meeting—just as I had to accept the fact that he existed. I would have preferred it if he hadn't, but at least his existence made sense of things. That logical puzzle went around in my brain, but I felt nothing. There must be something wrong with me, I thought: I should feel something, anything. I was sleepwalking. I was taking steps forward in some kind of unconscious agreement with myself, without having any sense of what or why—or of where that "forward" might lead.

John Julius asked if I'd like to see Bath. I didn't know what Bath was—only that it was a strange name for a place. So I said yes. "No" would have been argumentative and troublemaking, and might have made him ask what I would like to see. I wouldn't have been able to answer.

The drive to Bath took two hours—a long way for a day trip. I wondered if he was trying to put distance between us and the rest of his life. I hoped he wouldn't ask me if I'd read the books he'd sent: three volumes of his mother's autobiography, and one volume of his father's, and each December a new little pamphlet called *A Christmas Cracker*. I hadn't opened any of them.

I had a strange sense of dislocation as I watched my father drive us west down the M4. Dad never drove. Someone always had to drive him: Betty, Paddy Lynch, Cici, Gladys, chauffeurs and taxis. It hadn't occurred to me, before that day, that there was anything unusual in this. Suddenly, as I sat in the passenger seat of John Julius's silver-blue sedan, Dad's kingliness seemed demanding and grandiose. Despite his title, John Julius was more solidly a part of the real, democratic world.

In Bath, we drove to a car park: a dreary, randomly aligned expanse of asphalt and concrete. A tall woman with white hair walked to meet us.

"This is Mollie," said John Julius.

"Hello," I said politely. He didn't explain who she was, beyond that. It was obvious she wasn't his wife. She was beautiful and elegant in a rangy, tweed-trousered way.

There was something furtive, I thought, about meeting in a car park. I wasn't sure whether I was the one being discreetly kept away, or Mollie was. Perhaps because we were both peripheral, we didn't have to be hidden from each other. I wondered, suddenly, if I was just an excuse that allowed John Julius to meet up with Mollie. If he'd really wanted to spend the day with me, why was he bringing her into it? I took it as a slight. He must love her very much, I decided, to drive such a long way just to see her for lunch.

They took me to the Roman baths. I didn't know the Romans

had been in Britain, and John Julius didn't think to explain it to me. So I didn't quite understand why the baths were ruined, or why we were looking at them at all. I felt muffled, as if nothing I was seeing was quite in focus, and whatever sounds I heard seemed to come from far away. The information coming into my brain was fuzzy and jumbled. I couldn't bring it together to mean anything.

I thought he was relieved when he finally dropped me back at the house on Cheyne Walk. I was a duty he'd performed nobly, and it was a good thing I was a semi-secret. I had been an embarrassment to him just by being born; and I was an embarrassment in myself, now. I felt stupid, nonfunctioning, American. My clothes, which I'd liked till that day, were all wrong. I'd worn my best outfit, which Anjel had bought me during the Ryan time: a gray wool skirt, cream shirt and jacket, and Maud Frizon boots—but they were two-tone cowboy boots in cream and magenta, and the cream part, which was canvas, was stained blue from the day I'd been caught in the rain wearing jeans.

When I got up to my birdcage room and took off my jacket, I saw that it was smeared with red all down one side. So was my handbag—a canvas Sportsac with short handles that tucked into my armpit. A red pen had leaked, right through the canvas. The jacket was ruined; the ink would never wash out. I cut a strip of cotton— the cream-colored shirt had come with a matching piece of fabric to tie around the neck—and glued it to the handbag over the red stains.

I could have bought a new bag. Sportsacs weren't expensive, and Anjel wouldn't have minded. I didn't. The bandage kept the red ink off my clothes, and no one would see it if I kept that side next to my body. I was more or less able to hide it when I unshouldered the bag and set it down. I felt defensive about my bandaged bag—which Anjel must have sensed, as she never questioned it. She would look at it doubtfully, and I would pretend not to see and brazen it out. The bandage got messier as the edges, which I never sewed down, pulled away from the glue. Still, I kept it. It was damaged, but that didn't make it worthless. I had fixed it, and even though I hadn't done a great job, it was good enough.

"How can you be spending so much money?"

Anjel was furious, standing over me where I sat on the purple-carpeted floor eating my dinner and watching *Top of the Pops* on the tiny TV, with punk bands like X-Ray Spex and British singers like David Essex that nobody in California had ever heard of. It was September. The decision had been made that I would stay with her and Jack in London through the autumn.

I knew I'd been spending too much, but I couldn't help it. The tutors who were teaching me my American schoolwork were scattered all over London, and I was taking five or six taxis a day. I was trying to be frugal, not buying things for myself beyond what was necessary, but in less than a week the envelopes of ten twenty-pound notes that Tim, Jack's cook, gave me were gone.

"Do you think you're some kind of princess? You can't go on a bus or tube like everybody else?"

Joan had told me what bus to take to her flat, and where to find it, but I'd never been on a tube train. I didn't know how to read the maps.

"I always had to go everywhere on public transport," she said, and stormed out.

I felt a rush of panic. What if Jack said I couldn't stay because I was too expensive? I knew he had lots of money, but that didn't mean he had to spend it on me. And if he did say that, what would that mean for Anjelica's relationship with him? I didn't want to be the cause of another breakup between them. She belonged with him, it was obvious, and I was virtually holding my breath that this time it would last. He was being very generous in letting me live with them—with her. And could I be spending so much that it was a lot even for him? The last thing I wanted to do was make him think I was a burden. I was doing my best to be sweet or, best of all, invisible.

Jack was working long days on *The Shining*, and at the same time he was editing a movie he'd directed, *Goin' South*. He went back and forth over a horse farting: taking out the sound effect and putting it back in, obsessively. Anjel was walking on eggshells around him. I remember only two flashes of the Jack who used to cannonball into the pool with Jen and me, the Jack who joked and played: his delight when he got a special suitcase just for his shoes, and a day when he slid into the chauffeur-driven Daimler, where Anjel and I were waiting for him, with the words, "Here I am, girls—a symphony of autumnal browns."

When Jack was given a week off from filming, he decided he wanted to see Ireland. The three of us flew to Dublin, got into another Daimler limousine, and headed west. We stopped for lunch in pubs, we walked on the quay at Dingle and along the cliffs of Moher, but mostly we just drove. And near the end of the week, we reached St. Cleran's.

We went up the back drive, where the lampposts still stood, and up to the Big House. The lions that had flanked the door were gone. Firewood was stacked high around the columns. It seemed deserted. We peered through the dining-room window. The Japanese wallpaper was still there, the birds swallowed up by the shadows.

"Stop!" called Anjel to the driver as we passed the Little House courtyard on the way out. The black iron gates were closed.

She got out of the car and stood in front of them, gazing into the courtyard. I followed her. Jack stayed in the car.

Inside, all was the same as I remembered it. The courtyard didn't look mistreated, as the Big House did. The gray stone was warm, the grass in the center circle had been mowed, the white statue of Punch was still there. But I'd never seen the gates closed before.

I hadn't wanted to stop, hadn't wanted to get out of the car. I did, because I felt I ought to do what Anjel had done. She wasn't the only one who had lived there. I wanted to lay claim to St. Cleran's. I was entitled to feel as anguished, as exiled, as she did. Suddenly I felt that even when I had lived in the Little House, I'd been her ghost.

Anjel put her hands on the iron bars and curled her fingers through them. So I did too. I wished she would just let go. I wanted to get back in the car, wanted to get away from this horrible feeling of being shut out. But I couldn't, not as long as she stayed standing there, holding on to the gate.

A figure appeared from a side doorway, wearing a ragged green jumper. His shaggy, steel-gray curls looked familiar. It was Paddy Coyne. He stared—and started running toward us.

"Anjelica! Oh Jaysus. And Allegra, is it? Ye're back. Ye've come back. How are ye?"

He was crying. He'd never spoken so many words together in all the time I'd known him. He told us he was the only one there; the people who owned the Little House were away, and nobody lived in the Lynches' house on the other side of the courtyard. All the while, he was hauling the gate open.

Anjel was in tears, like Paddy. I should be also, I knew, if I had any heart, but I had felt my tears dry up, like a blast of dry hot air into the space just below my eyes, right at the moment Paddy reached us. When I walked through the gate onto the crunching gravel, I felt a spell break. The past was gone, lost. The unraveling yarn of Paddy's sweater pinned me to the present like a captured moth. I felt like myself again: not caring much about anything, but so aware of how I was supposed to be that it stung.

In Dublin, we went to see Nurse in the little terraced house that Dad had bought for her. She was nervous as she welcomed us in—because Anjel and I had come into her world, or because of Jack's fame, I didn't know. She sat us in the living room and disappeared to make tea. The sofa and chairs had plastic covers on them, as if they were still in the shop. I felt a disapproving snobbishness rise up, like a succubus taking me over, and I loathed myself for it. This was Nurse, who had looked after me so devotedly, who had gone anywhere I'd been sent without protest: to New York, to Cuernavaca, to Gloom Castle. Her stalwart, unchanging presence had made everything normal for me. How dare I judge her for something so trivial as a lapse of taste in how she kept her house?

But there it was. I couldn't unthink the thought. I felt awkward hugging her. I had nothing to say. Anjel was talking, laughing, crying, appreciating the details of Nurse's new life as she winkled them out of her. I had nothing to give: no interest, no appreciation. I could feel that Nurse was hurt that I was so cold, though of course she did her best to disguise it. Why couldn't the part of me that was loyal and grateful get back inside that standoffish body and make it do what I wished it would: smile, make a fuss of her, show her that I knew how much I owed her and that I loved her still?

I remembered how cavalier I'd been when, at Cici's house, I didn't even realize she'd been sent away. Since then I'd lived in places that Nurse, I thought, would barely be able to imagine. I wasn't, anymore, the little motherless girl whom she had looked after and loved. I could look after myself now; I didn't need anybody. But how could she know that? I was recognizably me: bigger and spottier, but my long blond hair was the same, my blue eyes, my stolid body.

I felt like a pretense, a walking shell: the shape and shadow of me, the brain of me, but a blank space where the heart should be. I wondered, suddenly, if I'd ever really had one. Who would I cry never to see again? No one. I could outlast any loss now. It scared me—mildly, as much as I could be scared by anything less than a raging beast or a plane crash—that I was so empty.

I saw Nurse one more time, two months later, when she came to England for Tony's wedding to Lady Margot Cholmondeley.

I remembered Margot—Nurse always called her Lady Margot—from the times she'd come to stay at St. Cleran's. I was rather in awe of her, with her soft voice and her cloud of coppery hair, like a woman in a Vermeer painting. She was beautiful in a way totally unlike any of the women I knew. She didn't wear makeup or fashionable clothes; she wore flat boots instead of high heels. She seemed not to care what people thought of her, and she was never at a loss for something to do. I envied her ability to interest herself as much as I admired her talent for creating beautiful things. Her pencil drawings were delicate, perfect likenesses; and at St. Cleran's she had made a group of puppets. I had watched her as she worked on them for days in the Little House: building skeletons of wire, forming the papier-mâché into perfectly pointed noses and curvy mouths, painting them with vivid expressions. When the trunk from Ireland arrived at Gloom Castle, I had hoped to find them as much as I hoped for my treasure chest. But they weren't there.

The wedding took place in the chapel at Margot's family home, Cholmondeley Castle. Anjel and I went, without Joely. Zoë came from Rome, and Danny from his boarding school somewhere in the English countryside; Dad flew in from Mexico, without Maricela. Tony arranged it so that Danny and I stayed at Cholmondeley with Dad, while Anjel and Zoë were billeted at a neighboring house. Dad was given the bedroom the Queen used when she came to stay.

I played backgammon with Dad on a clattery Turkish board, sat in while he and Buckminster Fuller discussed philosophy, and listened to Margot's brother, David—who had the absurdly glamorous title of the Earl of Rocksavage—play the piano, very well. My piano lessons had finished when I left Cici's house, and I knew that I would never, never have been as good as David. This was the standard, I thought, by which John Julius must have judged me: an aristocratic English standard. I had been even more of a disappointment than I thought.

Nurse stayed on the top floor—the servants' floor—along with

Margot's old nanny. For the two days that we were both at Cholmondeley, I didn't go in search of her, didn't sit and talk with her. It
was as if she were someone I'd met once or twice, no more. That selfishness and ingratitude that I'd blamed myself for when she was sent
back to Ireland—blamed myself a little unfairly, I had decided—I
showed it all, truly, that weekend. I barely gave her a thought. As if I
owed her nothing.

Except for the wedding itself, she stayed upstairs. She never came
to find me; I'm sure she felt it wasn't her place. She was as substantial
as a ghost: less, maybe. I couldn't comprehend, anymore, what she'd
once meant to me.

After the ceremony, we sat for a photograph: Dad and his four
children. It was the first time the five of us had ever all been in the
same place at the same time. This is my family, I thought: the Hustons. Zoë wasn't in the photograph, which meant, to me, that John
Julius mattered as much as she did, or as little. Despite our odd
histories, Danny and I were part of the core. The Irish band De Dan-
nan played, and Tony had chosen songs in honor of each of us: "The
Kerry Dance," for Anjel and me, and "Danny Boy" for Danny. We
were brothers and sisters, and Dad was our father. I never felt I was
second best to him. I was as much his child as any of us.

16

"Allegra doesn't want to go back to L.A.," Anjelica said to Helena on the phone—at least, as Helena remembers it. "She won't come out of the room. Her hairbrush is full of hair. And Jack's gone crazy. You've got to come."

My hairbrush probably was full of hair; and my bed wasn't made; and some days I didn't even open the curtains. For Anjelica—as it would have been for Mum—it was evidence of an unhealthy mind.

Going back to L.A. meant going back to Gloom Castle. I had been giving my address as 1315 Angelo Drive when I filled out immigration forms, but it had been a kind of holding zone for those times when Anjel's life was too unsettled, or she was out of town. Now I realized that that was where I would come to rest.

I had loved running through the house with Collin, taking the three steps at each end of the minstrels' gallery in one leap down and then up again, chasing him down the spiral staircase in the back, doing cannonballs off the high retaining wall into the pool. Without him, it was entirely different: a cavernous, echoing house, dark and tired from not having enough people in it. I felt trapped. The road down the mountain was miles long, and steep, and most of the neighbors were over seventy.

I no longer slept in the room next to Aunt Dorothy and Uncle Myron's room, the room that had been Cici's. I had my own room, at the farthest end of the house. I think it used to be Stephan's. Mostly I sat on my bed watching TV or reading.

The previous spring, in the interlude between Ryan and Jack, I had decided to get thin, so I'd read books while pedaling furiously on Aunt Dorothy's abandoned exercise bike in the back attic. I used to play canasta with Uncle Myron, but his Parkinson's disease was getting so bad that cards were hard for him (though he still drove himself to his rental-car office every day). When Aunt Dorothy had friends from the Beverly Hills Women's Club over to play bridge I sat at her elbow at a folding table in the cavernous living room, the ceiling twenty feet above, the vast picture window half a basketball court's length away. The ladies all had perfect lipstick and motionless hair, and they didn't talk much except to bid and score. Their painted nails clicked on the cards; the ice clicked in their glasses; the glasses clicked on the laminated coasters. Occasionally the silver end of one of Aunt Dorothy's special bridge pencils clicked against the engraved silver binding of the score pad. "It's one of the great games," Dad had once said about bridge. "Every intelligent woman should know it." I couldn't imagine myself ever being one of those women.

I hated my room, with its hairy grass wallpaper and furniture inset with mud-green leather. I hated our dinners at six-thirty, with stringy meat and soggy vegetables, and Aunt Dorothy squirming minutely as she tried to get her toe on the buzzer under the carpet to summon the maid to clear the plates, and Uncle Myron turtlelike opposite her, silent except when he suddenly came out with incomprehensible strings of letters, which were the initials of some phrase that I was supposed to be able to figure out.

I'd become sullen. I was tired of being nice and acting the perfect granddaughter. I almost resented Aunt Dorothy for having opened her house to me; I didn't like having to feel grateful to be living in someone's house. I hated the way she was rich but behaved like she was poor: buying cheap cuts of meat, Scotch-taping a rip in a Japanese screen, jamming a fake jewel into her antique Chinese necklace and twisting the filigree around it with a screwdriver. And hating it made me feel mean-spirited and ungrateful.

One morning, she came into my room. I was still in bed, reading.

"I had a terrible dream last night, Allegra," she said. "I dreamed you'd stolen my diamond ring."

This was a gigantic marquise-cut diamond set in platinum, which she kept in a hollowed-out shoe tree in her shoe closet.

"I didn't," I said. I couldn't take this seriously.

Aunt Dorothy clicked her tongue against the back of her top teeth. It was one of her habits that drove me crazy, just like her way of answering the phone with "Hay-lo-oh"; and saying "ah-hah-uh" deep in her throat as if she were gargling and practicing opera singing at the same time; and never asking a direct question but always saying "I wonder if . . ."

"Well," she said, "it would set my mind at rest if you'd open that closet so I can see it's not there."

"That closet" was a door I kept locked, mostly to hide my little shrine of John Travolta pictures. I also kept my coin cabinet in there, with its few little disks of gold—wanting to feel that it was valuable enough to be locked up, even though I knew it wasn't. Hanging on the rail were some old clothes of mine that had come in the trunk from Ireland.

"Why don't you just look where you keep it," I said. "You'll see it's there."

"That's not it, Allegra," she said firmly. "I need to see inside that closet to put my mind at rest."

I knew perfectly well the dream was a fiction. I couldn't be angry; it was too transparent. I pitied her for letting her curiosity humiliate her. I could see her making up her own certainty as she went. The further I pushed her, the further she'd go. I didn't have the stomach for it.

I fished my keys out of my bag, unlocked the closet, and dropped to my knees to fold up the magazines with the John Travolta photographs. I felt her behind me, not quite wanting to crane her neck into the closet and not prepared to push me aside to move closer. I thought I could actually feel the wave of anticlimax crash against the back of my neck.

I pulled open the drawers of my coin cabinet one by one. Most were empty.

"Okay?" I said. "It's not here."

I could have hidden twenty rings in the rest of the closet and she'd never have known.

"Thank you, Allegra," she said, and went out.

Two years later, when she gave my things away in my absence— some clothes, the portfolio of Halsman photographs of my mother— I realized that she felt that as long as my things were in her house, they were actually hers.

Helena came to London for Christmas and made a deal with me. If I agreed to go back to Gloom Castle, I could stay with her on weekends and help her run her new roller-skating club, Skataway.

Skataway had started when I was in London and Helena had had a birthday party at a roller rink in Reseda, in the depths of the San Fernando Valley. She had, she told me, been a champion skater as a teenager. The first friends she invited protested, so she just told people to meet her on a street corner and bring socks. When it was over, so many people begged her to do it again that it turned into a regular Monday-night event. Many of Helena's friends were actors, singers, and musicians, so the paparazzi staked it out. That was where the roller-disco craze of the 1980s began.

Helena was fierce about her rules. No cameras; no alcohol or drugs, because they were dangerous if you were on skates. Nobody was allowed in uninvited, and if you were there, you had to wear skates. There was usually a knot of fans outside the door, and I'd see the flashes pop when Cher, or Don Henley, or Jack arrived or left. For most of my life, I'd felt peripheral; now here I was at the center of the in crowd, at Helena's right hand. I had the run of the DJ booth and the area marked PRIVATE and felt second in importance only to Helena herself. Plus, I could skate. I wasn't brilliant at it, but I didn't fall and I could dance. Finally my body felt integrated with my head and my spirit. I wasn't uncoordinated and incompetent anymore; I was smooth.

Someone brought the football star Jim Brown one night. Helena didn't know who he was, but she was told that he was bad news. When he asked if he could become a member, Helena came straight out with it.

"They told me you threw a woman out the window," she said. I would never have had the guts to say something like that to anyone.

"That was the past," said Jim.

Helena made up her own mind about people. She was very clear about who she thought was a good person, and who wasn't. I watched her at the door of the Reseda Roller Rink and thought of Saint Peter: letting the good people in, and consigning the rest to the outer darkness of a parking lot in the San Fernando Valley.

"Okay," she said to Jim, "you can become a member."

"I'll be your door guard," he said. "You get any trouble, I'll be there."

If anyone tried to crash the door, Jim would materialize out of nowhere, huge and intimidating. The longest conversation I had with him was when I sold him a Skataway T-shirt—size small—but every week when they called a pairs skate, Jim would glide up beside me and link his arm in mine.

I loved telling Aunt Dorothy about this, and about my friend Miguele Norwood, a teacher from Detroit who taught me to skate, because both Jim and Miguele were black, and I knew she didn't approve and she couldn't say it because then she'd be admitting she was prejudiced. Best of all were the nights when Miguele or the dancer Charles Valentino gave me a lift home. Now she had to think of me alone with black men in cars—beat-up cars at that, because neither Miguele nor Valentino had money. I knew she worried that I'd be found dead in a canyon, or knocked up with a black baby, and what would she tell Dad then? I had no sympathy. That was my revenge. If she didn't want secrecy, fine; I'd be honest.

I knew too that by any standards other than mine and Helena's, all this was very unsuitable for a fourteen-year-old. I was out skating with celebrities till midnight on a school night; and after that, often as not, I'd go on to Carlos 'n Charlie's nightclub, where we'd have the private VIP area. If I ordered a frozen strawberry margarita, they served me. We danced till two, which meant I didn't get back to Gloom Castle until two-thirty. Valentino would lift me above his head and spin me around, and I'd try to point my toes and arch my neck to look graceful. If Anjelica was there he'd lift her up and spin her around too. I couldn't quite identify, or allow myself, the hurt I felt as I watched them. I knew I didn't look as graceful as she did.

My schoolwork didn't suffer. I was taking classes one or two years ahead of my grade level anyway. I wasn't getting into any trouble. Nobody was offering me drugs, older men weren't taking advantage of me, and I knew that if anyone did try to, Helena would throw them out on their ear. The rest of the week, I sat in my room reading and watching TV. Without Skataway, I'd have gone so far into my shell that I might never have come out again.

I even arranged to get school credit for roller skating. Since seventh grade I'd been getting doctor's notes to excuse me from PE on the grounds of "arthralgia of the lower extremities exacerbated by exertion"—in other words, growing pains. Helena knew I needed exercise, and she made sure I got it. Whenever she saw me sitting and chatting, she'd scold me: "Stop socializing! You gotta skate. It's schoolwork!"

I spent Friday and Saturday nights in the Father O'Sullivan Suite, as the maid's room of Helena's house was called, after Jack's family priest from New Jersey. Usually Roberto would drive me to her house, but I loved it when Helena picked me up at Gloom Castle in her microscopic shorts and strappy high heels and leotards, because she was a creature totally outside Aunt Dorothy's frame of reference. It amused me to see Aunt Dorothy have to swallow her prejudices: about class, about clothing, about what I'm sure she thought were Helena's dubious morals. I knew how wrong she was. I knew that if there was anyone in my life I could rely on, anyone who was completely upright and true of heart, that person was Helena.

She was so discreet that, though I spent almost half the week with her, I never knew anything about her private life. She listed people by first name in her address book, and if their last name was famous—like "Dylan"—she put only an initial. (It was Anjelica who told me who "Bobby D" was.) To me, with my tangled ego in relation to the famous people I knew, it was amazing to understand how, for Helena, despite her starry circle of friends, her own self was enough.

Once she picked me up from school, and I was furious. I hated her to see me in my uniform with its drooping polyester pleats, knee socks, and horrible crepe-soled shoes.

"Allegra," she said severely. "Who cares about the outfit."

I did. I felt like a pretender now when I was wearing that uniform: the good Catholic schoolgirl, the levelheaded misfit in my sister's life. We were all pretenders there. One girl, who was fifteen—with braces, I couldn't get over that—used to meet her flying instructor in motel rooms.

When I was with Helena, I felt like myself. She took me everywhere with her: to casting auditions, to Jack's business manager's
office, to her electrolysis appointments, to the garment district where
she was having T-shirts and satin bomber jackets made for Skataway,
up to Marlon's house, where I sat on his bed and played chess with
him. I was her prodigy. She loved that I was smart, but I never felt
that I had to be. All she expected of me was loyalty, honesty, good
sense, and high standards. For the next year and a half, when without her I would have slowly twisted into craziness alone in my room
in Gloom Castle, she kept me sane.

Marlon had a way of arriving unannounced just as we were
getting ready to leave for the roller rink, on a little electric scooter.
His body, when he sat, was an equilateral triangle, with his beautiful head and falcon's nose at the apex, and his spreading bulk below.
It looked funny perched on the scooter. The scooter was silent, and
Marlon moved as silently as a prowling panther, so I never knew he
was there until he materialized a few feet from me, near the photo of
him in his youth that hung on the wall: black-and-white, in profile,
staring through a rain-drenched window. His voice was so quiet you
had to lean into the sound waves to hear it, and tune out the rest of
space and time. It was a game of his, to make us late. He awed me;
but Helena awed me more, by being stronger than him and shooing
him out.

I knew we made a strange pair: Helena with her street smarts
and her clothes falling off her, and reserved, bookish me. I typed up
lists of members' names, in three categories: those who were allowed
to bring one guest, those who could bring three, and the special few,
with red membership cards, who could bring as many people as they
liked. I cut the necks out of my T-shirts so that they slipped off my
shoulders, the way she did. I tucked up long skirts into my underwear to make miniskirts with bustles on the hips, the way she did. I
slept in silky negligees—castoffs from Helena and from Cici—and
on weekends wore them all morning, the way she did.

I helped her with the script she was writing, at a table below that photo of Marlon by the rainy window, and learned about the lives of prostitutes and street people. She called me her secretary, and I felt needed.

At the end of the school year, some friends and I decided to make a funny tape about our class, using snatches of songs. Most of my contributions were a bit obscure for high-school girls in 1979—Bob Marley, Aretha Franklin, songs I knew from the compilation tapes called "Jack's 20s thru 70s" that played constantly at his house. Then, after we finalized our script, I realized that my eight-track tape of Stevie Wonder's *Songs in the Key of Life* was useless for our purposes. The store wouldn't exchange it because it was a discount version. I convinced Aunt Dorothy to take me to Tower Records, where I knelt down and secretly, I thought, swapped my discount tape for a full price one.

The only difference was a strip of yellow on the label, instead of a strip of white. I told myself that it wasn't really shoplifting, because I was exchanging like for like, not stealing anything. The album was the same; who would even look for that strip of color? I planned to come back another day and officially exchange the full-price eight-track for the LP.

As I walked out to the parking lot, where Aunt Dorothy was waiting for me, a security guard took my wrist and said, "You'll have to come with me."

I got off with a lecture. It was humiliating, but the worst of it was being caught shoplifting—which, really, I knew it was—with a monogrammed Rolls-Royce as my getaway car. I looked like a little rich girl. It was true to some degree, I knew, but still I felt a gulf between appearance and reality. I wore the same three dresses in rotation; my shoes were hand-me-downs from Anjelica and Cici; my allowance was barely enough to cover basic toiletries. I didn't have enough money to buy one album so as not to disappoint my friends. I felt poor, even barren. I almost wished I really was, so that my inside would match my outside—and I knew what a hypocrite I was.

I was terrified that Aunt Dorothy would tell Dad—or Helena. She didn't. I decided she must think it would reflect badly on her, since I'd never done anything like that before. Dad might ask why I'd felt I had to steal, and then she'd have to admit how little of the child support he paid her actually got spent on me. I was a bad lawbreaker: consumed with guilt, nervous of being caught, glancing about shiftily before fumbling my exchange, sauntering so nonchalantly to the door that it must have been obvious I'd done something wrong. As much as anything else, my total incompetence convinced me not to try anything like that again.

"You need only to look around you, to see the wonder, to know that a higher Being must have created it," said Sister Charles, who had made me her pet. With her Irish accent, cropped gray hair, and sensible skirts, she reminded me of Nurse. But she was larger and sturdier, and she had an ownership of her place in the world, whereas Nurse was blown about by the gusts of the Huston family drama. God was her invisible ballast.

I envied her that unshakable stability, and her golden vision of the world, so perfect and intricate and orderly. That wasn't what I saw. I saw randomness, indifference, cruelty, and pain. There was no benevolent hand directing it.

In Ireland I'd had to memorize the catechism word for word: no "of" where a "to" should be, no "a" for "the." Southern California Catholicism didn't require that kind of precision, but we did go to chapel every Friday, and the familiar ritual was comforting. It threw a line back to my earlier self, my earlier life, and strung the fragments together. Belief in God seemed warm, a sanctuary. It would assign me a place in creation that was uniquely and perfectly mine.

The year before, I had written out a prayer that I would meet John Travolta, and he would fall in love with me. Even though it had lots of "Please, God"s in it, I felt that it was incomplete, so I finished it off with the entire "Our Father," even including the last line, "For thine is the kingdom and the power and the glory," which nobody in Ireland had ever used. I'd heard it on a TV commercial, intoned by a majestic-looking Indian gazing into the sky. I was afraid that leaving it out might be God's excuse for not granting my prayer, while putting it in, even if it didn't really belong, surely couldn't offend Him because it was so complimentary.

After a few days the one prayer seemed paltry. So I wrote out another, this time in red pen to show how strongly I felt, and all in careful capitals in case God couldn't read my regular handwriting. I knew it was ridiculous even as I was writing it, but still it felt good. I was doing something to try to take control of my life.

I folded the papers into little squares. The thought jumped into my head that if God had trouble reading anything other than capital letters, He might have trouble reading inside the folds—but what could I do? I wanted to keep the prayers on me at all times; I didn't want Aunt Dorothy, or anyone else, reading them. As I didn't wear a bra yet, I slotted them into my underwear—which meant that I had to wear underwear to bed too. The paper became cottony with the oils from my skin.

After a few months, I was keeping them just for form's sake. There was no sign of John Travolta, so obviously God—if He existed— wasn't interested, and I was losing interest myself in someone who could make a movie as ridiculous as *Grease*. Maybe it was the thinning of my crush that made me careless.

In London, I borrowed Jack and Anjelica's bathroom when they were out, since mine didn't have a tub. Drowsy from reading in a cloud of stephanotis bath oil, I heard the front door open and leaped out, grabbed my bathrobe, and ran upstairs. Only when I was putting my clothes on ten minutes later did I realize that I'd left the prayers on the edge of the washbasin. I tiptoed downstairs, hoping Anjel wouldn't confront me. I thought she'd take a dim view of the whole thing, and tell me I was an idiot—which I knew I was. The bedroom door was closed. I sidled into the bathroom, which was right beside it, and there were the prayers, where I'd left them. Unfolded. Read.

I picked them up and ran back upstairs. I refolded them on their fragile creases and slipped them back against my skin. But they didn't sit right anymore. They seemed to itch, as if the fingers that had touched them had left a toxic residue. After a few days, I buried them deep in the kitchen garbage. I'd been exposed for having a crush on a dumb guy, but what stung the most was that Anjel would think me credulous for writing prayers to a God who didn't exist.

As I sat in chapel at school, still not believing but once again wishing I did, I wondered whether I should ask for Confirmation. A number of girls were preparing for it, and the smooth, tracklike progression of their days appealed to me. I had never made my first Communion, though I'd seen Jackie and Caroline Lynch in their bridelike first Communion dresses, and I wasn't at all sure that I'd ever been baptized. Probably not, I figured, since I was the product of an illicit love affair. My lack of real belief relieved me of any spiritual qualms about taking Confirmation when I had never been cleansed of original sin; the problem was that I wasn't sure if the nuns knew what an atheistic upbringing I'd had, or if I'd have to produce certificates of some kind. I certainly couldn't ask Sister Charles, since then I'd have to tell her that the man who she still thought had made her favorite film wasn't really my father.

I decided not to say anything about Confirmation. If I wouldn't be taking it as a sacrament, why would I be taking it? There was no point in taking a sacrament based on a lie.

At least I could pray, properly this time. Whether God existed or not, there was no harm in praying. But what to pray for? A mother, a proper father, a normal family life? They were too far beyond what I knew—if I suddenly had those things, I wouldn't be me anymore. So I prayed for belief, and prayed as if I believed, putting full passion into the silent words in my head.

I didn't feel them rising to heaven. They just echoed in the cavern of my skull.

17

At Cholmondeley Castle, during our two days of gentle collision for Tony's wedding, Dad had drawn pictures of the place he was building in Mexico. It was outside the town of Puerto Vallarta, beyond the reach of the coast road, which turned inland to avoid the mountains. Foreigners weren't allowed to buy coastal property in Mexico then, so he'd bought a ten-year lease from the local Indian community. His face glowed as he described how the buildings were designed to melt back into the jungle. It disturbed me that he was, so bluntly, planning for his death—and so soon. When he described the buildings disappearing into the jungle, I saw his body merging into the earth.

I went to Las Caletas—"the little coves"—for the first time the Easter after I came back from London. I was longing to see it, this Swiss Family Robinson enclave that Dad had built. I wasn't living with Cici, so I wasn't so torn between her and Dad as I used to be; and as the years went by, Maricela was becoming as irrelevant to me as I was to her. I wanted to spend time with Dad, to reestablish the relationship we'd had. I wanted to prove to him that John Julius's appearance in my life made no difference to my love for him.

At Puerto Vallarta airport I was met by a woman named Joan Blake, who described herself as Gladys's secretary. Gladys was living at Las Caletas with Dad. There was no telephone service there, so Joan was the anchor in town, with a CB radio for communication. We drove on a narrow two-lane road through fields and into town, which was just as I remembered it: a grid of cobblestone streets with tendrils climbing up the hillside. We carried on out the other side, toward the beaches where Cici and her gang had loved to go, past Mismaloya where Dad's set for *The Night of the Iguana* stood deserted and crumbling into the jungle, just as he'd designed his new home to do. Finally we came to a little fishing village called Boca de Tomatlán.

There was a makeshift café on the beach: a few tables and a refrigerator of soft drinks. Open boats—*pangas*—slid slowly up and down the swells, anchored to buoys, motors slung up at their sterns. A few men pulled in nets, with fish flapping inside the twine. I heard Joan asking for Armando or Javier. Their names were like an incantation, the boatmen who could carry me to Dad's new kingdom beyond the waves.

I think it was Javier that day. A *panga* drew up at the little wooden jetty, and I got in. There were a few boards across it for seats, and fishing nets lay in the V-shaped keel. It was a weathered, creamy white. I could see the linenlike weave of the fiberglass through the syrupy paint.

Joan waved as Javier revved the motor and we headed out of the cove. Pelicans perched on the rocks and dived after fish. Low, dark green trees, tangled with vines, furred the steep hillsides all the way down to the rocky shoreline. I gripped the plank to stop from bouncing as the *panga* bumped across the corrugated water.

The salty air was thick, rich with the smells of damp greenery and fish. As I breathed it in, I felt I was drinking it, slaking a thirst for the expansive wonder of the world. Here was space and freedom. A sour-sweet whiff of gasoline spiced it as Javier gunned the motor into the open bay.

We passed a finger-shaped cove, tiny and deep, with a scrap of beach gleaming white in the sunlight like a buffed fingernail. I longed to take a picnic there one day. The coastline was almost uninhabited: one house at the long beach called Las Animas, "the spirits"; the village of Quimixto, thatched huts clinging to the hillside and a big brick house on an outcrop into the water. For half an hour the boat bumped on, the motor droning, the wind warm in my face, a double spray of white feathering at the bow.

I knew we'd reached Las Caletas when Javier pointed the boat toward shore. There was one perfect, secluded little beach, with a thatched house set in a cleft of hillside; then a small point of rocks, then another beach, shallower and longer, with a patch of flattish ground beyond, planted with flowering bushes and traced with brick pathways. I almost couldn't see the houses. Their red-tiled roofs were already mottled with lichen, and they had no walls, just screens that shimmered phantomlike amid the lush tangle of greenery.

Anchored about twenty yards offshore was a blue *panga*. As Javier gunned the motor to run us up on the beach I saw the name painted on the side of its bow: *Allegrita*.

Dad appeared from among the bushes, wearing a pajama-like outfit of thick white cotton that stopped above his ankles. He looked brown and healthy: not strong, but hale. His step was light, as if the warm brick of the path shot energy up into his bare feet. He stepped down onto the sand to hug me. Instantly I loved this new incarnation of him. This was where he belonged: still king of his domain, but a small and cozy domain, with nobody to impress, luxurious with fruit and flowers instead of valuable artworks and hot and cold running servants, and edged by the protected water of the bay.

"Welcome to Las Caletas, honey," he said, his arm around my shoulders. "I'm glad you've come."

Danny had been there during construction; Tony and Anjelica had never seen it. It warmed me to be the first of Dad's children to come and stay in his new home.

I slept in Gladys's house, since the guesthouse on top of the hill wasn't finished yet. Though the houses were close together, you couldn't quite see one from another. There were big sheets of sailcloth on runners under the wide eaves to draw closed at night, and terra-cotta fireplaces for warmth. We could find one another or disappear, as we liked.

As well as the two beds in Gladys's L-shaped room, there was a crib. She had just adopted a little girl: Marisol.

Marisol was less than two, Gladys was over sixty. The story I was told—I can't remember who told it, but not Gladys—was that a friend of Gladys's had wanted to adopt a baby, and Gladys had gone in search of one for her. She'd ended up at the Puerto Vallarta brothel, where Marisol was pulled out from underneath a bed. Her mother was happy to give her up, especially to a promising future in America. Then the friend in New York said no: this little girl was too old. Gladys couldn't leave her at the brothel, so she kept her.

Gladys adored her. She was a round little thing, always laughing. For the week that I was there, she hardly ever cried. She loved it when I bounced her on my lap and tickled her. I'd never played with a toddler before, and I fell in love with her too. She could barely talk, so it didn't matter that my Spanish was broken. I was surprised that Gladys had called her by a name so like Maricela's, since I knew that she disliked Maricela; but I never asked her why. Perhaps it was the name her mother had given her, and Gladys hadn't wanted to change it.

Dad swam in the mornings, and we played backgammon, and

he sketched me while we talked. His gaze felt like a caress, sweeping softly over my face, and his pencil was an honest recorder. He didn't want a pose; just me.

Talk was easy here: about books mostly, and the doings of Las Caletas. I didn't feel interrogated, as I always had in the Beverly Hills Hotel; I was here for a week, not one of those crammed afternoons which were too long and too short at the same time. Our words were shot through with sunlight and airy with the breeze that came off the salt water and through the screens and the fat, shiny hibiscus leaves outside. Often he'd play with some new pet: a boa constrictor called Lechugita, an ocelot, a ring-tailed *tejon*. In the background was the constant crackle of the CB radio, turned down low until we heard Joan's voice saying, "Joan to Las Caletas. Joan to Las Caletas. Come in, Las Caletas." There was a generator to power a walk-in fridge— unlike the other houses along the coast, which had no electricity— but no phone, no newspapers, no television. The CB was our only connection to the outside world.

We had one strange, trivial disagreement, when Dad told me how a local worker had let him down with the excuse that his mule was pregnant. He shook his head in condescending amusement at how the man could be so stupid as to think anyone would believe such an excuse.

"Maybe it's in the translation, Dad," I said. "He probably said *burro*. It's a donkey. It could be pregnant."

"No, honey. He said, his mule. And everyone knows mules are sterile."

Dad didn't speak Spanish. I knew he had no idea what the man had actually said. Nor did I, but I was prepared to give him the benefit of the doubt. Dad wasn't. I realized that he'd clutched on to this idea of the thick-witted, colorful locals, and he wouldn't let it go. He always insisted he loved Mexico and loved Ireland; but he loved the Mexicans and the Irish like children. When, at school in L.A., I wanted to take Spanish for my foreign language because it would be more useful, he insisted I take French because, he said, it was the language of culture and civilization.

(He didn't really speak French either. Anjel has memories of following him, cringing with embarrassment, through hotels as he cast "bone-jure"s right and left, like a king scattering coins to the populace.)

As we talked and played, we'd hear a *panga*, which was the signal that Archie, a jolly Hawaiian chef, had arrived from Quimixto. An hour or so later Archie rang a bell and we all came together for lunch, the only meal we shared: Gladys, Dad and I, and usually an ex-CIA agent named Bill Reed, who lived down the coast at Las Animas and was helping Dad write his autobiography. Maricela didn't join us. She was Dad's personal attendant; she had no interest in anyone else. She tolerated other people only because he wanted us there.

I felt closer to Dad at Las Caletas than I ever had. I loved this idyllic place that he had created as much as he did. I felt loved too: he had named the *panga* after me.

I was fifteen, and finishing eleventh grade. I'd taken all the twelfth-grade classes Marymount had, English more than once. Sister Colette agreed there was no point in my going back for the final year of high school. I wouldn't graduate with the seniors, which was fine by me; I didn't care about things like that. I got my high school diploma by mail.

I took the exams I needed for college entrance, and applied to a few in a halfhearted way, because it was the thing to do. I didn't want to go to college aged sixteen—I knew I wasn't ready for that social world. I didn't know what I did want to do, though. I could carry on living at Gloom Castle—and it would be easier with a driver's license, which I could get in August, when I turned sixteen—but it wasn't an appealing prospect.

Dad was about to leave for Budapest, to film *Escape to Victory*

with Sylvester Stallone (I could never hear his name without thinking of Marlon's practical joke), Michael Caine, and Pelé. The story was
based on a real incident, in which the Nazis had organized a soccer
match between some prisoners of war and their guards, but the script
was pretty silly. Dad was doing it for the lark. In Ireland, he'd always
watched the World Cup, and Pelé had been the star of four of them.
Dad wasn't impressed by many people, but he was impressed by Pelé.

He arranged for me to work on the film as a production assistant. I was excited, and nervous. I'd come to rely on Helena for moral
support, a sort of lodestone for what was right in the world. Dad
wouldn't give me that; he'd judge me, and find me wanting if I was
wanting. He liked people to be sure of themselves, and not just good
at what they did but the best. How could I be that, right off the bat,
doing something entirely new?

Maricela, obviously, would be no comfort. I was trying hard to be
her friend, but I couldn't read her. Sometimes she seemed to accept
me, even like me; other times I thought she hated me, or just wished
I didn't exist. She told Dad that I stole things from Los Galovan,
when all I'd done was borrow a facecloth to wrap my special acne
soap in. Gladys would be in Budapest too—without Marisol, who
had to take second place to Dad—but her quiet reserve was ironclad.
She wasn't someone to turn to if things went wrong.

My ticket arrived from the travel agency. I'd be flying alone. As
the date closed in, I started to panic. I couldn't back out; Dad would
despise me for a coward. Something, some accident, would have to
save me from going. I wished for one of those earthquakes or car
crashes that teenagers wish for, the kind that only harm other people
but throw everything into disarray.

If I break something, I thought, I won't have to go. I wasn't
brave enough to throw myself down the stairs or jump from a great
height—which I'd have to lie about anyway, and I knew I was a bad
liar. Maybe, I thought, I could break my finger. I laid the pinkie of my
left hand on the bookshelf, and brought a rock of turquoise down on

it, which a friend of Dad's in Mexico had given me for Christmas. It hurt—but the skin was barely red, and the bone wasn't even close to breaking. I smashed the turquoise on it again, harder, and harder again. I could feel the muscles of my right arm seizing up, trying not to hurt my finger even as I tried to break it.

This is ridiculous, I thought, staring at my sacrificial finger. There's no way I'll ever be able to break it. And if I do, what am I going to tell Dad? That I've broken the little finger of my left hand and that means I can't come? Even a broken arm wouldn't do. It would have to be a broken leg. Which would mean I couldn't roller-skate either, so I'd be marooned even more gloomily in Gloom Castle. And if I can't break my finger, what chance on earth would I have of breaking my leg anyway?

So I got on the plane.

My room at the Budapest Hilton connected to Dad's suite, but mostly I kept the door closed. He was tired and went to bed early after a day on set; we ordered room-service dinners independently. He didn't keep tabs on me, or set any rules. I was responsible for myself—in effect, living on my own.

Grown-up though I was from hanging out at the skating rink, I hadn't had a boyfriend, hadn't even had a date. I had an impossible crush on Teihotu Brando, who lived in Tahiti and spoke only French; when he visited his father and came down to Helena's house, all I could do was gaze at him. My French still didn't go much further than the songs I used to sing with Sister Annunciata.

Then a guy called John turned up at the rink. I never knew his last name, what he did, where he came from. Week after week I looked for him to arrive, and skated with him. One Monday he came to Carlos 'n Charlie's afterward, and sat beside me on a sofa. He was wearing a tight T-shirt with a picture of a nautilus shell over the left nipple. I traced it with my finger. He held up a menu in front of us and kissed me, soft little touches of the lips.

I felt very grown-up, making out on a sofa in a nightclub. I was self-conscious, but not ashamed. This was the kind of thing I imagined Anjelica doing with Ryan, or Jack, at places like Studio 54.

The next day Helena and I were working on her script in our negligees when Anjelica stormed in from next door.

"You little tramp! How dare you?"

That was all she said. I was on the point of tears, but so stunned that they couldn't fall until my brain started up again.

"She shouldn't've yelled at you like that," Helena said calmly when the air settled down again. "But she's right. It looked trashy."

Suddenly I saw us on that sofa: unremarkable John, and me a little girl thinking she was cool. I knew instantly that Helena would never have done anything like that, though I couldn't quite shake the thought that Anjelica might have. If she had, she had the sense to be ashamed of it.

I ignored John the following Monday, and I never saw him again. I think Helena banned him without telling me.

In Budapest, I was suddenly grateful to Anjel. There was a girl on set whom Dad referred to with patient pity as "the company law." When I heard it, I felt a twisting in my guts. I could have been that without even knowing it.

When the two months of filming were over, I stopped in London to spend a week with Tony and Margot. It was my sixteenth birthday.

"What are you going to do now?" asked Tony.

Dad had suggested I go to Perugia and learn Italian, and had even taken me there during a break in filming. The prospect of being alone in Italy, unable to speak the language, terrified me.

"Go back to L.A., I guess," I said. "Work for Helena."

Tony had stayed at Gloom Castle and come skating; he knew the shape of my life. I could see he was concerned by my aimlessness. He didn't want me to fall into the sinkhole of the lost children of Hollywood.

"You always said you wanted to go to Oxford," he said. "Why don't you apply?"

I'd forgotten that I used to say that when I lived in Ireland. In that moment, I remembered. Suddenly I had a purpose—and it was my own purpose, recovered with Tony's help. He lent me his old flat temporarily, the same one I remembered visiting with Mum. It was around the corner from Maida Avenue, and the canal with its flower-topped houseboats, and John Julius's house on the other side.

John Julius had been to Oxford. Maybe Mum had talked about Oxford to me.

John Julius took me to lunch often, and one day we went back to his house on Blomfield Road. On the blue-painted front door was a bronze plaque of two clasped hands and the word NORWICH. It was, he told me, from the Norwich Union insurance company. I thought of the little blue-and-white enamel box I had, with cursive letters on the top: *A trifle from Norwich*. A tourist souvenir from the city. When it came to me in a small, unannounced consignment of Mum's things, it was empty. He must have given it to Mum with a present inside.

In the hall, on a bureau, was a piece of pre-Columbian art: a laughing Jaliscan dog like the ones Gladys had. Instantly I felt at home. On another bureau, on one side of a window, was an enormous glass case containing the front half of a St. Bernard emerging from about six inches of doghouse.

"I found it in a junk shop." John Julius had seen me staring at this incredible object, so out of keeping with the elegant good taste of everything else (though the Roman bust on a column did have a panama hat on it). The other things in the hall Dad might have had; this, never.

"I keep looking for the other half, the rear end disappearing into the doghouse," John Julius said. "I think of putting it on the other side of the window."

I thought this was as funny as he did. Not everyone would, I realized. Our sense of humor was the same.

As he talked, footsteps thudded down the stairs. A tall, Tiggerish figure in corduroy trousers bounded into view and smothered me in a hug.

"Allegra! I'm your brother, Jason!"

He said it as if it was the most wonderful surprise. And it was, to me. I thought I was a problem, an outpost in John Julius's life, something to be, if not quite ashamed of, then discreet about. In public, he was my godfather, I was his goddaughter. Discretion suited me fine. I didn't want to have to explain him any more than he wanted to explain me.

That wasn't how Jason saw it at all. I was his sister; there was nothing more to it than that. There was no reservation in his delight: no doubt, no resentment, no duty. I felt like the gift he'd always wanted, tied up in a big red bow.

His older sister, Artemis, had sought me out at Gloom Castle, and come for an awkward dinner. I'd changed in the year that had elapsed since then. With Artemis I'd been reserved, still unsure about whether I wanted this other family. When I met Jason, I'd committed myself to following John Julius's path to Oxford, which had been Artemis's and Jason's too. Gradually I found myself pulled into their embrace. A few years later, when Artemis had a daughter, she asked me to be Nella's godmother and gave her the middle name Allegra. And when, at the age of six months, Nella was rushed to intensive care with a mysterious infection, I sat shifts beside her hospital bed as one of the family, holding her hand. Her little body was red and massively swollen, with tubes coming out of all parts of her. She looked like a little prizefighter—too strong to die. I brought in a cassette machine and played Chopin nocturnes to her, as my mother had played them for me.

Jason and Artemis had no truck with the "godfather" rigmarole. I was their sister, in public as well as in private. My American accent, and my name, created confusion. Often I'd have some explaining to do.

Where are you from? people would ask me at parties. What does your father do? How many brothers and sisters do you have? Sometimes I used one father to base the answer on, sometimes the other. And then I'd regret the choice, because the next question was easier with the other one. I'd feel myself becoming shifty, volunteering either too little information or too much. I devised a short version, which was Dad and the Hustons, and a long version, which included the English side. Whatever I said, I felt I was lying.

Even so, it seemed natural to plan on staying in London once I finished at Oxford. Moving back to L.A. would have been like cutting off half of my family, half of myself—and anyway, both Tony and Danny were in England. In L.A., I didn't fit in; being there exhausted me, for I knew I wasn't really being myself, even though I wasn't sure what this was. In my mind, Southern California had become a glittering, sunlit hellhole of blandness and hypocrisy and worship of fame. I know now, from reading Mum's letters, that the sprawling fakeness of L.A. depressed her too.

In London, Mum had found a city which allowed her to forge her own identity, to cut her own path through it. She didn't have to be "John Huston's wife" there, and I didn't have to be "John Huston's daughter"—or John Julius Norwich's either, since I was still a half-kept secret. An American in London has fewer pressures to conform than an English person does. Despite my family there, I always felt American. When I visited the United States, I felt English. Being an outsider was comfortable now. I was different, and I didn't mind looking—or sounding—that way. It took the pressure off.

I loved the irreverent stories John Julius told about his family—mine. His grandfather, he said, had been the venereal-disease specialist to the aristocracy, including King Edward VII; and our royal ancestor William IV was famous for nothing but having nine illegitimate children and no legitimate ones and a head shaped like a pear. Illegitimacy ran in the family, evidently—which made me feel a legitimate part of it. His mother, Diana Cooper, whose mother was the Duchess of Rutland, was notoriously not the daughter of the Duke of Rutland but of a local lothario named Harry Cust—in whose house the grandmother of Mrs. Thatcher, the prime minister, is said to have been a parlormaid. Mrs. Thatcher's round, unearthly blue eyes could have been Diana's eyes, Harry Cust's eyes. One night at dinner with Jason and Artemis at the round table in the basement of the house on Blomfield Road, with the many volumes of history he'd written lined up on a shelf behind him, John Julius delightedly recounted for us the moment when he'd approached Mrs. Thatcher's daughter at a party and said something like, "Isn't it funny, we're cousins!" He got the impresion that her mother wouldn't find it funny at all.

I was torn, in the secrecy of my heart, between my two families. Could I really have two, or did I have to choose between them? Without question Jason and Artemis felt like my brother and sister. I'd had practice in picking up a brother, with Danny. It was the same with Jason: almost instantaneously we were comrades, we turned to each other for help, support, advice. Once I tried to bring my two families together, giving a dinner party when Anjelica was in London to make *The Witches*, and inviting Jason. It wasn't a success. So I let them stay separate, and I lived in two different families as two different selves.

I still didn't think I felt about John Julius the way a normal daughter feels about a father. He was more like a favorite uncle, who took me to the theater and the opera, to lunch and to dinner. It had seemed a bit thin at first—not enough for a father and daughter—but I didn't know how to ask for more, or even what that more might be. Then I realized that in fact I didn't want anything more. I hadn't grown up with John Julius as my father; knowledge and experience were two different things. It was a relief not to feel we had to create some kind of backdated relationship. Gradually, we built a closeness without a name. I never called him Papa, like Jason and Artemis did. Occasionally people who knew the truth would refer to him as my dad and I corrected them instantly, probably rudely, in a kind of panic, before the thought could be allowed to settle. John Julius could be accurately referred to as my father, though the combination of words still rang a little strangely in my ears; but I had only one Dad.

18

"Hello, honey. This is your father."

I'd answered the phone in the flat John Julius had rented for me. It was the spring of 1981, less than a year after the summer in Budapest. Hearing that voice, I sank into the little flowered boudoir chair beside the telephone table. I knew something terrible was wrong.

I'd never picked up the phone and heard Dad's voice. Always it had been Gladys, saying, "Your father would like to speak with you."

"Hi, Dad." I waited for the blow to fall.

His voice was somber, its music minor and descending. "Honey, Gladys is dead."

Gladys was ageless, not old. She was never sick. I could hardly believe she was gone.

"She went to lie down yesterday evening," Dad continued. "She never woke up." His voice was nearly breaking.

They were in New York, preparing to shoot *Annie*. Again, Marisol had been left behind in Mexico.

I'd seen Gladys just a week before, on my way back to London from L.A. I hung up the phone and booked a ticket back to New York. I wanted to be with Dad. Gladys had been his rock, his Helena. He was unmoored without her, uncertain of his days.

"What about Marisol?" I asked him when I got there. She'd been my first thought. Gladys had had her for only two years. She was three years old. Too young to remember the kind, sphinxlike woman who took her on, in defiance of all reason, and loved her so.

Dad saw Marisol as his charge now, because Gladys had brought her into his world—just as I had become his charge when my mother died. A friend of Gladys's in New York had already offered to take her. Dad had refused.

"She's a Mexican," he said, when I asked why. "She'll always be a second-class citizen in the United States. It will be hard for her to amount to anything here."

I didn't believe it, and I was shocked that Dad did. Did he really believe that American society would refuse to let Marisol be anything but a maid, just because her skin was brown? Was prejudice against Mexicans so powerful that even a wealthy New York upbringing, and bright little Marisol herself, couldn't overcome it? It made no sense to me.

"She'll stay at Las Caletas," he said. "Maricela will adopt her."

Four words. I swallowed them and felt them gnawing like a hyena at my guts.

Maricela had hated Gladys in her feral way. It was obvious to everyone except Dad, who affected not to notice. Like Aunt Dorothy, he was a master at shaping the world to his will. To him, this solution was the most natural thing in the world. Just as he had welcomed me into the Huston fold, he welcomed Marisol, and that was the best in him. But I had had Nurse; Marisol had nobody. That was the worst in him: he refused to consider other people's realities if they didn't chime with what he decided was right.

I'd never once seen Maricela show affection for Marisol. I should take her, I thought. At least I love her. And I knew I wouldn't have to worry about money; Dad would support us. But I had no idea how to look after a little one, and I didn't know what my immediate future held. I'd failed the Oxford entrance exam once, and was preparing to sit it again. How could I go to Oxford and take Marisol with me?

I knew Dad would have none of it. And though I felt passionate—at least about the barrenness that I feared faced Marisol with Maricela as her keeper—I didn't think I could argue passionately, because the arguments he'd use against me were already undercutting my own certainty that it was the right thing to do. I felt ridiculed even for thinking of it. If Dad dismissed Gladys's friend for wanting to bring Marisol to New York, how much more ridiculous was it for me, aged sixteen, to pretend to be able to look after her in London?

So I held my tongue, and let the guilt sink in.

Danny and I met up at Las Caletas every Christmas now, and often at Easter and in the summer as well. Marisol was there, a little figure following the caretakers around, but we couldn't play as we used to. She was growing up into a girl whose only language was Spanish. Now that she could talk and wanted to, I couldn't talk to her.

Danny was as golden as he'd been at St. Cleran's, full of adventure, laughing at every scrape he got into. To begin with, we stayed side by side, in the two bedrooms of the guesthouse on top of the hill. Then, one night, I found a scorpion under my pillow. I moved into his room and slept in the other twin bed. There was no strangeness between us, even though we'd shared so little of our lives.

Age separated the four of us into two and two, with an eleven-year gap between Anjelica, who was a year younger than Tony, and Danny, who was two years older than me. I felt a sweetness in Danny's and my relationship with Dad that I suspected had been lacking for Tony and Anjelica. From what they'd told me, he'd judged them almost cruelly, riding them hard to be accomplished, and was stingy with praise.

Dad was simply happy that Danny and I came to Las Caletas; that was, almost, enough for him. Dad worried that Danny wasn't turning out to be the well-read man he wanted him to be, and during one weeklong visit, he and I made a list of the hundred books an educated person should know. This, of course, turned out to be a list of classics, dotted with some of Dad's favorites like Eric Newby and Kipling. Once we'd completed it, Danny's shortcomings were less glaring. Dad hadn't read many of the books on the list, and neither had I.

One Christmas Eve, Danny and I were sitting on the beach watching the sun go down when I was suddenly certain that we'd both got Dad the same present. We had: a book of photographs of Paris in the 1920s by Brassaï.

There was no way we could get into town to buy something different. If we were to find anything else, we'd have to find it here, in this unadorned little compound of buildings, and the jungle around us, which was quickly getting dark. We'd have to make something.

I looked around and saw the foot-thick piece of heavy Styrofoam that Miguel, who worked there, used as a raft to paddle out to the *panga* where it lay at anchor. "How about a float for his snorkel?" I said. "So we can see where he is."

We decided to cut off a corner of the Styrofoam raft and carve a whale.

The sharpest tool we could find was a steak knife. We kept at it hour after hour, taking turns when our tired hands couldn't saw away any longer. Blisters rose on the insides of my knuckles. The waves crashed lightly on the sand, glittering in the moonlight. Occasionally we'd hear a thudding splash: a manta ray leaping out of the water. They were enormous creatures, flat and diamond-shaped, dark gray shadows of themselves. I could hardly see them when they jumped, even though the moon was full and my eyes, accustomed to the night, saw the rocks and trees in sharp, unearthly detail.

It was past midnight by the time we finished our whale, fat with a fluked tail curling over his back. The contours were rough because of the nubbly Styrofoam, and we smoothed them the best we could. We found some red paint and stuck a sign into the whale's back with a toothpick: MOBY JOHN.

The whale looked rattier by daylight than it had in the moonlight, but still I was proud of it. I hadn't made anything for Dad in ten years, and I dared this only because it was a joke, and a last resort. Danny and I had made Moby John out of love for Dad, and I figured that if he didn't appreciate it, that was his failing, not ours.

Dad looked bemused when he opened the wrapping paper. He picked up the whale and turned it this way and that: the crude red paint, the jagged saw marks on what should have been the smooth curve of its tail. I saw them all too—and they didn't matter. It wasn't supposed to be art, or even craft. It had been made from a piece of garbage with a steak knife.

We tied it onto his snorkel when he went into the ocean later that day. It didn't work very well; it tipped over and lost its sign. I knew he wouldn't use it again and that it would quickly find its way, with Maricela's help, into the trash. I didn't mind. I was, for some reason I couldn't fathom, euphoric. I felt it was the best Christmas present I'd ever given anybody. The night Danny and I spent making it would be a beacon for the rest of our lives.

But as the years went by, I felt my hold on Dad's tenderness slipping. Though he boasted about his daughter who went to Oxford, I sensed some disappointment: I was too ordinary. When I brought my boyfriend to Las Caletas one Easter, Dad didn't like him. Though he never said so outright, I sensed that Dad had a living model of who he wanted each of us to be: Tony, a Buckminster Fuller–type intellectual; Anjelica, a combination of Greta Garbo and Grace Kelly; Danny, who loved diving, another Jacques Cousteau or Ramon Bravo; and me, an admired social figure like the beautiful, charming, intelligent, cultured Marietta Tree, to whom he had once proposed and who had turned him down. He too should have been a painter, a true artist; though he loved filmmaking, he despised it, just a little, for being a carnival occupation.

Of all of us, only Anjelica was living up to his hopes. She had been cast in *Prizzi's Honor* even before he signed on to direct it. When they were preparing it, she went to Las Caletas, taking two friends with her. I thought that was cheating, as if she wouldn't be able to bear the remoteness on her own. The photographs of the three of them were beautiful, all taken in the glow of sunset, with flowers in their hair and cocktails in their hands—but that wasn't my Las Caletas. Mine was a refuge, almost sacred in its solitude. I didn't think it ought to look like Acapulco.

Somehow, the pleasure Anjelica took in her visit to Las Caletas robbed me. Of the four of us, I had been there by far the most, and, I felt, loved it the most, in the way it was supposed to be loved. Of course I wasn't in her photographs; I hadn't been there at the time. But in my eyes, the completeness of the photographs seemed to imply that I'd never been there at all.

And then, the next time I visited, and the *Allegrita* came to pick me up at the Boca, I saw it had been repainted. It was the *Anjelica*.

Nobody mentioned it. I wondered if it had been a figment of my imagination that it had ever been the *Allegrita*. I said nothing to Dad, nothing even to Joan Blake. I didn't want anyone to know how deeply hurt I was. Dad would just dismiss it, tell me I was being silly; and maybe I was. The change was inevitable. I had had my few years of topping the league table; but the truth was that I could never be as beautiful, as beloved, as extraordinary, as Anjelica.

Anjelica only went to Las Caletas that one time. She never knew that her boat used to be mine.

In May 1985, on the last day of my last term at Oxford, I found a phone message on the board in the porters' lodge: "Call Anjelica." Dad had been taken to hospital again—as he was, from time to time, because of his emphysema. This time, along with the breathing trouble, he'd had a heart attack.

"I'm worried, Legs," she said. "I don't know if he's going to make it."

That night I went to a friend's twenty-first birthday party, ball gowns and black tie, champagne and a dance floor set out over the lawn. Two or three times I borrowed the phone and called L.A. Dad was in intensive care, but he was still alive. I didn't go to bed. I got on a plane early the following morning.

This time it was Jack who lent Dad a house to recuperate in. It was high in the mountains above the beach, beyond Malibu. I'd never known Jack to go to that house; I didn't understand why he even had it—maybe just for more walls on which to hang his exponentially increasing collection of art. There was a pair of small, blue-green Picassos on the wall of the living room, which had the same unused air as all the movie-star living rooms I knew.

Dad was, for the first time, on a permanent oxygen feed, like a leash. Someone had to wheel it around after him whenever he moved. He hated it, of course; it marked the end of snorkeling, of wandering around Las Caletas—maybe even of Las Caletas itself, for him. Two hours' flight from L.A., plus nearly two hours by *panga* and car: his doctors would be a long way away.

Suddenly Maricela went to Mexico, leaving Danny and me in charge of Dad for two weeks. I felt very daughterly, in the importance of my mission. I was twenty. The *Allegrita* had become the *Anjelica;* maybe this would give me an opportunity to regain some ground. Every four hours someone had to perform on him a procedure called cupping: he lay on one side, then the other, and we rhythmically tapped over his lungs with cupped hands, to loosen the mucus. I liked doing it: it gave me pleasure to look after Dad in this vital, intimate, wordless way.

Maricela's departure was unexplained and bizarre: she never left Dad's side. And to leave him at a time like this, when his health was so precarious and his mood so brittle? I asked him why she'd gone. He didn't want to tell me, it was obvious, but evidently he couldn't think of a convincing lie.

Marisol had been playing on the beach with a friend. The friend's mother had seen sexual knowledge in her that a little girl shouldn't have. As a result, they had discovered that a man who was working at Las Caletas had been abusing Marisol.

I felt sick. Tears stung my eyes. I hated myself for having been such a coward when Gladys died—afraid of Dad's ridicule as much as of the responsibility of looking after a little girl. If I'd taken her then, this would never have happened. I realized that my fault was small in the scheme of things, but it was mine.

"Of course," said Dad dismissively, into the silence, "her mother was a whore."

I stared at him, dumbfounded. His face held its customary sage-like certainty, which had always told me that Dad knew best. This was his judgment: born of eight decades of accumulated wisdom of the world. He had spent his life telling stories of human nature. Sexual looseness was in Marisol's genes. Dad wasn't inclined to blame the man; he seemed to think that what Marisol had done while playing with her friend came to her naturally. If she had been abused, the abuse was her fault.

"Dad, she's seven!" I couldn't believe he was saying this.

"Well." His voice was curt. The subject was closed.

He would have listened to a psychologist, a child behaviorist, a Jungian or a Freudian analyst, an anthropologist—even a judge or a cop or a private detective. Maybe, even, a mother. He wasn't so self-obsessed that he thought he knew everything; he loved to learn new things, and his face came alive as he listened to people whose knowledge he respected. But there was no middle ground. Either he, the expert, was pronouncing, or another expert was.

There was no point in arguing. He wouldn't listen to me.

Here my memory cuts out. Did I yell at him, furious as I was, or did I just leave the room? Probably I turned and walked out, and that's why I don't remember it. I feared discord: the tiniest disagreements left me shaking. I would have been prouder of myself if I'd hauled him over the coals. Not that it would have changed his mind—but he deserved at least a little discomfort. He had insisted on keeping Marisol in Mexico, where nobody truly cared about her; and this was the result.

That was the break. What had happened to Marisol could have happened to me; or, in a better world, my life could have been hers. I'd had the luck, but I was powerless to help her. She was beyond my reach.

Dad had wrenched my entire moral universe off its bearings—which showed me, in a dawning of consciousness, that I had one, and that it wasn't his, wasn't anyone's but my own. Until that moment, I'd accepted everything. I might have grumbled inwardly, or sulked alone in my room, but I didn't question the fundamentals. People made mistakes, of course, or were forced by circumstances into courses they might not have freely chosen, but it was my role to understand, and forgive, and make the best of what they decreed for me.

Not this time. But if I unpicked all the strands, the assumptions that led to Dad being able to say such a thing—with no twinge of sorrow for this little girl who had already lost two mothers, and no sense of his share of the blame—I'd never be able to look at him, love him, again.

⌒⌯⌒

Exactly at this time, Dad was contacted by a journalist who had interviewed him for *Playboy*. The interview was published in the issue that had nude photos of Madonna, so its sales were astronomical; and on the strength of it a biography was commissioned. The writer asked Dad for his authorization. Dad—newly leashed to the oxygen machine; angry, depressed, and bored—agreed.

Some time later the biographer came to interview me in London. I didn't want to talk to him, but I felt that, as Dad had authorized him, I had no right to refuse. I wasn't as smart as Anjelica was; she managed to put him off for two years without ever saying no.

"Is it true that your mother was decapitated in the car crash that killed her?" he asked me.

I knew the cause of death was "head injuries"—I had seen the death certificate a long time before. Occasionally those words had come back to me, a vision of my beautiful mother with her head smashed through a windscreen, or on a dashboard. There was blood in her hair, but her serene face was perfect, even with the impact of death.

"I don't know," I said. My tongue stumbled on the words. The image was obscene to me; I knew Mum had died violently, but I couldn't bear to think of her torn apart. "Why do you ask me? I was four."

And then came the next question: "Who is your father?"

I didn't answer. That was the last time I felt I had something to hide.

John Julius turned sixty just before the book was to be published, with its newsworthy revelation that he was my father. So we arranged a photo in the gossip column of the *Daily Mail*: the Viscount Norwich with his wife, Mollie (John Julius and Anne had finally divorced a few years previously), and his three children:

Artemis, Jason, and Allegra. So normal as not to require any explanation at all.

I stopped choosing one father or the other on which to base an answer to those chatty questions. I started to say, "I have two." The more often I said it, the more confident I felt, the richer for having two. I developed my own shorthand to distinguish them: "my father" and "my dad."

19

I didn't go to Las Caletas the following Christmas. The Christmas after that, 1986, Marisol wasn't there. She'd been sent off with Maricela's mother to Guadalajara, or Mexico City, or somewhere. Dad never had to see her again.

(I never saw her again either, nor could find out what happened to her. Eventually, when the time came for her to receive her inheritance from Gladys, Maricela said she didn't know where Marisol was—and Gladys's estate went, unclaimed, to the state of West Virginia.)

Dad went to Las Caletas against doctor's orders. Zoë came with Danny, and Tony was there too. Anjelica wasn't. Tony's wedding would remain the only time when Dad and his four children were all together.

Dad was due to start filming *The Dead* in less than a month, with a script written by Tony, and they were putting the finishing touches to the script, the casting, the design. I was edgy, waiting for the blowup between Dad and Tony, afraid of what it would do to Dad's health. They'd always found something to argue about. I remembered Tony picking up an apple, an orange, and a banana in the dining room at St. Cleran's and juggling them after lunch; I thought it was fantastic, and couldn't understand why Dad was incandescent with rage. The only other time I'd seen Tony at Las Caletas, he and Dad had argued so vehemently about how to score gin rummy that Tony had packed his bag and left for town. For as long as I'd known him, Dad had complained about Tony in a tone of wounded worry. Each seemed to feel let down by the other. It was a miracle, I thought, that they'd made it to the edge of shooting *The Dead*, and I prayed in my atheistic way that they'd make it to the other side.

Dad rarely came out of his bedroom into his sitting room, where we'd spent so many days talking, making our list of the hundred essential books, playing backgammon, and in the last few years watching football and baseball on TV. The satellite dish ruined the hazy progression of days which I had loved so, the sense of being suspended in a pocket in time as long as I was at Las Caletas; but for Dad, drifting toward death, it anchored him to the world. When he was with us, at lunch, he seemed unusually introspective, even glum. I put it down to sadness at the knowledge that, after this holiday was over, he would never see Las Caletas again. However long he lived, the doctors would forbid him to go anywhere so remote, and I sensed that he'd used up all the defiance he had in coming this time. He was very frail. His skin was translucent, as if it was thinning away.

I'd found a pair of turquoise dice in London, about three inches on a side. I'd spent all the money I had on them, and I was thrilled because I thought they were the perfect present for a gambler, a backgammon player, who had collected beautiful things. They were the kind of object I could imagine displayed on a table in St. Cleran's.

I gave them to him on Christmas morning, in his bedroom. Danny and Zoë and Tony and I had gathered there, because he was too weak to walk up the hill to the living room where the tree was. I saw confusion on his face when he unwrapped them, as if he couldn't understand what they were.

"They're giant dice, Dad," I said. "They're turquoise. Aren't they beautiful?"

He threw them on the bedspread. They barely rolled, for their corners were square.

"They're not really for playing," I said feebly. "But don't you think they're beautiful?"

"Yes, honey," he said with effort, but I could see it was an automatic response to the pleading look on my face. He'd moved beyond the reach of useless, beautiful things.

By the end of the day, his unresponsiveness had shaded into a staring blankness. I didn't recognize what was happening. I'd never been with him when he'd been rushed to hospital, and I'd imagined his collapses as something more dramatic, like the collapses of Mr. Smallweed in *Bleak House*. There was no clutching at his chest, no wheezing for air. Just a closing of the shutters over his consciousness.

The following morning it was obvious that he hadn't improved. Tony got on the CB to Joan, in town, and she phoned the airlines. They were booked solid. She managed to get three seats—only three—for the following day. The rest of us would have to wait two days more.

Zoë and I talked often. Dad was dying, we knew; and we both felt that the constant in and out of hospital was killing his spirit as much as the emphysema was suffocating his body. I don't remember which of us said it first, but we felt the same: "We should just let him die here, in peace, in this place he loves."

Tony was furious that we could even consider it. Danny, characteristically, agreed with his mother and me and agreed with Tony too. But what Zoë and I felt was irrelevant. Dad was being taken away, and the only point at issue was how to get him from Las Caletas to the airport.

There was no stretcher, and we doubted he'd be able to sit up in the *panga*. His mind was too fuzzy from lack of oxygen to understand what was going on. He would need a chair—an armchair, that he couldn't fall out of. The only one we could find was a heavy, carved thing, with a leather seat and thick square legs. A couple of strong men picked it up with him in it, and waded into the waves. They wedged it between the thwarts of the *panga*. And so Dad left Las Caletas on a throne, with Maricela and Tony on either side of him, holding his arms.

Zoë, Danny, and I stood on the beach and watched until the *panga* was out of sight. It grieved me to see him go so blank and dopey, like a baby, with no power left to him even to say good-bye. I wondered if he'd come to Las Caletas hoping that the ordeal of the last few years might end quietly, without drama. That hadn't happened. The atmosphere was tense and excitable, with constant CB conversations to Joan in town, and Tony furious at Zoë and me for wanting to allow Dad what we thought was a good death. An Irish proverb that Dad loved counseled one to die by the sea.

Looking back on it, I'm not so sure as I was then. Dad had launched Anjelica's career with *Prizzi's Honor*. *The Dead* would, he hoped, launch Tony's; and after that he planned to act in Danny's first feature as a director, *Mr. North*. I was already on what looked like my life's path, working in publishing, an appropriately Marietta Tree–like occupation. I think the intense desire to see all his children set was what gave him the strength to last so long.

It felt wrong to see Dad so rarely, and only when he was sick. Even that last Christmas, which was meant to be a celebration, tailed off into the usual routine of the VIP floor of Cedars-Sinai. Was I abandoning him in favor of my English family? Tony, Anjelica, and Danny were all working with him, in his business; I wasn't. I used to describe myself as the family rebel, the only one who'd completed university and held down an office job, but it was bravado. Dad didn't need me. Anjel was there to see he was well taken care of, and to bring him food from the best restaurants when hospital food was getting him down. It was I who needed him: needed to be a good daughter to him, in return for his greatness of spirit in taking me in and loving me.

The phone call came in late July 1987, as I worked in my minuscule office halfway up the grand staircase of a Georgian building in Bloomsbury, which I loved for its west-facing window and because it was mine.

"You should come now, Legs, for his birthday," Anjel said. "If you want to see him before he dies."

His birthday was August 5. Mine was the twenty-sixth. When I was little, I'd seen this cradling of our birthdays in the same month as a sign of destiny.

Anjel was in Newport, Rhode Island, acting in Danny's film, *Mr. North.* Dad had been there too, as a nominal producer, though Robert Mitchum was playing the part Dad was too frail to play. The nearest hospital was in Fall River, Massachusetts, nearly an hour's drive away.

I didn't feel any great pleasure from him in seeing me. Another sickbed visit: my duty to him, made because I'd been summoned, not because I'd come of my own accord. It was true. The same sense of duty was in his welcome. I was pained, even more than I had been by the sight of the *Anjelica,* by the erosion of the closeness we'd had. Now that Las Caletas was in effect gone, it was up to me to pull its spirit around us: the long peaceful mornings, the delicate threads of appreciating each other through pencil and backgammon and talk.

We were all there except Tony. In his hospital room, I gave Dad a birthday present of fur-lined slippers, which I'd bought when I got to Newport. They turned out to be half a size too small. We didn't exchange them. It was an unspoken admission that by the time the cold weather came, his feet would no longer need warming.

"We won't feel guilty, Legs, that we'll be relieved when it happens."

We were alone together in a car again, Anjel driving, me beside her. The summer sun was bright on the low clapboard buildings, broken by the nearby ocean into a million prismatic strands that flashed through the town like a web. She was smoking, as she usually was. Even with Dad dying of emphysema in his hospital room, she and Danny would have to retreat to the corridor for a quick cigarette. Each time I heard the sound of her breath as she drew smoke into her lungs, I felt my heart beat fractionally faster.

"No," I said, loving her for trusting me enough to say that. "We won't."

I saw tears in Anjel's eyes. She saw tears in mine. She smiled. It was our pact.

The routine of hospitalizations was grinding on all of us: Dad and Maricela, Anjelica and me. The first one, when she'd picked me up from school and driven me to Cedars-Sinai, had been almost ten years before. They were getting more frequent. Tony and Danny were there for some of them; but it seemed that Anjel and I were there for them all. Anjel was first on the scene, then she'd phone me in England and I'd get on a plane. I got to know the particular intensity of her voice saying "Hi, Legs" when she was calling with the same wrenching news. She had taken the place of the loving, conscientious daughter that, for two years or so, was mine. She'd been wrapped up in the complications of her own life and distant from him during those years; now I'd moved away to try to make a shape of mine.

"He hates this," she said. "He'd never have wanted it. He'll be glad when it's over."

I knew she was right. Dad was fed up with the duty of staying alive.

On my birthday, back in London, I gave my contractual month's notice that I was quitting my job. I had a feeling that Dad would die in November. My plan was to work out my notice, good girl that I was, then go wherever he was in late September and stay with him until the end.

Two days later, the phone call came. "Legs, it's me." Anjelica was crying. "He's gone."

I hadn't called him in those two days. I didn't know how to say, I've quit my job so I can be with you until you die. None of us spoke of his death to him, nor he to us. I'd been dogged by a wild notion that he'd be annoyed at me for tossing in my career, even for his sake. So he never knew that I'd given my notice and was coming to be with him.

I'd been waiting for the moment of Dad's death for ten years. I thought I'd be calm, able to handle it. Instead I couldn't stop crying. I felt untethered, like an astronaut on a space walk whose cord has come undone. It took all my concentration to get myself home, get to the airport, change planes in New York. I tried to tell the flight attendants I needed help, but I was trying to communicate across such a vast distance that they didn't understand me.

In Providence, I was the last person off the plane. I could barely find my shoes, my carry-on bag, my handbag, and collect it all to me. My power—the energy force that held my atomized self together—had gone.

There was no one at the gate. It was late; the airline staff had gone home. Dimly I walked through the empty airport and found an escalator going down. At the bottom was an echoing marble hall, deserted. I didn't know what to do.

Then I saw a figure in a camouflage jacket walking toward me: Harry Dean Stanton. His long, sunken face shone to me. He was also in *Mr. North*, and he'd insisted on coming to the airport for me. Behind him was Anjelica.

We went to the baggage carousel. There was nothing there. In my daze I hadn't realized I had to clear customs in New York, so my suitcase was still there.

I slept in Anjel's little rented cottage that night. The next day Nancy Reagan phoned to offer *Air Force Two* to take Dad's body back to L.A.

Anjel broke out laughing when she hung up the phone. "It's a good thing he's already gone back so we don't have to refuse," she said. Nancy's father, a brain surgeon, had operated on Dad's mother; but Dad despised Ronald Reagan as a McCarthyite fellow traveler, a posturer, and a panderer. Nancy, for all her adoration of Ronnie, never held it against Dad. She kept inviting him to the White House, and he kept refusing. He would have been livid if we'd accepted anything that was Reagan's to give.

His business manager called, and his lawyer—the evil-hearted Henry Hyde. I could see Anjel, on the phone, starting to lose her temper. Suddenly she calmed, as if a breeze had lifted her and erased the frown between her eyes.

"I heard Dad's voice," she said when she hung up. Her eyes were gleaming, as if she'd experienced a miracle. "'Rise above it.' You know how he always used to say that? 'Rise above it.'" She imitated his honeylike voice. "I didn't just remember it, Legs. I heard his voice saying it to me."

I rode in the limo with Anjelica and Jack to the Hollywood cemetery. It was the old cemetery, laid out in the nineteenth century, with Paramount Studios across the street. Dad's mother was buried there.

Jack and Anjel weren't exactly together at that point, so it surprised me that he came with us. But he had adored Dad, and Dad him. "I'd like to have one of that litter," Dad used to say about Anjelica and Jack. Anjelica had turned to him, and he was there.

He wore his usual dark glasses. I thought they were inappropriate for a funeral: too casual and recreational. Then we stepped out of the limo into an explosion of flashbulbs. I ducked instinctively; it was like gunfire. I wanted to close my eyes against them, but if I did I'd stumble. Anjel had put on sunglasses too, I noticed. I understood: sunglasses were the flak jacket. They let you move through the firestorm unscathed.

Inside, Dad was lying in a coffin on a dais. His head rested on a cream satin pillow, which was badly out of character for him. The lower half of the coffin lid was closed over him, as if maybe his lower half wasn't there or had to be hid. The St. Bernard in the glass case in the hall of John Julius's house popped into my mind. The sacrilegious thought made me smile, and I felt a flood of affection for both my fathers, together.

Dad's face was smooth. Alive, his face had been full of changing expression. The furrow between his eyebrows would flash in and out as he concentrated, or leaned forward with interest. Now it was the deadest part of his face. His cheeks were rosy; later, Anjel made a crack about the makeup artist having had too heavy a hand with the rouge. I wished I could take a Kleenex and pat it off. When Dad had campaigned against the colorization of black-and-white films, he had talked about them as if they were babies; people had cut them and mangled them, and now Ted Turner wanted to dye their hair. Here he was, my poor dad: they had colorized him.

I leaned down and kissed his forehead, as I used to do when I said good night to him in Mexico. He felt hard—not as cold as I'd expected, but hard like wood. I tried to make myself remember that foreheads are hard, they're bone under the skin, but still the nerve endings in my lips missed the infinitesimal pillowing that the pulsing of blood would have made there. It wasn't creepy or upsetting: it was like kissing a statue of Dad, the way you kiss the statue of a saint. I thought of the foot of Saint Peter in the Vatican, which Dad had taken me to see: the sculpted lines of the toes worn away by the millions of lips that had brushed across them. I imagined the abrasion of my kisses on Dad's forehead: lines in living flesh smoothed away over ten years—what for stone took centuries.

It wasn't him: not the body that I had hugged, not the hands that had sketched me. The eyes that had interrogated me or delighted as I made an unexpected move at backgammon were sealed under embalmed eyelids. He was gone—vanished, just like Mum.

Seeing his body made it no different. I hadn't seen Mum's dead body, of course, and I never asked what was done with it. I have no bodily memories of her—of touching her, of being hugged by her. Who she was, and the substance she was made of, are two entirely separate things to me. If Mum is buried somewhere, I didn't want to know; it would locate her somewhere definite and unyielding, away from me. I knew, as I looked down at his Dad-less body, that I'd never revisit Dad's grave.

Anjel told me that they'd held a Quaker service for Mum: no priest or prayers, just a gathering of friends who stood to speak as they were moved to words. Dad's service was the same. His agent and oldest surviving friend, Paul Kohner, who owned the house in Cuernavaca where I'd had the piñata birthday so long ago, gave a eulogy in his thick Swiss accent. I don't remember what he said, what anyone said, what I said, just that I stood and said how I'd loved him.

Tony, Anjelica, Danny, and I walked out with our arms linked. It was only the second time we'd all been together. I felt that we were strong. In his leaving, Dad had united us.

"Dad wouldn't want to be put in an ugly funeral-home urn. We should find a nice box to put him in."

Anjel and I were sitting at her kitchen table, in the little pink house off Beverly Glen Boulevard that Jack had bought for her. It was full of objects I recognized from St. Cleran's, including Dad's silver cigar boxes. They looked too small to contain the ashes of a giant.

"How big a box do we need?" I asked.

Anjel looked at me. "I don't know," she said. "I guess we should ask." We started to laugh.

Anjel called the funeral home and asked. It was surreal, taking notes on the size of our father's ashes as if we were taking dimensions for a refrigerator.

The box we liked best, casket-shaped and decorated with cameos, was slightly too small. We didn't see how we could leave a bit of him out—even to bury some of him and scatter the rest. So in the end we let them put him in a funeral-home box. As long as it wasn't actually an urn, we decided; he would have thought that was cheesy.

When we arrived for the burial, they handed us a package wrapped in white paper, like a box of See's chocolates without the ribbon. Anjel took it, then handed it to me. My arms sank under the weight. I hadn't expected it to be so heavy.

"It's bronze," said Anjel. She smiled. A thread of light flew from her eyes to mine.

Dad's mother's grave was marked by a bronze plaque set in the grass, just as his would be. Rhea Gore Huston. Next to it was a small hole in the turf. Anjel set the box in the hole. We threw earth onto it, each of us in turn. The white paper still shone through.

"Good-bye, Papa Bear," Maricela said. She had said nothing at the service. She had nothing to say to the living; only to him.

Tony wandered down to the lake and played Irish melodies on a tin whistle as Anjelica, Danny, Zoë, Maricela, and I watched the gravediggers fill in the hole.

Afterward, Anjelica took us all—Maricela and her sister too—to the property she'd just bought in central California, a few hours' drive from L.A. At its center, on a small hill, was a little adobe house, and another building next to it which she called the bunkhouse. There were two lakes, which Jeremy had put in—he'd bought there first, and brought Anjel.

It was bare, dry land in the foothills of the Sierra Nevada—but we could walk down to the Kaweah River to swim off the summer heat. Later Anjel would plant a beautiful garden down the slope, lush with flowers and fruit trees, and put in a fountain and shady arbors. Pale purple water hyacinths would grow over one pond, like a shimmering carpet. She brought in horses and chickens, and bought another little house so that there would be enough room for all of us to come and stay.

We hid out there, playing backgammon, reading magazines, and talking about Dad. He never saw this new St. Cleran's, but his painting of Saint George and the dragon hung there already.

At the Directors Guild tribute a week later, Harry Dean sang a song of the Mexican revolution. My Spanish was better by now, and I could understand a good deal of it: it was a celebration of bravery and victory against the odds. Horses featured in it, and comrades, and the sun and the stars. Harry's voice caught and slid between the notes, as it always did—and I could hear that the barbs of emotion were in his heart, not just in the music. He had played poker with Dad, and made *Wise Blood* with him. His song that afternoon was the tribute Dad would have loved beyond any words of praise.

At the end, we played Dad's father's recording of "September Song," which Anjelica and I had chosen. It was an old, crackly recording; and Walter's voice was old and crackly too.

> *"Oh, the days dwindle down to a precious few*
> *September, November . . ."*

Those were the years in which I'd known Dad. It grieved me that my timing had been bad: to have been born too late to know him in the prime of his youth and health, to have quit my job too late to spend those last precious days with him. It tore me apart that I had been so conscientious in returning to London and hadn't just stayed in Rhode Island with him. Why had I thought his death would come in November? He was tired: of the relentless rigmarole of his collapsing body, of being too weak to do the things he loved. He dreaded another turn in hospital. That he had managed to make

The Dead was a miracle—one he wouldn't be able to repeat. When he saw his friends, in those last days, he bade them—as he had not used to do—a formal good-bye.

I am certain he chose his time to go. It was still August, the month of his birthday and mine.

20

John Julius still wears the slippers Mum needlepointed for him. Whenever he mentions her to me—which he does easily, with no restraint or regret—he calls her "your darling Mum." But they weren't together anymore when the car crash killed her. She had fallen in love with a new man. John Julius tells me that she had, he thought, finally found true happiness.

That man, whom I've never met, was driving. He was, apparently, from Jamaica, and not used to driving on the French side of the road. The story I've always heard is that, when the car hit a pothole and jounced up, out of control, he instinctively yanked the wheel to turn it off the road and instead turned it into the path of an oncoming truck. Mum took the full impact. His injuries were minor. He survived.

Mum didn't have time to make the baby book she'd planned for me. I found a little cache of things for it: my hospital tag, showing my name as "Allegra Soma"; a clipping from *The Times* of "'The Night Sky in August"; a photo of John Julius as a little boy in a sailor hat on a ship (probably the Admiralty yacht, as his father was First Lord of the Admiralty); and, pressed flat in separate pieces of tissue paper, a small yellow rose and a much larger red one. I'm sure John Julius sent them to her.

And there are thirteen scraps of paper, little notes that she wrote on whatever was to hand, recording my first smile, the day I discovered my hands, the week I perfected my crawling, my first few teeth, the first time I stood alone and my first step, my first words (which included "a very clear 'Hello' in greeting to 'Dolly' as she was gathered up to play with"), and my favorite: "July 19th: I realized today for the first time Allegra was calling me by name."

I called Mum "Mamam" then. When Anjelica told me this, I felt a tingle of memory so faint that it might have come from the farthest reaches of space. I felt my lips, without conscious intention, moving in the shape of the word; and warmth bled through me. Probably I called Mum that only for a short time, and grew out of it before she died.

Mum called me "the Empress" in her letters to John Julius. She told him about my progress, but the reports are dutifully informative rather than intimate. All those milestones that she recorded for my sake—she doesn't mention them to him.

I can see her passion for him trickling away. After that brutally blunt letter to the poste restante address in France, the sweet deliriousness with which she used to write to him is gone. She has reread his two-volume history of the Norman kingdom in Sicily, and kicks herself that she didn't do a better editing job on the manuscript. He arranges for her to be a panelist on a BBC television cultural commentary show called *Three After Six*, on which he has appeared. She reminds her friends that he is an expert on Venice and many other things, in case they know of media or lecturing work that might suit him. They go on holiday to Norway, with me, just before I turn two. And after that, the letters fade. Months, then years, pass between them.

And here chance flings a dart into me: her last letter to John Julius, written in January 1969, the month she died, was written from St. Cleran's. Why did she go there? I don't know; she doesn't say. The letter is chatty about doings: Dad getting his Irish citizenship, Tony going fishing, a book she's read, a beautiful little piece of pre-Columbian art that Gladys gave her for Christmas. I'm pleased to see that Mum was fond of Gladys—that Cici's war with her was hers alone.

She calls John Julius "dearest" again and signs with the initial R, as she used to. There has been some reconciliation, after—I guess—an estrangement between them. Mum's writing slopes forward again, as if yearning for him—in the few letters before, it became rounder and more upright, as if she was attempting to speak clearly to someone who may not hear. That "dearest"—it comes as a gift to me. I didn't want Mum to go to her death with coldness in her heart for him. She wouldn't have wanted to either; I know it would have mattered to her.

It shines from her letters: Mum didn't want to hate. She didn't want to hold resentments. She always forgave. She wanted to think only the best of people, to hold only the best wishes for them in her heart. Every lover became a dear friend; the shape of her love changed, but not the substance. Rereading her letters to John Julius, I found this, from Christmas 1963, in the letter where she describes herself as "enormous with secrets"—in other words, with me.

"So much of the St. Cleran's nightmare to me," she writes, "is the impossibility of helping John. He grows ever more to me a being in suffering and distress: I can feel his aimless, abortive reachings towards me and I feel so trapped in such a variety of emotions, none of them free of suspicion or temporizing. It is so hard to see one's duty, somehow. I come back to the children with a sigh of relief. That, at least, is simple and whole-hearted."

I think Mum's heart was always torn, from the time she was a little child. She never knew ease of spirit. From the slashing vortex that was Grampa to the hurricane that was Dad, she juggled loyalty and hurt and tried to live up to the perfection both men demanded of her. In her letters to John Julius, she is harsh on herself. She worries, a little, that she may have told him too much of her past. "I am vain and envious and self-pitying," she writes. "I don't even know whether indulgence in such self-castigation isn't purest proof of monumental egocentricity and selfishness." It's not true! I want to shout to her, across the dimensions that sever us. That you can even think so proves you are not.

But to write that to him is a release for her, and a flowering. Her diary was sporadic because it was written for her eyes only, and she couldn't believe that she mattered enough to herself to keep it up. Written to another person, her sensations and thoughts and perceptions take on meaning. She bares herself to John Julius. She can be imperfect in his eyes—she positively wants to be. He will love her not for her flaws or despite them, but anyway. She felt that he loved *her*. Of all the men she had been with, my father was the one who helped her become whole. That, maybe, is the secret of why he is my father, and no one else.

The pain of losing Mum is caught up in the splendor of coming to know her. Her greatness of spirit, her generosity and intelligence and warmth and grace: I knew all this, always, but I knew it at a remove, as mortals know goddesses. Though it wrung my heart to read her letters, they gave me another gift: the sense of holding Mum herself in my hand, and coming upon odd resemblances between us. A woman says to her at a first-night party, "But you are always a bit bored." It isn't really boredom, but a lack of interest in glitter and adrenaline: a sagging disappointment when she finds the core of an evening, a play, a book, hollow. I recognize that in me. She describes "the sort of pulverizing death I used to feel ten years and more ago, when I went to places and parties in the shadow of John, and felt invisible." That was me too.

Yes, I lost her too soon. But what better mother could I have asked for? Whatever I have of her in me is the best of me. I was lucky in my two fathers, but I was luckiest of all to be her daughter.

I was in my thirties before I dared walk on Maida Avenue again. I drove past it often during the eighteen years I lived in London, on my way to and from John Julius's house or taking a shortcut to the M1. I could see the number 31 painted in gold on the window above a black front door on the right-hand half of the second building from the corner of Warwick Avenue. If I was on foot, I kept to the streets in front and behind; and if I went to Hsing, John Julius's favorite restaurant on the corner of Edgware Road, I made sure to turn off Maida Avenue before the brick mansion blocks gave way to white stucco semidetached houses, the second half of which held number 31.

Then I made an appointment to meet someone who was staying at number 26. "Can you come here?" he said.

"Sure," I answered with my heart racing.

I didn't know how I'd react to being on that street, with its slabs of stone paving heaved up by the roots of the giant plane trees, the street that my mother's new car had been parked on, the street where, in the last photo I have of her, I'm holding her hand. I had never been back to a place where I'd been with her—other than Tony's flat, and that was so full of his personality, his life, that the wisps of her long-ago presence were overpowered and beyond sensing. Gina had moved decades before; so had Leslie Waddington. I was more comfortable keeping my loss without shape. If I was in a specific, Mum-connected place, I might see the gap in space where she was supposed to be.

Like a totem I wore Mum's ring, which Anjelica had given me for my twenty-first birthday. Anjelica had always worn it. I thought it was one of the most beautiful things I'd ever seen: a gold panther crouched in the delicate gold branches of a tree, with diamond blossoms. I thought of the panther as crouching on his pile of diamonds. She had pulled it off her finger on the spur of the moment in the Star of India restaurant, and I slipped it onto mine quickly, before she had a chance to change her mind. Mum had bought the ring as her own gift to herself when she got engaged to Dad.

Number 26 was one of the white stucco houses, like number 31. I couldn't avoid it, couldn't keep to the far end of the street that didn't look like the Maida Avenue I remembered. This is silly, I thought. It's a street, a house. Everyone in the world has to revisit places where someone they lost once lived.

I parked on a road behind, walked up Warwick Avenue, and turned right, to the second house. Number 31 was blocked by a solid steel gate between the pavement and the front path. Beside it was the brass box of an entryphone.

I couldn't look at it: so cold, so impersonal, so excluding. It seemed to divide those who belonged in that house from those who didn't. A plain front door invites you to walk up the steps and press the bell; that entryphone asked for a password that I didn't have. It was unbearable to stand there as a stranger—a stranger to my own amputated childhood and the world my mother made.

The tree, I thought. In that last picture of Mum and me is one of the thick-trunked plane trees. We're walking away from the house— to her car, I guess, without knowing why I think so. The tree blocks the line of parked cars from view. Its deeply ridged bark is stalwart, indestructible. I wanted that tree to be there. I needed it to be.

I battled my memory, forcing it to give up the tiniest peculiarities of the shape and bark of that tree, so that I'd know it in the crowd. The trees are close together; I wasn't sure which one it was. If the person who took the photo was standing at the foot of the front path, which they probably were, it would be the second tree to the east. Was it that one? It had a pair of burls where my right hand would touch it—I didn't think those burls were in the photo. Maybe it was the next one, or the one before. Suddenly I was relieved that I couldn't tell exactly which one it was. It would have been like a gravestone, and I'd have collapsed in front of it in tears—which would have been embarrassing on a public street, and besides I had a business meeting in five minutes.

Happiness rushed through me with the knowledge that the tree—whichever one it was—was still there. There are no gaps where one might have died and been cut down. No saplings. All old giants, with leaves as big as plates, just as I remembered them.

I had never wanted to get married, except for the party. If we had a wedding, I'd think idly, my whole family would have to come: the Hustons and the Coopers, and who knows who else from my past. The more I thought about it, the thirstier I got for this to happen. But at the price of getting married: of asserting a future that might not come true, of tempting fate? And besides, Cisco didn't propose.

Cisco Guevara is a Rio Grande whitewater rafter, champion country-and-western dancer and storyteller, with a long braid of hair down his bull-strong back and an ever-present black cowboy hat that looks like no other hat, because it's been shaped by the river. In London, restaurants fall silent when he walks in. Nobody looks exotic in London except Cisco.

"Mum would have loved Cisco," said Tony—for the same reasons that Dad would have loved him: his deep knowledge of the natural world; his ironic sense of humor; his colorful history and sense of adventure; his uncompromising, almost unconscious insistence on always being himself. Dad would have delighted in the fact that Pancho Villa married Cisco's great-aunt, that his grandmother ran a brothel–cum–gas station in Chihuahua, and that his father was a thermonuclear engineer who worked on the hydrogen bomb. Mum, the political idealist, would have been proud that her grandson shares an ancestor with the legendary Che.

When I found I was pregnant, the plan formed instantly: a christening instead of a wedding—a big party, to which everyone would have to come. A baby was a far better reason to haul them to Taos. He would be here, a fact in himself, and that's what we would celebrate. No promises that could be broken. No curdling of hopes.

So on June 8, 2003, I sat with Cisco and our eight-month-old son in a rubber raft covered with feathery juniper boughs, bunches of plastic grapes and trailing vines and sunflowers, and glittering tin *milagros* of hands with eyes in the palms and hearts on fire. The walls of the Rio Grande Gorge rose hundreds of feet above the river: tumbled black basalt formed by the lava of ancient volcanoes nocked with buffalo grass and Apache plume, and here and there burly piñon trees and gnarled junipers which were saplings when the Spaniards first came here five centuries ago. I knew of eagles' nests upstream and downstream; and I'd seen owls in the gorge, which reminded me of Nurse. Owls were her favorite creatures. We used to call them *oolas*, the Irish word.

I wore a pleated, flowing, blue-green Fortuny-like dress, and a crown of gold laurel leaves. Around the crown of Cisco's hat was a garland of wildflowers. The little boy on my lap wore a white Chinese outfit that my oldest friend, Kate O'Toole, had given him, and a lei of plastic marigolds.

Behind us, two guides who worked for Cisco each rowed one oar. They wore wildflower garlands too. It was a low-water year, fortunately; I hadn't thought of what we'd do if the river had been raging, as it might well have been in early June. That day it flowed in soft, purling eddies through the deep-cut artery of the parched high desert of northern New Mexico.

As we floated downstream, I looked over to the far shore. A year or so before, a homemade wooden cross had been planted there: a *descanso* to honor a teenage boy who had died one night trying to swim the river. Usually you see *descansos* by the side of the road, covered in plastic flowers, hung with toys and tinsel and beads: not grave markers, but little shrines to beloved sons, brothers, fathers, daughters, who died at that spot. If my mother's car had crashed in New Mexico instead of in France, I thought suddenly, she would have a *descanso*, with her name on it perhaps, and words like *amor* and *muerte*. It would mark the place where her spirit had left her body. Each bright flower that I fixed to the cross would be the earthly shape of a kiss that I sent toward her cheek, her hair, her forehead. I imagined her there, on that other bank, the lines of her face and hands traced in the particles of pollen and dust by the lowering rays of light.

She has no gravestone. Her ashes were sent to her father, and for the year that I lived in Grampa's house, I didn't know they were there. When the house burned to the ground, with Grampa in it— aged eighty-nine, and well on his way to a hundred—the remains of Mum disappeared into the smoke. Now she is nowhere, and every where.

"As I went down to the river to pray . . ." My friend Tara's voice rose, singing the Southern spiritual, for which she and I had written new words to welcome Rafa. Her voice was joined by more voices, at first a ragged choir, hardly enough to imprint the air. As we came closer, they grew stronger, the words lapping against the canyon walls, tucking into the spaces among the boulders.

We rounded a bend, and I saw them all: Tara, in another pleated, water-colored dress hitched up above her Teva sandals, high on a rock like an Arthurian priestess, and below her, on the dusty beach, more than a hundred people: John Julius, Artemis, Jason, and my godmother Gina, who had all come from London; my mother's friends Jay Hutchinson, who had come from Boston, and Lillian Ross, who had come from New York; Anjelica, Tony, and Danny, all four of us together again—not as unusual as it once was; and all of Cisco's closest family. His sister Ana had come from Atlanta. His mother, Luchi, sat in a camp chair, a long clear tube running from her nose to a silver canister of oxygen behind her.

Everyone held a sunflower. That had been Anjelica's idea. In researching Saint Raphael, her nephew's namesake, she kept seeing sunflowers. They grow in northern New Mexico, but not until later in the summer, so she FedExed a hundred and fifty long-stemmed sunflowers to me the day before the ceremony.

From behind a rock a procession emerged, led by Tony, wearing an animal skin draped over one shoulder and a shoulder-length wig of black curls like Charles II. He carried a tall staff. This apparition was his surprise for me: a christening in the river demanded a John the Baptist.

Dad would have been apoplectic with anger. I loved it, because it was something only Tony would have done.

Behind Tony walked Anjelica, in yet another Fortuny-pleated dress. Behind her came Joan Buck and Cisco's niece Ana, wearing two more of the dresses—all in different shades of water and fog. They were Anjel's costumes from *The Mists of Avalon*, and because there were five, another layer of ceremonial was added: attendants.

At that moment my head filled so full of sound and sight and memory, and the man next to me and the little boy on my lap, that I couldn't take in any more. The voices dissolved, though I could still see mouths moving as the song was sent into the sky. The faces merged, so that I could hardly tell one from another. I felt the gift surge toward us—so many people coming from so far away, my friends and family adding their own ideas into the ceremony, so that it became richer and more wonderful than I could ever have made it on my own. It lifted us up above the water, the three of us, into a protected, temporary little realm of pure happiness.

A banner wobbled up into sight above the singing faces: blue velvet edged with fringe and tassels, with my son's full name in gold: Rafael Patrick Gerónimo Niño de Ortíz Ladrón de Guevara.

Rafael because we liked the name, and the short version Rafa. Patrick, because it had always been my favorite name, and Irish. Geronimo, at Anjelica's urging, because he was born on San Geronimo Day, which is the feast day of Taos Pueblo and a celebration of thanksgiving for the gifts of the gods. All the rest is Cisco's surname, commemorating a long-ago battle in the reconquest of Spain from the Moors. When Rafa was born he was an elfin creature, with pointed tufts of hair on his ears, and he looked around the room very deliberately, as if to decide whether he really wanted to commit himself to being here. Naming him was frightening, like pronouncing a sentence that might someday prove to be unjust.

As we floated to the shore, Anjel waded into the water. The pleats of her dress swirled around her knees, the gray-purple of an evening sky with a storm blowing in. She reached to take Rafa and handed him to Tara, who set him on her shoulders. The attendants ranged themselves around her. Suddenly Jeremy, Anjelica's old friend, rushed into the water, thigh-deep, holding the banner with Rafa's name on it. Tony was with him, holding the other pole. They raised the banner behind Rafa, who sat calmly chewing on his plastic marigolds and surveying the crowd—"just like the Queen Mother," as John Julius said later.

None of this was rehearsed, or even planned. When I'd first thought of having a christening, my only idea was to do it in the Rio Grande, and have the three of us arrive by boat. One by one, people added their inspiration: Anjelica, the sunflowers and the *Mists of Avalon* dresses; Joan Buck, the garlands of flowers and my crown; Bruce and Kim, each taking an oar; Tara, the singing; my friends Annapurna and Janet, the decoration of the raft and the gold-lettered banner; Jeremy, holding the banner where it belonged; and the indescribable vision that was Tony.

And one more, someone that none of us expected: a guy who had been sitting drinking by the river when we arrived. It was a public place; we couldn't ask him to leave. So we explained what we were doing, and asked him if he wouldn't mind turning down the *norteño* music on his truck radio. He obliged, and I forgot about him.

We had asked Cisco's friend Steve Harris to officiate, since he's a minister of the Universal Life Church. He has the narrow face of Ratty in *The Wind and the Willows*, with lively eyes and a droopy mustache, and the waterlogged look of a lifetime boater. Just as he pronounced Rafa's name, a voice echoed off the cliffs: "Don Rafael!" It was the drinker, following an old Spanish custom. Because of him, Rafa has the right to call himself *don*, the Spanish equivalent of "sir."

Anjel gave a heavily Catholic sermon on the meaning of Rafa's three names—she went to the nuns in Loughrea too. And then Louie Hena, an elder of Tesuque Pueblo and Cisco's closest friend, baptized Rafa in the Tewa language with an Indian name: Tseh Shu Ping, Flying Eagle Mountain. I can see Flying Eagle Mountain— better known as San Antonio Mountain, a freestanding dormant volcano—from my kitchen window, and I think of it as Rafa's mountain. It's very round, with a concave groove in the center of its horizon. The Tesuque people say that its top is shaped like the outspread wings of an eagle. I see a giant loaf of Irish soda bread, just like a hill in Connemara called Roundstone. Louie had no idea how he pulled my past and present together when he gave Rafa that name.

Louie spoke in Tewa, and then in English, of the spiral patterns of the universe: in the eddies of the river and the currents of the air, in the whorl of hair on the crown of Rafa's head. Nothing is linear, he said. Life and time circle back on themselves, joining up, making new patterns. There is no beginning or end. Only the movement of energy.

I felt, for the first time, at the center of the spiral. Rafa pulled my family together around me, into one. It would have been impossible, once; now it was natural, beyond question. I didn't have to do anything, be anything in particular: just me, just there, a daughter and a sister, and now a mother too.

At the party afterward, John Julius commandeered the piano when the band took a break, and he and Jason sang 1940s songs.

John Julius danced until his face was the same color as his salmon-colored shirt, bending Tara backward till her hair touched the floor. Rafa spent most of the evening in his auntie Anjelica's arms. And my favorite moment of all came the next morning at breakfast, when Danny and Jason—who had never met before they came to Taos—slapped each other on the back and said, "My brother!"

I go to London a few times a year, and stay at John Julius's house across the canal from Maida Avenue. The room I sleep in is on the top floor, at the same height as my room in Mum's house, level with the treetops. Far below, I see the black-painted iron railing and the potted geraniums on the roofs of the houseboats. Often Rafa comes with me, to visit his Grappa.

Every visit, I take Rafa to the zoo on the Water Bus, boarding at the same place in Paddington Basin where Mum and I, or Nurse and I, used to board. Ducks and swans paddle in circles, as they did forty years ago. Everything is the same: the little island where the three canals meet, the shouts of the boatmen as they stride along the roofs of the narrowboats, the thudding cough of the engines, the dark mustiness of the brick-lined tunnels squeezing the boats so tightly together that you might touch a passing one with your palm.

Often John Julius walks with us to the canal basin to see us aboard. As the Water Bus rounds the little island and heads east down Regent's Canal, he crosses the arched, blue-curlicued footbridge and walks home along the paved towpath on the inside of the black railings, a few feet below the level of Blomfield Road.

"Grappa!" Rafa shouted the first time he saw him there, only a few feet away on the far side of the window glass. "Grappa!"

Seeing his little face at the window, John Julius waved. Rafa waved back, thrilled that someone could walk on land at the same speed as we chugged along on water.

"Mama, there's Grappa!"

They are so alike: bright-eyed and charming, quick-witted, energetic, open to the world. Artemis wrote to me that Rafa is the incarnation of John Julius. It made me intensely happy that she saw it. It would make Mum happy too.

Is it the ordinary we remember, or the extraordinary? Fondly I think Rafa will remember me pushing him on the swings, or singing a lullaby to him at night, or holding his hand while he learns to skateboard. But perhaps what will stick in his mind is me in a fury flinging his Legos out the front door into the night, or driving too fast, or throwing a tantrum at the dust and cobwebs.

I am aware of creating his sense of me—a feeling of extraordinary power and extraordinary powerlessness. I determine the quality of his days, but I have no control over which parts of those days etch lines in his memory. Nor, I guess, does he. I don't know why I remember the things I do, and not others. Surely I had times of intense happiness with Mum, the kind that adults make mental notes to remember. I feel closest to Mum not in my memory, but in that photograph taken on Maida Avenue, where I'm holding her hand.

Acknowledgments

This book grew out of a magazine article I wrote for *Harper's Bazaar*, UK, titled "Daddies' Girl." Thanks to Catherine Fairweather and Sharon Walker at *Harper's* for commissioning it.

I thought I'd said all I had to say in eighteen hundred words. Three people encouraged me to expand the article into a book:

Barbara Leaming has been the most wonderful friend to me for twenty years. I've edited six of her books, and she reads everything I write. Her generosity of spirit and tireless encouragement have made me a writer. Her unerring instinct for what isn't there, and her willingness to be brutal and force me to find it, produced many of my favorite passages in this book.

My sister Artemis Cooper and my stepmother Celeste (Cici) Huston added their voices to Barbara's. If it hadn't been for their vision and belief in me, I might never have embarked on this intimidating project.

My father John Julius Norwich, and my brothers Tony Huston, Danny Huston, and Jason Cooper gave me their wholehearted support, as did Mollie Norwich. Most important, my sister Anjelica Huston, who could be forgiven for trying to dissuade me from revisiting a difficult time in her life, gave me her blessing and said only, "Be kind"—and then, when it was written, gave me the title for the book.

I am grateful for the trust they all put in me, as for the thousands of kindnesses and pleasures and close moments I've shared with them all.

Helena Kallianiotes and Sonali Wijeyaratne harangued me for years to write a book instead of screenplays, as did my first agent at Curtis Brown, Nick Marston. James Navé, my partner in the Writing Salon, gave me the confidence to trust my imagination as a writer, and showed me how to encourage it to come out to play. In addition to my family and to Barbara Leaming, who gave this book her tireless imaginative engagement from inception to finish, David Parker, Joanna Briscoe, Lara Santoro, Rhonda Talbot, Tara Lupo, Elizabeth Burns, Diana LaSalle, Arron Shiver, Annapurna Sydell, Stephen Boucher, Joan Juliet Buck, Kate O'Toole, Robert Mack, and Helena Kallianiotes read various drafts of the book and gave me valuable feedback. Rhonda also recommended Nick Flynn's wonderful memoir *Another Bullshit Night in Suck City*, which inspired me to try different ways to tell my story and broke an impasse that might well have defeated me.

My editor, Sarah Hochman, and my agent, Elizabeth Sheinkman, put their faith in me with very little to go on. From the start, Sarah understood the kind of book I wanted to write. Her keen editorial eye made the book far better than it would have been without her—but more important, her encouragement, and a judicious hand with the whip, kept me on track during the most difficult times in the writing. David Rosenthal and Victoria Meyer of Simon & Schuster gave the book their powerful support. I'd also like to thank Gail Winston of HarperCollins for her enthusiasm at an early stage, which bolstered me enormously and helped me to refine my ideas.

I am grateful to David, Marquess of Cholmondeley, for storing Mum's letters, and to Gina Medcalf, Jaqueth Hutchinson, and Lucio Garcia del Solar for sending me letters my mother wrote to them. Lucio, Anjelica, Joan, and Cici also found photographs for me. Beth Filler at *People* magazine helped me track down a vital image. I'd also like to acknowledge the generosity and help of Gigi and Harry Benson, Magnum Photos for the Philippe Halsman estate, the Norman Parkinson estate, and especially the Richard Avedon Foundation.

This book was largely written at two coffee shops in Taos, New Mexico. Thanks to David Stewart and the staff of Wired?, especially Corinna Jang; and to Marc and Jennifer Campbell and the staff of Mondo Kultur north, especially Mary Esther Winters.

My son, Rafa, kept my nose to the grindstone with remarks like, "You know that book you're writing, Mama? Have you finished it? No? I thought so!" The happiness he and his father, Cisco Guevara, have brought me made this book possible.

Finally, thanks to Rafa's friends Teva Leshem and Kendra Gibson—and their mothers, Jenny Lancaster-Leshem and Babs Costello—without whom this book could not have been written at all.

About the Author

Allegra Huston was born in London, and raised in Ireland, Long Island, and Los Angeles. She has worked with Chatto & Windus publishers in London, and Weidenfeld & Nicolson, where she was editorial director from 1990 to 1994. A freelance writer and editor for over ten years, her work has appeared in *The Times*, the *Independent*, the *Tatler*, and *Harper's Bazaar* (all in the UK), in French *Vogue*, and in the United States in *People*, the *Santa Fean*, and *Mothering*. She is co-director of the Writing Salon, a workshop retreat for writers held annually in Taos, New Mexico, and in other places around the world. She lives in Taos with her son, Rafa, and his father, Cisco Guevara.

Love Child
By Allegra Huston

Introduction

"This is your father." With those words, Allegra Huston's life changes forever: at age four, she joins the household of John Huston, acclaimed film director, actor, and estranged husband of Allegra's mother, recently killed in a car accident. Allegra slowly adapts to the vastness of her father's Irish estate, with its frenetic orbit of efficient servants, starstruck flatterers, and concerned caretakers of this timid little English girl.

Soon Allegra's life shifts again: she becomes an American, first living with her grandparents on Long Island and then with her father and stepmother in Los Angeles. Then another short sentence changes everything: "You were a child of love." Allegra meets her biological father, a British lord named John Julius Norwich, who was her mother's lover during her strained marriage to John Huston.

Increasingly benumbed and confused about her origins, Allegra clings to her older sister, Anjelica Huston, a rising star in Hollywood. Anjelica spirits Allegra off to the lavish retreats of her two boyfriends, Jack Nicholson and Ryan O'Neal. As she grows up, Allegra quits Hollywood's deceptive glamour and moves to London, where she slowly gets to know her biological father. Through her two fathers' memories and her mother's correspondence, Allegra finally finds the mother she barely remembers, discovering touching parallels between a daughter's life and a mother's hopes and dreams.

Discussion Questions:

1. *Love Child* begins with two dramatic scenes from Allegra Huston's childhood: learning of her mother's death and meeting John Huston in a smoky hotel room. What emotions are conjured up in these two opening scenes? What role does memory play within each scene?

2. Allegra describes several episodes of gift-giving: the bicycle she received at St. Cleran's, the belt Cici made for her new husband, Allegra's beach glass picture, and "Moby John," the Styrofoam whale that Allegra and Danny improvised for their father. What expectations, disappointments, and other emotions seem to be wrapped up within each of these gifts?

3. What does Allegra learn about her mother's life, her marriage, and her dreams from reading her old letters? How is she able to piece together a relationship with her mother through reading and writing?

4. "I felt, in myself, bog-ordinary. My skin itself was tired by my chameleon life." (90) What does Allegra mean by her "chameleon life?" What toll does it take upon her mood, her aspirations, and her relationships? In the end, does Allegra seem "bog-ordinary" in her memoir? Why or why not?

5. Consider each home in which Allegra spends her childhood: Maida Avenue in London, St. Cleran's in Galway, her grandparents' Long Island home, Uncle Myron and Aunt Dorothy's

"Gloom Castle," the Euclid Street rental in Los Angeles, Cici's light-filled house, Jack Nicholson's hillside home, Ryan O'Neal's Malibu beach house, and Allegra's stay in a London flat during the making of *The Shining*. What does Allegra's description of each home reveal about its owners? In which of these houses does Allegra seem most—and least—at home?

6. Compare the two scenes in which Allegra meets her fathers: first as a young child in London, then as an adolescent in Los Angeles. How does Allegra react differently to each meeting? What expectations—and disappointments—does Allegra bring to her first encounter with John Julius Norwich? How are they able to formulate a unique relationship, what she calls "a closeness without a name"? (245)

7. Allegra meets many strong male personalities in *Love Child*. What comparisons does she make between John Huston and the other kinglike men in her life—Grampa, Jack Nicholson, Ryan O'Neal, and John Julius Norwich?

8. Throughout her memoir, Allegra worries that she doesn't have "ownership rights" to her identity, and particularly to her relationship with the mother she barely remembers (152). How does this anxiety of ownership reveal itself in her memoir? With whom does Allegra feel she has to compete for ownership over her parents? How does she resolve this conflict?

9. Revisit the photographs at the center of the book. What story does each photo tell? What do these images add to the experience of reading *Love Child* and which relationships especially come to life within these family portraits?

10. Although Allegra grew up in a very glamorous world, many of the experiences, emotions, and uncertainties she expresses are common among ordinary families. Additionally, she forged loving bonds with "family members" who weren't blood relations, as with her brother Danny. What scenes in *Love Child* were you especially able to relate to?

Enhance Your Book Club:

1. Host a movie screening for your book club! Let your book club members vote on which of John Huston's movies to watch together: *Prizzi's Honor* (starring Anjelica Huston and Jack Nicholson), *Annie*, *The Maltese Falcon*, *The Night of the Iguana*, *The Misfits* or his last movie, *The Dead*. Watch *Chinatown* to see John Huston and Jack Nicholson light up the screen together; *The African Queen*, Huston's most popular film, starring Humphrey Bogart and Katharine Hepburn; *The Man Who Would Be King*; or *The Treasure of the Sierra Madre*.

2. One theme in *Love Child* is the uncertainty of memory. Ask your book club members to bring a childhood photograph to your meeting. Have each member explain the photograph and discuss what he or she remembers and doesn't remember from the day it was taken.

3. During your book club meeting play songs by Bob Dylan, Allegra and Anjelica's favorite singer in *Love Child*. Sing along to "Knockin' on Heaven's Door," like the sisters used to!

4. Visit Allegra Huston's website, www.allegrahuston.com, to read more of her writing, including the original *Harper's Bazaar UK* article that inspired *Love Child*.

5. Visit losriosriverrunners.com and see photos of the Rio Grande Gorge, where the christening of Allegra's son Rafa took place, and get a taste of Allegra's life in New Mexico.

Author Questions:

Tell us how you came to write *Love Child*. How did you decide to write your story, and what shape did it originally take?
Someone asked me recently, "How long did it take to write *Love Child?*" "Two years," I said. Then he asked, "How long did it take to get up the courage to write it?" That made me laugh, it was so unexpectedly perceptive. I made a guess: ten years.

The idea of writing a memoir lay at the back of my mind for a long time, but I didn't really let it come out until after I wrote "Daddies' Girl" for *Harpers Bazaar UK*—and I wrote that because I woke up one morning wanting to write about how lucky I feel to have the family I have, though a stranger might pity someone with my history. I'd never wanted to write something that would come across as "poor me," but I did want to tell my story honestly, because I thought it might give courage to people in similar situations. The day I realized I had a happy ending for it—my son's christening, when all my family came together—was the day I knew I'd write the book.

The dubiousness of memory—particularly what you can and cannot remember about your mother—is a strong theme in your memoir. How were you able to channel those few memories of your mother? Did those memories come to the page naturally, or did you find them difficult to access?
I had always had my little trove of memories from the time before Mum died. I knew them well, they seemed secure—and the fact that I had them gave me courage to attempt to write a memoir. I thought

it would be easy to write them down, but it wasn't at all. Suddenly I wasn't sure of details I'd always been sure of; things didn't add up; I started embellishing because the memories seemed so thin, but everything I wrote was dead on the page. I panicked. I thought, how did I get a contract to write a memoir when I can't bloody remember anything? But I was settled in at my favorite coffee shop, curled on a sofa by the window, and I couldn't give up, so I did an Imaginative Storm exercise: I wrote for ten minutes about what I couldn't remember. That freed me from having to be exact. I realized that the book was not supposed to be an accurate record of trivial events—this wasn't the Cuban Missile Crisis! I hoped that if I was honest and didn't try to gloss over the gaps and contradictions, readers might find connections with their own memories.

Please tell us more about finding and reading your mother's correspondence, which feels so crucial to the memoir. Do you think you could have written *Love Child* without drawing upon her letters?

Even though *Love Child* arose from an article about my two fathers, I knew that my mother and her story were central to it. Ten years ago, I had thought about writing a book "in search of my mother." I would certainly have written *Love Child* even if I hadn't had Mum's letters, but it would have been impoverished; it would have been "all about me," and I wanted it to be about Mum, too. I wanted to come to know her, and I also wanted to memorialize her so that she wouldn't be forgotten in Dad's shadow. I didn't know that Mum's letters to John Julius existed when I decided to write the book—and they are, for me, the book's heart. I was very disappointed when I wasn't able to dig up more letters that she had written to her family and friends, but I think in the end the one-sidedness of each correspondence proved to be a bonus. I couldn't be an objective observer of the back-and-forth, like someone watching a tennis match; I was plunged into the subjective experience of either receiving or writing the letters.

Your memoir has so many moments of doubting your creativity as a child—and yet now you have written an acclaimed memoir!

How do you reconcile the tentativeness of your youth with your adult accomplishments? Do any of those childhood uncertainties persist?

You bet they do! I've started another book, and it's like reinventing the wheel. I have no idea if I can do this. I look at *Love Child* and it's as if it was written by someone else—someone who knew what she was doing. I have to remind myself that when I was writing it, I felt like I didn't know what I was doing then either. I'll always be the kind of person who doubts myself; I am fascinated by and sometimes yearn to be one of those confident people who think they can do anything but I never will be (and the truth is, that mindset can get you killed). I just have to keep putting the doubts to one side and taking things one step at a time. I tell myself the least I can do is try, and I'll find out later whether it's any good or not. The end—a good book—is so far away it's out of sight.

As you wrote in your memoir, Anjelica heard your father's voice while trying to plan his funeral: "'Rise above it.' You know how he always used to say that? 'Rise above it'" (266). Were you able to put your father's motto to use while writing *Love Child*? Was there anything you have had to "rise above" in writing your family's story?

I think "Rise above it" is a very good motto for living generally. Don't waste time on what's not important. Don't get sucked into the drama. Get on with it: don't dwell on the past. Be a big person; be generous of spirit; be the person you'd admire. I think our whole family has had to do a fair bit of "rising above" the complications Dad left us, as well as the difficulties that beset us all by virtue of the fact that we're human: family dynamics, cruel circumstances, disappointments and crushed hopes, clashing needs and agendas. I, personally, have had to rise above my feelings of inferiority to my sister Anjelica, not to mention feeling sorry for myself because I lost my mother so young. I try to say to myself, when I'm angry or depressed over something, "How can this be a good thing?" Or if not that, what am I grateful for? I'm lucky that I live in a very beautiful place, so if all else fails I can look up at the mountains or west across the vast horizons, which remind me of the ocean. Stars and moon are good too.

Your memoir chronicles so many moves from country to country, and the evolving national identity you cultivated as a child and as an adult. How do you view your nationality now? Do you see yourself as belonging to many countries, or primarily to one?

I see myself as part English and part American, with a dash of Irish thrown in, and a pinch of Italian from my mother's ancestry. Because I had three different accents as a child my voice tends to change according to what country I'm in. The American never vanishes, but I still say "cahn't" even at home, and once in Ireland someone said to me, "You sound like you never left!" When I was living in England as an adult, I always felt American there and English whenever I was in the United States. Now that I've lived back in the United States for eleven years and have a family here and an investment in the local culture of Taos, I feel more American. Still, one of my goals is to establish a pocket of British slang in northern New Mexico, so that in a hundred years linguists will puzzle over people saying things like, "Ee, *ese*, I'm knackered."

The last scene of the book—when all sides of your family came together for Rafa's christening—makes for a very moving conclusion. Do you see this event as the climax of your search for family and belonging?

Yes, I do. I didn't at the time, of course, but when it came to thinking about a book and the shape of my life, that fantastic event was the natural climax. Moments like that are fleeting, but the fact that they happen is enough. Memory makes them eternal (and photos help). The search doesn't actually end until you die, so Rafa's christening was the climax only to that particular strand of my story. It's the beginning of another story one.

Love Child ends, "I feel closest to Mum not in my memory, but in that photograph taken on Maida Avenue, where I'm holding her hand" (286). What details in that photograph stand out for you? Why is it so special for you?

It's special because it's the last photo, taken only weeks before Mum died. Maybe less. The way she's looking back over her shoulder; the way I'm walking on ahead, regardless. The fact that she's holding my hand. If she hadn't died, those details wouldn't be so charged with meaning. It's also the only photo that exists of the two of us where I'm a conscious person, not a newborn baby. That's important to me—it proves, somehow, that I did actually know her.

In your acknowledgments, you thank Anjelica Huston for providing the title _Love Child_. Did you have any reservations about showing your work to family members? Did they show any hesitation in supporting your decision to write about the family?
As I wrote in the Acknowledgments, the only hesitation any of my family showed was that pause before Anjel said, "Be kind." I had no agenda for revenge or "justice" when I wrote the book, so I knew I would be kind—but I would also be honest, as scrupulously honest as I could. I worried most about Anjel, Cici, and John Julius, because I knew some of their actions would be open to ungenerous interpretations, but the only way to protect them from that would be not to tell the story at all. I felt that the value of telling the story outweighed the risk and that if I told it with love and understanding and lack of judgment, maybe that would encourage readers to suspend judgment, too—and not just about members of my family. Very often, people are just doing the best they can in tough circumstances.

Of course I was nervous when I finally sent the manuscript to everyone, even though I'd gone through it specifically looking for anything I thought might offend or hurt someone needlessly. I sent it to them all at the same time, in the same e-mail. Fortunately they all loved it and are supporting it 100 percent. The very few corrections they asked for were minor and factual.

Now that you have written the story of your life so far, what is the next unwritten chapter, the next challenge to embrace?
I'm superstitious about talking about things before they happen, so I don't want to say anything beyond that I'm working on another book. The greatest challenge of all is raising my son to be a confident, generous, engaged, happy person.